Pollution and Property

Comparing Ownership Institutions for Environmental Protection

Environmental protection and resource conservation depend on the imposition of property rights (broadly defined) because in the absence of some property system – private, common, or public – resource degradation and depletion are inevitable. But there is no universal, first-best property regime for environmental protection in this second-best world.

Using case studies and examples taken from countries around the world, Professor Cole demonstrates that the choice of ownership institution is contingent upon institutional, technological, and ecological circumstances that determine the differential costs of instituting, implementing, and maintaining alternative regimes. Consequently, environmental protection is likely to be more effective and more efficient in a society that relies on multiple (and often mixed) property regimes.

The book concludes with an assessment of the important contemporary issue of "takings," which arise when different property regimes collide.

DANIEL H. COLE is M. Dale Palmer Professor of Law at the Indiana University School of Law at Indianapolis, where he teaches and writes about the law and economics of property, natural resources and environmental protection. His publications include *Environmental Protection in Transition* (coedited with John Clark, 1998) and *Instituting Environmental Protection: from Red to Green in Poland* (1998), which received the prestigious AAASS/Orbis Polish Book Prize in 1999.

Pollution and Property

Comparing Ownership Institutions
for Environmental Protection

Daniel H. Cole

CAMBRIDGE
UNIVERSITY PRESS

PUBLISHED BY THE PRESS SYNDICATE OF THE UNIVERSITY OF CAMBRIDGE
The Pitt Building, Trumpington Street, Cambridge, United Kingdom

CAMBRIDGE UNIVERSITY PRESS
The Edinburgh Building, Cambridge CB2 2RU, UK
40 West 20th Street, New York, NY 10011-4211, USA
477 Williamstown Road, Port Melbourne, VIC 3207, Australia
Ruiz de Alarcón 13, 28014 Madrid, Spain
Dock House, The Waterfront, Cape Town 8001, South Africa

http://www.cambridge.org

First published 2002

Printed in the United Kingdom at the University Press, Cambridge

Typeface Plantin 10/12 pt   *System* LaTeX 2$_\varepsilon$ [TB]

A catalogue record for this book is available from the British Library

ISBN 0 521 80637 2 hardback
ISBN 0 521 00109 9 paperback

For Marysia and Stefan

Contents

Preface

The basic environmental problem is to prevent the overuse and abuse of "environmental goods," including clean air, water, and wildlife, by controlling access and use. As control implies the assignment of private (individual or common) or public rights and duties with respect to otherwise open-access resources, this book posits that *all* approaches to environmental protection ultimately are property-based. On this view, even government regulation constitutes a property-based approach to environmental protection. Regulations impose private duties with respect to the use of environmental goods, and in doing so necessarily create concomitant public rights of enforcement. Consequently, the choice in environmental protection is not *whether* to take a property-based approach but *which* property-based approaches to use under various circumstances.

As to the latter question, there is no universal, first-best property-based solution to all environmental problems in all circumstances. This book assesses the utility of public, common, and private property-based approaches to environmental protection, and finds them all useful but within limits. Each has advantages and disadvantages, which may be maximized or minimized, respectively, depending on the ecological, institutional, technological, and cultural circumstances. One property system may work better than another in one set of circumstances, but compare very poorly under different conditions. No single property regime is demonstrably superior to all others, in all circumstances, across all dimensions of policy concern.

That conclusion should not surprise anyone. Yet much of the existing literature on relations between property and environmental protection either presupposes or argues normatively in favor of one property system or another, regardless of circumstance. This book, by contrast, seeks to describe relations between property and environmental protection more realistically, in their full complexity. Thus, its purpose is largely positive. The book also offers some normative arguments in favor of *multiple* property systems and admixtures of property systems. In part, those arguments constitute resort to a default position because of the difficulties inherent in predicting which property systems are likely to work best in different settings. The variables are too many and the *ex ante* uncertainty too great to reliably predict which approach would work best, except in the easiest – and, therefore, least interesting – cases. In more interesting and important cases, society's decision to impose some property regime (or admixture of regimes), rather than some other, for environmental protection remains "in the nature of a social experiment."

This work has roots in various disciplines, including law, economics, political science, and anthropology. Unfortunately, the increasing specialization of academic disciplines has created a situation in which the property literature of one field often goes undiscovered – or worse, ignored – by scholars in other disciplines. This is not invariably the case, of course. There are scholars who regularly cross disciplinary boundaries in search of what is worthwhile and useful, from whatever source. I count myself among them. Although I am first and foremost a legal scholar, I do not believe that a narrowly conceived legal analysis of relations between property systems and environmental protection would be either illuminating or very interesting. At the same time, I sense that an economic analysis of environmental protection devoid of considerations of law and other institutions, technology, ecology, and culture, is likely to be quite sterile and unrealistic. By combining legal and economic analysis, along with some lessons from anthropology – in short, by undertaking a New Institutional approach to the problem of environmental protection – this book's *comparative institutional analysis* will hopefully prove to be more robust and realistic.

My thinking about the relations between property systems and environmental protection has been influenced by many writers, but three above all others: John Dales, Dan Bromley, and Elinor Ostrom. J. H. Dales's *Pollution, Property and Prices* (1968) is a classic work in the environmental economics literature, but arguably should be even more influential – and for more reasons – than it is. Professor Dales is universally acknowledged as the originator of transferrable pollution rights as an environmental policy instrument. Ironically, he was not. An economist at the University of Wisconsin–Milwaukee named Thomas D. Crocker (1966, p. 81) recommended the very same thing in 1966, two years before Professor Dales published *Pollution, Property, and Prices*. Professor Dales's fame is justly deserved, however, because he first analyzed tradeable pollution rights in a systematic way. In any case, there is much more to *Pollution, Property, and Prices* than tradeable pollution rights. It is in the best tradition of economic analysis – rigorous but realistic, analytical but humane, even humble. It is, in brief, a very wise book about the power and, just as importantly, the limitations of economic analysis for describing and resolving environmental protection issues. And its unique influence on my own thinking about those issues is manifest throughout this book, beginning with the title, which I chose in part as a tribute to Professor Dales.

Daniel Bromley is another economist who has greatly influenced my thinking on environmental matters. His book *Environment and Economy: Property Rights and Public Policy* (1991) first started me thinking about a comparative property systems-based approach to environmental protection. In contrast to many economists, Professor Bromley treats the law – and property law in particular – seriously, as an institution that shapes economic behavior. His analysis is, consequently, more nuanced and realistic than much of the economic literature on environmental policy.

I also owe a sizeable intellectual debt to the political scientist Elinor Ostrom, whose book *Governing the Commons* (1990) opened the eyes of so many scholars in various disciplines to the continuing role of common property systems in the contemporary world. In particular, her systematic, comparative institutional approach to assessing property regime choice for resource conservation has provided an extraordinarily useful framework for analysis. My approach, though perhaps less formal than her own, owes a great deal to her process for analyzing property problems and solutions.

This book was written, in almost equal measures, in Indianapolis, USA and Cambridge, UK. I owe several debts of gratitude in both locations. In Indianapolis, I am grateful to Dean Norman Lefstein and my faculty colleagues at the Indiana University School of Law at Indianapolis, who provided me with the means and the time, including successive Summer Research Fellowships and a six-month sabbatical in 2000, to research and write the book. Several colleagues and friends at IU, including Nicholas Georgakopoulos, Andy Klein, and Florence Roisman went above and beyond the call of duty, providing helpful comments on drafts of several chapters or the entire book.

In Cambridge, I am grateful first and foremost to Malcolm Grant, who arranged visitorships for me in the Faculties of Land Economy and Law from June to December of 2000. Malcolm possesses an almost unique combination of admirable traits: he is at once an accomplished scholar, an exceptional administrator, and a very kind person. Several of his colleagues on the Law Faculty and in the Land Economy Department were instrumental in helping me sort out various issues relating to this project. I am grateful especially to Simon Deakin, Timo Goeschl, Ian Hodge, and Joanne Scott. In addition, I want to thank Sanjay Peters of the Economics Faculty for being such a good friend and mentor in all things Cambridge.

While in Cambridge, my family and I resided at Clare Hall, of which I am proud to be a Life Member. I would like to thank Clare Hall's former President, Gillian Beer, and the entire staff of the college, especially Elizabeth Ramsden, for making our stay in Cambridge so pleasant and memorable.

At Cambridge University Press, I am profoundly grateful to my editor and friend Finola O'Sullivan, who nurtured this project with great care and enthusiasm. Finola's assistant Jennie Rubio has also been extremely helpful, as has my copyeditor, Hilary Hammond.

Several individuals outside of Indiana University and the University of Cambridge, including Daniel Bromley, John Dales, Robert Ellickson, and Richard Lazarus, provided helpful comments on various chapters of the book. I am especially indebted to my friend and frequent collaborator, Peter Z. Grossman, who, to paraphrase Franz Joseph Haydn, is among the very best economists I know either personally or by reputation. Peter provided much needed encouragement as well as critical commentary on every chapter of the book. Finally and above all, I am eternally grateful to my wife, Izabela, and children, Marysia and Stefan. This book could not have been written without their constant support and love.

This book is the product of several years' thinking about the relations between environmental problems and property systems, which began when I was first invited, in 1996, to contribute an entry on "New Forms of Property: Property Rights in Environmental Goods" to the *Encyclopedia of Law and Economics* (2000). Since then, I have published several articles relating, in one way or another, to this topic. Each of those earlier works has found its way into this book, although none completely in its original form. Sentences, paragraphs, sometimes whole sections of previously published works are scattered here and there, throughout the various chapters. I am grateful to the following journals for providing permissions to reprint: Duke Environmental Law and Policy Forum, for "Clearing the Air: Four Propositions About Property Rights and Environmental Protection," *Duke Environmental Law & Policy Forum* 10 (1999); Indiana Law Review, for "The Importance of Being Comparative: the M. Dale Palmer Professorship Inaugural Lecture," *Indiana Law Review* 33 (2000); and Wisconsin Law Review, for "When is Command-and-Control Efficient? Institutions, Technology, and the Comparative Efficiency of Alternative Regulatory Regimes for Environmental Protection," *Wisconsin Law Review* (1999) (coauthored by Peter Z. Grossman).

Table of government documents

INTERNATIONAL TREATIES

Kyoto Protocol to the United Nations Climate Change Convention, Dec. 10, 1997.

STATUTES

Clean Air Act, 42 USC §§ 7401–7671q (1970).
Colorado Revised Statutes §§ 38-30.5-107, 109 (1994).
Endangered Species Act, 16 USC §§ 1531–1544 (1973).
Florida Statutes Annotated 70.001(2), (3)(e) (1995).
Indiana Code § 32-5-2.6-7 (1984).
Internal Revenue Code, 21 USC § 1 et seq. (2001).
Michigan Compiled Laws 336.11 et seq. (1995, repeated 1994).
Michigan Statutes Annotated 14.58(1) et seq. (1994).
Texas Government Code Annotated 2007.041, 2007.002, 2007.003 (1995).
Uniform Conservation Easement Act (Supp. 1995).

BILLS

S. 1180, 105th Congress; 1st Session (1997).

LEGISLATIVE HISTORY

Environment and Natural Resources Policy Division (1993), Library of Congress, 103rd Cong., 1st Sess., *A Legislative History of the Clean Air Act Amendments of 1990*, Washington, DC: US Senate Committee on Environment and Public Works Print.
Environmental Policy Division (1974), Library of Congress, 93rd Cong., 2nd Sess., *A Legislative History of the Clean Air Act Amendments of 1970*, Washington, DC: US Senate Committee on Public Works Print.
Environmental Policy Division (1978), Library of Congress, 95th Cong., 2nd Sess., *A Legislative History of the Clean Air Act Amendments of 1977: a Continuation of the Clean Air Act Amendments of 1970* (1978), Washington, DC: US Senate Committee on Environment and Public Works Print.

REGULATIONS

26 CFR § 1.170A-14(h)(3)(ii) (Nov. 23, 2001).

49 CFR § 171.15 (Nov. 23, 2000). Immediate notice of certain hazardous materials incidents.

Chicago, Ill., Gen. Ordinances, §§ 1650, 1651 (1880).

Department of the Interior, Fish and Wildlife Service 2001, *Endangered and Threatened Wildlife and Plants; Final Determination of Critical Habitat for Peninsular Bighorn Sheep*, 50 Fed. Reg. 8650.

Environmental Protection Agency 1986a, *Emissions Trading Policy Statement; General Principles for Creation, Banking, and Use of Emission Reduction Credits*, 51 Fed. Reg. 43,814.

Environmental Protection Agency 1986b, *Emissions Trading Technical Document*, 51 Fed. Reg. 43,837.

Environmental Protection Agency 1993, *Final Rule on the Acid Rain Program*, 58 Fed. Reg. 3,677–78.

Revenue Procedure 92-91, Oct. 29, 1992, 92 Fed. Reg. para. 46,595.

CASES

ENGLAND

Attorney-General *v.* Antrobus, 2 Ch. 188 (1905).

Attorney-General *v.* Sheffield Gas Consumers Co., 3 De G.M. & G. 304 (1853).

Blount *v.* Layard, 2 Ch. 691, n. (1891).

Burmah Oil *v.* Lord Advocate, AC 75 (1965).

Grant *v.* Duke of Gordon, III Paton 679 (1776).

Sisters of Charity of Rockingham *v.* The King, 2 AC 315 (PC) (1922).

AMERICA

Alliance for Clean Coal *v.* Bayh, 888 F. Supp. 924 (SD Ind. 1995).

Armstrong *v.* United States, 364 US 40 (1960).

Atlanta Processing Co. *v.* Brown, 227 Ga. 203 (1971).

Babbit *v.* Sweet Home Chapter of Communities for a Greater Oregon, 515 US 687 (1995).

Boone *v.* United States, 944 F. 2d 1489 (9th Cir. 1991).

Briggs & Stratton Corp. *v.* Concrete Sales & Servs., 29 F. Supp. 2d 1372 (MD Geo. 1998).

Buck *v.* Bell, 274 US 200 (1927).

Cabinet Mountains Wilderness *v.* Peterson, 685 F. 2d 678 (DC Cir. 1982).

Christy *v.* Hodel, 857 F. 2d 1324, 1334 (9th Cir. 1988), cert. denied sub nom.

Christy *v.* Lujan, 490 US 1114 (1989).

City of Chicago *v.* Commonwealth Edison Co., 24 Ill. App. 3d 624 (1974).

Commonwealth *v.* The Barnes Foundation, 159 A. 2d 500 (Pa. 1960).

Detroit Edison Co. *v.* Michigan Air Pollution Control Commission, 167 Mich. App. 651 (1988).

Dolan *v.* City of Tigard, 512 US 374 (1994).

Douglas *v.* Seacoast Products, Inc., 431 US 265 (1977).

COURT BRIEFS

1   Pollution and property: the conceptual framework

This chapter describes the theoretical relations between pollution and property and provides a framework for the analysis that follows in subsequent chapters. Sections 1 and 2, respectively, rehearse and critique the conventional but too simplistic notion that environmental problems are at bottom property problems. In fact, the structure of property rights *and* environmental problems are both largely consequences of other factors, most notably transaction costs, which in turn are substantially determined by institutional and technological circumstances. Section 2 illustrates this point by describing an ideal, frictionless economy, in which well-defined property rights are clearly *not* a precondition to optimal environmental protection. In a world of zero transaction costs, the optimal level of environmental protection would be attained regardless of the existence and initial allocation of property rights. This is not to argue, however, that the structure of property rights is irrelevant to environmental protection. As I will show in section 3, where I take readers from the ideal world of perfect markets and costless transacting to the real world of imperfect institutions and costly transacting, the structure of property rights can significantly influence environmental performance, and has done so throughout history. Section 3 introduces the "tragedy-of-open-access" model and discusses one of its most important but often overlooked implications: that all means of averting the tragedy, including regulatory measures, are property-based. Section 3 also attempts to clarify some terminological issues in defining property rights, and frames the task for subsequent chapters, which is to compare how alternative property systems differentially effect environmental protection in various institutional and technological circumstances. Finally, section 4 sets forth the organizational structure of subsequent chapters.

I   Things that are unowned receive the least care

Scholars long ago recognized that the nature, extent, and allocation of property rights can significantly affect rates of resource depletion and degradation. In the fourth century BCE Aristotle observed that whatever "is common to the greatest number has the least care bestowed on it" (Aristotle 1941, § 1262b34–5). His observation has resonated throughout history, and today is understood (after Hardin 1968) as "the tragedy of the commons."

Despite Aristotle's early warning, many environmental goods never have been subject to private ownership for a variety of economic, technological, political, and cultural reasons. Writing 350 years after Aristotle, the Roman poet Ovid (1992, p. 111) put these words in the mouth of Dædalus: "Though he may possess everything, Minos does not possess the air." Indeed, according to Roman law, it was against natural law for any individual, even the emperor, to own the air or other socially significant environmental goods. The Institutes of Justinian, compiled 1,000 years after Aristotle, decreed "[b]y the law of nature these things are common to mankind – the air, running water, the sea and consequently the shores of the sea" (Grapel 1994, p. 50). In most countries, for most purposes, these environmental goods have ever since remained off limits to private ownership.

If we were to construct a syllogism, positing Aristotle's observation as a major premise and the rule from Justinian's Institutes as a minor premise, the conclusion would be that the commonly owned air, running water, sea, and seashore have the least care bestowed upon them. History, unfortunately, has too often confirmed this. In the absence of property rights to protect them, environmental goods have been abused, sometimes to the point of destruction.

Obviously, there is an important connection between pollution and property. But what is the nature of this connection?

II   If the absence of property rights explains pollution, what explains the absence of property rights?

It is frequently said that pollution and other environmental problems stem, in the first instance, from the absence of property rights in natural resources (or "environmental goods") (see, for example, Goodstein 1995, p. 1029). This reductionist assertion is repeated so often that it has become a truism. But it begs a further reductionist question: what accounts for the absence of property rights in many environmental goods? If some other factor is responsible for the lack of completely specified property rights, then the lack of property rights itself cannot be the ultimate "cause" of pollution and other environmental problems. This reflects a standard problem with reductionist arguments: at what point does the process of reduction end?

As economists know (at least since Coase 1960), property rights are not completely specified for all – really any – environmental goods because they are costly to define, sometimes *too* costly.[1] We might legitimately claim, therefore, that the cost of establishing property rights, rather than the absence of such rights, is the ultimate cause of environmental problems. But that only leads us to the next reductionist question: why are the costs of imposing property rights sometimes, but not always, too high? With this question we finally arrive at the twisted root of the matter: the economic, institutional, technological, and ecological *circumstances* that in large measure determine the costs of defining property rights in, and transacting over, environmental goods. Relations between pollution and property are ultimately determined by the economic, institutional, technological, and ecological circumstances that prevail at a given time and place.[2]

III   Property and pollution in an ideal (nonexistent) world

In a world of perfectly defined property rights, optimal environmental protection would be achieved automatically, but only if certain other preconditions were met. Interestingly, those preconditions would obviate the assumption of perfectly defined property rights.

Imagine a society characterized by a perfectly functioning market economy, with attendant institutions such as freedom of contract.[3] In this ideal economy, benefit and cost functions are fully known; a social welfare function is completely specified; information costs for all people in society are very low, so that the level of pollution and the distribution of costs and benefits are both always known; and transacting (including bargaining, policing deals, and enforcing contracts and property rights) is costless.[4] This is the world of the Coase theorem,[5] and in it social costs and benefits equal private costs and benefits.

In this ideal world, the optimal level of pollution control is attained automatically by virtue of the assumptions of perfect markets, nearly perfect

---

[1] See also Barzel (1989, p. 64).

[2] I am hardly the first author to recognize this (see, for example, Dahlman 1980, ch. 3).

[3] The description of the ideal economy in this section is adapted from Cole and Grossman (1999, pp. 895–6).

[4] To these assumptions, many scholars would add the further assumption that property rights are perfectly defined. But, as will be shown later, this assumption is unnecessary to ensure optimal efficiency and optimal environmental protection in a world of costless transacting.

[5] The world of the Coase theorem is not the world Coase was concerned to explain. He posited the "Coase theorem" (the label was coined by George Stigler) as a counterfactual heuristic device, to illustrate the importance of legal institutions in the real world, which is characterized by ubiquitous and often quite high transaction costs. See generally Coase (1960).

information, and costless transacting. Indeed, these assumptions ensure optimal environmental protection even in the absence of well-defined and efficiently allocated property rights. Because transacting is costless, participants in the perfectly functioning market will contract with one another to create, allocate, and reallocate entitlements to resources as needed to achieve and maintain optimal efficiency (see Cheung 1998 and 1986; Coase 1988, p. 15). Moreover, the assumption of perfectly functioning markets means that there are no market failures requiring or justifying corrective action by the government. In this circumstance, government intervention in the market for purposes of environmental protection is both unnecessary and undesirable. Any government-mandated pollution reductions could only reduce social welfare.

Apparently, then, well-defined property rights are not a necessary precondition for optimal environmental protection in an idealized, zero transaction-cost world. Nor are they a sufficient condition. As Steven N. S. Cheung (1998) has pointed out, the very notion of a property system contradicts the assumption of zero transaction costs because the existence of a property system necessarily implies the existence of substantial transaction costs (see also Dahlman 1980, pp. 138–9). Moreover, in a world of costless information and transacting, there would be no basis for choosing between capitalist and socialist organization of economic activity (Cheung 1986, p. 37).[6] This implies that the property regime itself is irrelevant to the attainment of optimal efficiency and optimal environmental protection in the idealized world of the Coase theorem. Cheung (1986, p. 37) and Coase (1988, p. 15) concur that, in a world of costless transacting, "*the assumption of private property rights can be dropped without in the least negating the Coase Theorem!*"[7]

IV   Property and pollution in the real, second-best world

If we inhabited the ideal world described in the preceding section, this book would end here. Environmental protection would be a nonissue; writing about it would serve no purpose. There is, however, much more worth writing about environmental protection and its relation to property systems, because the real world bears no resemblance to that ideal world. In the real world, with which the rest of this book is concerned, none of the conditions described in the previous section as necessary and sufficient for

---

[6] This is also an implication of Coase's (1960) own analysis, according to which the choice between market, firm, or government organization of economic activity depends on transaction costs.

[7] Italics in original. Barzel (1989, p. 55 n. 11) similarly notes that "[c]ostless transacting ... is a sufficient condition for clearly defining property rights, rendering redundant the requirement that property rights be well defined."

optimal environmental protection obtains, ever. Markets do not function perfectly; transacting is costly; the social welfare function is uncertain at best; and property rights are only ever imperfectly specified. This real world is so imperfect that there is little sense talking about, let alone striving after, theoretical "optima." As Ronald Coase (1964, p. 195) has observed, in our world all of the mechanisms for organizing economic activity – markets, firms, and governments – are "more or less failures." The best we can realistically hope for is to minimize the sum of market failures and government failures, rather than maximize any presumed social welfare function.

The tragedy-of-open-access model

In the twentieth century economists began to study systematically the relations between the absence of property rights and resource depletion in the real world – specifically, Aristotle's observation that goods held in common receive the least care. Jens Warming (1911), Scott Gordon (1954), and Anthony Scott (1955) each elaborated on Aristotle's observation in the context of unowned and overexploited fisheries. In 1968 Garrett Hardin, a biologist, provided the classic economic account of the depletion of open-access resources, including many environmental goods.

Hardin's "The Tragedy of the Commons" (1968) provides a useful starting point for analyzing the ties between pollution and property in the real world. Its thesis is that resource depletion and pollution problems both stem from the incentives created by open-access (nonproperty) regimes, in which no one can exclude anyone else from using a given resource. Hardin demonstrates the problem with the simple example of a pasture open to unlimited grazing by all cattle ranchers. Assuming that all ranchers who might use the pasture are rational, each will seek to maximize his or her individual benefits from the pasture. Each will ask, "[w]hat is the utility to *me* of adding one more animal to my herd?" In other words, they will conduct a cost-benefit analysis to determine whether adding an additional animal to their herd on the commons will provide a net gain or loss. The benefit side of the equation is "a function of the increment of one animal." According to Hardin, "[s]ince the herdsman receives all the proceeds from the sale of the additional animal, the positive utility is nearly +1." The cost side of the equation is "a function of the additional overgrazing created by one more animal." These costs, however, are not borne solely by the rancher who adds one more head of cattle; rather, they are spread among all the ranchers who use (or might use) the pasture. Thus, "the negative utility for any particular decision-making herdsman is only a fraction of -1" (Hardin 1968, p. 1244).

Adding together the component partial utilities, the rational herdsman concludes that the only sensible course of action for him to pursue is to add another animal to his herd. And another; and another... But this is the conclusion reached by each and every rational herdsman sharing a commons. Therein is the tragedy. Each man is locked into a system that compels him to increase his herd without limit – in a world that is limited. Ruin is the destination toward which all men rush, each pursuing his own best interest in a society that believes in the freedom of the commons. Freedom in a commons brings ruin to all. (Hardin 1968, p. 1244)

Even an exceptionally foresighted and other-regarding cattle rancher, who recognized the looming tragedy, would not likely forego the opportunity of adding one more animal to her herd. Against her inclination, she would add more cattle rather than conserve the pasture because in this state of nature – that is, in the absence of any property regime – she would be unable to enforce a conservation decision against other current or potential users. Why? Because any other rancher could come right along and exploit the opportunity she nobly bypassed, turning her conservation decision into a futile gesture. Being foresighted, she would comprehend this; and being rational, she would not consciously make the futile gesture.[8] Instead, she would do what she feels she should not do: add one more animal to the herd.

It is the sociolegal fact of open access – the inability of any user or group of users to enforce their management decisions against any other user or group of users – that obstructs conservation of the resource.

The absence of property rights likewise can lead to pollution. According to Hardin (1968, p. 1245), "[t]he rational man finds that his share of the cost of the wastes he discharges into the commons is less than the cost of purifying his wastes before releasing them. Since this is true for everyone, we are locked into a system of 'fouling our own nest,' so long as we behave only as independent, rational, free-enterprisers."

This process is not inexorable, however. The "tragedy" can be averted, but only if access to and use of the resource are somehow restricted.

Property-based solutions to the tragedy

Hardin (1968, pp. 1247–8) prescribes two means of restricting access and use, which he combines under the heading, "mutual coercion, mutually agreed upon." The first is privatization: convert the open-access pasture

---

[8] Some individuals may derive utility from making futile gestures. For such people it may be rational to forego adding another animal to the herd, even if they believed their gesture would be futile. But even if, say, 90 percent of all potential users of Hardin's open-access pasture were quixotic conservationists (which is an implausibly high figure), the other 10 percent could still decimate the open-access pasture, depending on the total size of the population and the size and fecundity of the pasture.

to private (but not necessarily individual) ownership. On a privately owned pasture, the costs of any decision to add an extra animal would be internalized by the pasture owner(s). They would continue to use the pasture but not to the point of destruction because, Hardin assumes, overexploitation would generate net costs for the presumptively rational pasture owner(s). Our foresighted rancher, who decided not to graze one more animal in order to conserve *her* pasture, would now be able to enforce her conservation decision. Because she now owns and controls that part of the pasture subject to her decision, no one else can lawfully come along and exploit the opportunity she has decided to forego. Assuming a reasonably cost-effective institutional and organizational structure for enforcing her property rights, her conservation decision would be not futile but rational.

Hardin's second means of averting the tragedy of open access is regulation, which may be either external (government regulation) or internal (self-regulation by the users themselves). Under this regime, the economic incentives favoring overexploitation might be reduced or eliminated through (self-)imposed restrictions on all herders. Assuming that the restrictions are enforceable and that penalties for noncompliance are sufficient, entry and use regulation would raise the (internal) cost of adding animals to the common, but no longer open-access, pasture.

Scholars have discussed and distinguished Hardin's two solutions to the tragedy of the commons, but almost all have failed to recognize that both are property-based: each involves the imposition of property rights on formerly open-access (or nonproperty) resources. This is obviously true of privatization, but it is also true of many forms of government regulation. A government can, of course, assert public rights by explicitly claiming the resource as public property. Most countries have done precisely this in establishing "national parks," "national forests," and other "public lands." In the United States, the lands owned by the federal, state, and local governments comprise 42 percent of the country's total area (Natural Resource Council 1992).

Explicit claims of public ownership are not the only way, however, by which governments establish public property rights in resources. Governments frequently impose public rights through the regulation of private resource use. When the government regulates air pollution, for example, it imposes a system of public rights and private duties with respect to the atmosphere. Whether it chooses to regulate with command-and-control measures (such as technology-based standards), transferable pollution rights, or other "market-based" approaches, the state imposes on air polluters a legally enforceable duty to comply with all restrictions on use of (what amounts to) the public's atmosphere. What distinguishes this regulatory approach from "privatization" is not the existence or non-existence of property rights but only the *type* of property regime imposed. Privatization converts nonproperty into private (individual or common) property. Government regulation typically (if tacitly) converts nonproperty into public/state property or some mixed form of public and private property. It may be objected that government regulation constitutes an exercise in *imperium* (sovereign authority) rather than *dominium* (ownership) (see Denman 1978, pp. 25, 29–30). However, this old Roman-law distinction marks little practical difference. Property and sovereignty are both forms of power – as Denman (1978, p. 3) puts it, "a sanction and authority for decision-making" – over resources.[9] Whether the state is purporting to act as sovereign or owner, the rights it asserts are in the nature of property.

A digression on the conventional typology of property systems

At this point, it will be useful to review the conventional typology of property systems, according to which there are four basic property regimes: private, common, state, and nonproperty (or open access).[10] In the law and economics literature, "private property" (*res privatae*) typically denotes property owned by individuals holding rights to use (in socially acceptable ways), dispose of, and exclude others from resources. "Common property" (*res communes*) refers to collective ownership situations, in which the owners cannot exclude each other, but can exclude outsiders. "Public" or "state" property (*res publicae*) is a special form of common property supposedly owned by all the citizens, but typically controlled by elected officials or bureaucrats, who determine the parameters for access and use. Finally, "nonproperty" or "open access" (*res nullius*) denotes a situation in which a resource has no owner: all are at liberty to use it; no one has the right to exclude anyone else. Strictly speaking, open access is not a property regime at all; it signifies the absence of any property regime.

---

[9] Marchak (1998, pp. 3–4) lists state and international regulations as separate "ownership regimes," distinct from outright public ownership of resources. Schmid (1999, p. 236) notes that "[r]egulation is not a denial of property rights, but rather a means of rights distribution."

[10] Michael Heller (1998) adds a fifth category, which we might refer to as "no access." This regime results when the right to exclude is held by so many people or organizations that no one can gain entry to use the resource. The result may be *under*exploitation of the resource, resulting in what Heller calls the "tragedy of the anti-commons." Whether this constitutes a separate category of property rights or is just a special form of *res communes* is an issue we need not resolve here. For present purposes, problems of closed access – the "tragedy of the anti-commons" – have no significance. Indeed, from an environmental point of view, closed access may in some cases constitute a boon, rather than a tragedy.

Table 1.1. *The conventional typology of property regimes*

State property	Individuals have *duty* to observe use/access rules determined by controlling/managing agency. Agencies have *right* to determine use/access rules
Private property	Individuals have *right* to undertake socially acceptable uses, and have *duty* to refrain from socially unacceptable uses. Others (called "nonowners") have *duty* to refrain from preventing socially acceptable uses, and have a *right* to expect that only socially acceptable uses will occur
Common property	The management group (the "owners") has *right* to exclude nonmembers, and nonmembers have *duty* to abide by exclusion. Individual members of the management group (the "co-owners") have both *rights* and *duties* with respect to use rates and maintenance of the thing owned
Nonproperty	No defined group of users or "owners" and benefit stream is available to anyone. Individuals have both *privilege* and *no right* with respect to use rates and maintenance of the asset. The asset is an "open-access resource"

Source: Bromley 1991, p. 31

One major problem with this conventional typology of property regimes is that it simply does not fit many real-world circumstances.[11] Actual property regimes invariably combine features from different ownership categories (see Feeny et al. 1996). Even fee-simple absolute landownership – the highest level of ownership an individual can possess in common-law jurisdictions – is always and everywhere subject to public rights of access, use, or control, including public utility easements, zoning authorities, and property taxes. The concept of *allodial* ownership, which refers to completely unregulated and unregulatable private control, is nowhere to be found in the world today, if ever it did exist.[12]

The academic typology of property regimes also differs significantly from the ways in which people ordinarily distinguish property regimes. In common parlance "private" property is not counterposed to "common" property as it is in much of the academic literature. Co-owned property, including joint tenancy, partnership, and corporate property,

---

[11] It is for this reason primarily that some scholars (including Hanna et al. 1996 and McCay 1996) offer more elaborate typologies of property regimes.

[12] As Dahlman (1980, pp. 70, 71 n. 3) explains, "There is no such thing as absolute ownership, not even in an economic system characterized by complete private ownership." Rights to use, exclude, and exchange "are attenuated in one way or the other in every known economic system." Coase (1960, p. 44) observes that "[w]hat a landowner in fact possesses is the right to carry out a circumscribed list of actions." And he doubts the very possibility of allodial rights by noting that "[a] system in which the rights of the individual were unlimited would be one in which there were no rights to acquire."

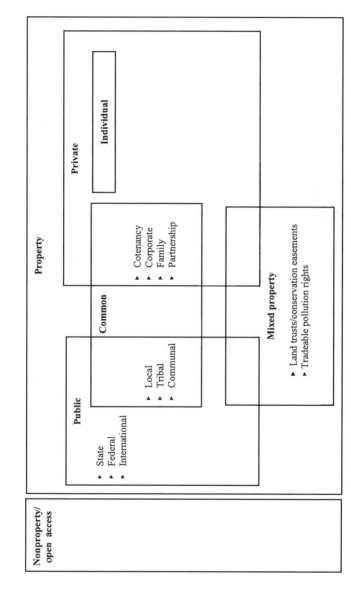

Figure 1   Relations among property regimes.

is usually referred to as "private," so long as it is not owned by the state or some public entity (see Denman 1978, p. 102). From another point of view, however, co-ownership simply denotes multiple individual ownership, with each co-owner possessing individual rights in, or attributes of, the resource (see Bromley 1991, pp. 25–6; Barzel 1990). Thráinn Eggertsson (1996, p. 161) suggests that the distinction between private and common (or, in his terms, "communal") ownership has less to do with the number of owners than with the comparatively free transferability of private property rights.

A more vexing terminological problem in the academic literature is the conflation of common property with nonproperty or open access.[13] This conflation is understandable because in the vernacular nonproperty resources are typically described as "commonses" or "common pools." Indeed, they *are* commonses in the sense that they are common to all; no one can exclude anyone else.[14] However, the labels "common property" and "open access" denote very different systems. They differ primarily in the size of the group entitled to access and use the resources (see Seabright 1993, p. 114 n. 1). In order for property to be common (*res communes*) rather than open access (*res nullius*) there must be at least two groups, one of which collectively controls the resource with the authority and ability to exclude the other (Ciriacy-Wantrup and Bishop 1975, p. 715; Stevenson 1991, p. 51). Daniel Bromley (1991, p. 149) claims that "[a] common property regime for the group becomes an open access regime for the individuals within the group." But this is not typically the case. In most (if not all) existing common property regimes, the individuals comprising the group of co-owners do not possess unfettered rights to access and use, as they would to an open-access resource; rather, the group collectively regulates the access and use of its own members. Bromley (1991, pp. 25–6) correctly notes, however, that "common property represents *private property for the group of co-owners* because all others are excluded from use and decision making."

Common property is also sometimes confused with public or state property. The state may be viewed as a group of co-owners, like partnerships, collectives, or villages. But those, such as Elinor Ostrom (1990), who write extensively about common property resources, seem to distinguish between state and common ownership based on the size of the ownership group and its location with respect to the resource. When a

---

[13] Cox (1985) and Bromley (1991, pp. 22 and 137) are among those who criticize Hardin (1968) and North and Thomas (1973), among others, for conflating open access with common property.

[14] Michaelman (1982, p. 9), for example, defines a "commons" as "a scheme of universally distributed, all-encompassing privilege."

group of self-governing villagers controls access to a fishery, for example, that is considered common ownership. But when nonusers, far removed from the village, control access and use, that is state or public ownership. Moreover, depending on the political circumstances and management practices, state or public property may more closely resemble individually owned private property than common property (see Eggertsson 1990, p. 37; Rose 1994, pp. 116–17; Denman 1978, pp. 3–4).

Another conceptual problem with the conventional typology of property regimes concerns the general neglect of a crucial question: just what specific rights and corresponding duties do the various property regimes entail? As Bromley (1989, p. 187) notes, those who write about property and property rights rarely are "specific about the content of those terms." Economists in particular often adopt (explicitly or implicitly) definitions of property rights that diverge significantly from legal definitions (see Cole and Grossman forthcoming a). Some facilely assume that private property means Blackstonian absolute dominion.[15] But as Harold Demsetz (1988, p. 19) explains, "full private rights, full state rights, full communal rights are notions that are very elastic with respect to the substantive bundle of entitlements involved."

Toni Honoré (1961) lists eleven distinct "sticks" in the *complete* bundle of property rights: the right to exclusively possess; the right to use; the right to manage; the right to the income; the right to the capital; the right to security; transmissibility; absence of term; the prohibition of harmful use; liability to execution; and the right to residuary character. None of these rights is strictly necessary, in the sense that one cannot be considered an owner of property without it. Even if one or more sticks are missing from a particular bundle, someone may still meaningfully be said to "own" property. It is not good enough, therefore, to recommend a certain property regime for environmental goods; one must also specify just what rights and corresponding duties that regime would entail (see Ostrom 1990, p. 22). Those rights and duties may well vary from one environmental good to another, or, with respect to any particular environmental good, from one context to another.

Although the problems arising from the conventional typology of property rights regimes are troublesome, especially when they are neglected, they do not become the ultimate concern of law and economics scholars, which is not the ownership regime *per se* but the costs of transacting

---

[15] Blackstone (1979, vol. II, p. 2) wrote of property as the "sole and despotic dominion which one man claims and exercises over the external things of the world, in total exclusion of the right of any other individual in the universe." Carol Rose (1998) has explained, however, that Blackstone could not have meant this literally, given the significant constraints on property he acknowledged in subsequent passages of the *Commentaries*.

(or refraining from transacting) over resources. The ownership (and management) regime is important only insofar as it impacts on externalities and transaction costs (see Coase 1960; Demsetz 1967; Dahlman 1979; Terrebonne 1993).

In view of the terminological confusions arising from the conventional typology of property regimes, which arguably reflect ideological issues more than real distinctions, the economist J. H. Dales (1968, p. 61) sensibly abandons the conventional typology. Rather than opposing private to common and public/state property, he merely refers to " 'property rights,' by whomever exercised." Depending on the circumstances, property rights may best be vested in individuals, groups (collectives or firms), or the state (on behalf of the public at large). The implication is that distinctions between individual, group, and state property tend to be more informative and less ideologically loaded than the conventional distinction between private and common property (also see Goetze 1987, p. 187).

This book relies on the conventional typology of private, common, and public property despite its manifest insufficiency, but with an important caveat: when I refer to public or private property, I should not be taken to mean *purely* public or private. There is no such thing as a pure or unadulterated public or private property system. As Charles Geisler (2000) has noted, all existing property regimes are more or less admixtures, comprising various individual, group, and public rights. A property regime can only be *relatively* public or private. Public/state property regimes are never unalloyed by private (individual or common) interests (see Huffman 1994). Similarly, private property is never devoid of public or common rights (see Dahlman 1980, p. 70). As Albert Church (1982, p. 93) has written, nominal "ownership is but one of the components of property rights in natural resources." So, when I refer to "private" property in this book, I do not mean allodial property, devoid of public rights, but property nominally owned by private individuals, subject to various group or public interests.

To the extent that all existing property regimes are actually admixtures of private, group, and public rights, we might legitimately conclude that all regimes really boil down to common property. Such a conclusion, however, would mask significant differences between actually existing property regimes. Therefore, I use the label "common property" only in its conventional understanding of property owned corporately or by a group of persons, who do not constitute a state agency.

The mere fact that I am compelled to parse these definitions is yet another manifestation of the insufficiency of the conventional typology of property regimes. Perhaps, in the end, we will be forced to conclude with

Dales (1968, p. 61) that the conventional typology must be abandoned in favor of a messier but more accurate description of property rights, "by whomever exercised."

Regulatory instruments as property-based regimes

Having rehearsed the basic structure of property systems, we now return to the treatment of environmental regulations as property-based solutions to the tragedy of the commons. There are, of course, a wide variety of regulatory instruments for averting open-access "tragedies." One environmental law casebook (Percival et al. 1996, pp. 154–8) lists twelve distinct regulatory approaches, including: design standards or technology specifications; performance standards or emissions limits; ambient or harm-based standards; product bans or use limitations; marketable allowances (which I refer to in chapter 3 as transferable pollution rights); challenge regulation or environmental contracting; pollution taxes or emissions charges; subsidies; deposit-refund schemes; liability rules and insurance requirements; planning or analysis requirements; information disclosure (e.g., labeling) requirements. The regulatory approaches in this expansive typology combine varying amounts of commands, controls, and economic incentives. But this categorization should not mislead us into thinking that certain regulatory approaches are "property-based," while others are not. They are all more or less property-based to the extent that they recognize or establish enforceable rights and duties in otherwise unowned resources. This may not be obviously true of pollution taxes, for example, but even they can be – and, perhaps, should be – viewed as a property-based approach, in which the government provides polluters with what amounts to an option to purchase limited rights to pollute. The key point is that those who are subject to the pollution tax have an enforceable *duty* not to pollute the public's atmosphere without paying the price set by the agent (the government) of the owner (the public).[16]

From a strictly economic perspective, conventional distinctions between "economic" instruments and command-and-control, for example, are immaterial. All approaches to environmental protection – from technology-based command-and-control regulations to effluent taxes, transferable pollution rights, and complete privatization – create economic costs and benefits that are distributed among polluters, the government and its taxpayers, and various other groups and individuals that comprise the "public." The only truly meaningful distinction between one

---

[16] This property-based conception of regulation is further elaborated on in chapter 2.

approach and another lies in their differential cost and benefit structures. On a practical economic level, the decision rule for choosing from among alternative regulatory approaches to attain a given environmental protection objective is their relative cost-effectiveness or regulatory efficiency: in a certain situation, how much pollution control or resource conservation would alternative property/regulatory regimes buy for the buck?

Criticisms of Hardin's allegory of the "tragedy of the commons"

Hardin's tragedy-of-the-commons model and his institutional mechanisms for averting the "tragedy" have been extensively criticized for conflating open access with common property (see, for example, Cox 1985; Taylor 1992; Dasgupta 1982, p. 13). What Hardin calls the "tragedy of the commons" is, in fact, a "tragedy of open access," to which common-property regimes may comprise a solution. This criticism is valid but facile. As I have already shown, open-access resources are conventionally referred to as "common pools" or simply as "commonses." Most importantly, Hardin's (1968, p. 1244) article makes crystal clear that the issue is open access, rather than common property: he writes about a "pasture open to all," not a pasture open to one group, but closed to all others. At worst, Hardin is guilty of an unfortunate choice of words. It would have been better if he had entitled his article, "The Tragedy of Open Access," which is how this book will hereafter refer to the central problem of environmental protection. This purely semantic quibble has no real bearing, however, on Hardin's analysis.

Hardin has also been criticized (by Berkes et al. 1989; Feeny et al. 1990; Feeny et al. 1996; Taylor 1992; McCay 2000) for preferring private and state ownership over common ownership. In fact, Hardin's analysis in "The Tragedy of the Commons" provides no basis for any such preference. His analysis calls for the creation of property rights where none previously existed, but does not suggest in whom – individuals, groups, or the state – those rights should be vested. In a later writing, Hardin (1978) lists private and state ownership (or "private enterprise" and "socialism") as the only two viable solutions to the "tragedy of the commons," implying that "common" property regimes (as defined earlier in this section) would not suffice. But nothing in "The Tragedy of the Commons" supports such a claim; and numerous empirical and theoretical studies dispute it (including Ostrom 1990; Bromley 1992; Hanna and Munasinghe 1995). In any case, as noted earlier, the appropriate distinction is not between common property and private property but between individual ownership – where a single person holds the right to exclude all others – and joint ownership – where no member of the group can exclude any other, but any single member of the group can exclude any and all nonmembers.

A more legitimate criticism of Hardin relates to his assumption that rational private owners would not knowingly overexploit their resources. This assumption is empirically and theoretically dubious. Empirically, individual private owners have often done exactly what Hardin assumes they would not do. Daniel Bromley (1991, p. 171) reminds us of the dust bowls that resulted when supposedly "'omniscient' private entrepreneurs" plowed up the American prairie against the advice of agricultural experts. More recently, in the 1990s private timber owners in the American Pacific northwest increased harvesting to unsustainable levels either to avert or to pay for junk bond financed hostile takeovers (see Power 1996, p. 138). According to economic theory, meanwhile, it is entirely rational for resource users to extinguish rather than conserve resources in some circumstances (see Gordon 1958). Colin Clark (1973a, pp. 950–1) has shown, for example, that the "extermination of an entire [animal] population may appear as the most attractive policy, even to an individual resource owner," when "(a) the discount (or time preference) rate sufficiently exceeds the maximum reproductive potential of the population, and (b) an immediate profit can be made from harvesting the last remaining animals." The outcome may not be socially optimal, but private property owners make decisions to maximize private, not social, benefits (see Clark 1973b; Larson and Bromley 1990; Schlager and Ostrom 1992). I will revisit this point in chapter 5, when reviewing claims that privatization of all environmental goods would lead to optimal conservation.

Even if all the criticisms leveled at Hardin's model of environmental degradation were true, his chief insight would remain nonetheless valid: open-access resources tend to be unsustainably exploited unless *some* property regime is imposed for their protection.[17] But which property regime? Open access may be replaced by a traditionally conceived private-property regime, in which entitlements to units of the resource are allotted to individual owners. Or the resource may be kept intact as common property, with entry and use restrictions imposed by some governing body. This governing body may be private, constituting collective self-government by the group of resource users *cum* "owners," or public, constituting state ownership or regulation.

---

[17] In addition to the criticisms discussed above, we might also fault Hardin for his advocacy of regulatory controls on human procreation (Hardin 1968, p. 1248). Interestingly, on this point most of his environmentalist critics are silent. In any case, the prescription of compulsory birth control is not central to his analysis of the problem of open access.

Which property-based approach?

Because all solutions to the tragedy of open access inevitably involve the imposition of property rights on previously unowned environmental goods, the choice in environmental protection is not *whether* to adopt a property-based approach but *which* property-based approach(es) to adopt. To what extent should the state assert public rights (*res publicae*) as opposed to vesting (limited or unlimited) private property rights in individual users (*res individuales*) or groups of users (*res communes*)? An adequate theory of property rights in natural resources must consider the full range of possible property-based solutions to the tragedy of open access, recognizing that, in this second-best world, no single regime is likely to be the first-best solution for every resource in every institutional, technological, and ecological setting. What is required is a *comparative institutional analysis* of various property solutions to the tragedy of the commons – not a comparison of some *idealized* theoretical institution against other, imperfect institutions but "a *comparative institution* approach in which the relevant choice is between alternative real institutional arrangements" (Demsetz 1969, p. 1).

Such an approach is entirely consistent with Coase's (1960, pp. 15–18) suggestion that efficiency is maximized sometimes by private market transactions, sometimes by transactions organized within firms, and sometimes by government regulation. As several authors (including Noll 1989; Komesar 1984; Eggertsson 1996, p. 166) have noted, every individual circumstance requires a comparative assessment of the costs of production, exclusion, and administration. A private property regime based on individual ownership may be appropriate in cases where the costs of governance are relatively high but exclusion costs are relatively low. Some form of common or state ownership may be preferable, however, in the converse situation of high exclusion costs and relatively low costs of administration. Finally, where the costs of either exclusion or governance would be extraordinarily high – reflecting, perhaps, the technological infeasibility of exclusion – or the resource itself is superabundant, open access may be inevitable, maximally efficient, or both (see Coase 1960, p. 39; Libecap 1989, pp. 13–14).

Stated as a rule (to be further elucidated in chapter 7): that property regime is best which, in the circumstances, would achieve exogenously set societal goals at the lowest total cost, where total cost is the sum of compliance, administrative, and residual pollution or consumption costs. Stating a rule is one thing, however; implementing it is another. As Gary Libecap (1989, p. 5) points out, society will not always, and may never, select the "best" property regime for conserving environmental goods: "examination of the preferences of individual bargaining parties and consideration of the details of the political bargaining underlying property rights institutions are necessary for understanding why particular property rights institutions are developed and maintained, despite imaginable alternatives that would appear to be more rational." This has obvious public choice implications that are explored in chapters 5 and 8 as they relate, respectively, to "free market environmentalism" and the "takings" problem.

Natural resources in most (if not all) countries historically have been subject to multiple and mixed property regimes. Some environmental goods, such as land, have been protected primarily (though not exclusively, and not at all in most socialist economies) by private (individual and common) property rights. Many other environmental goods, such as the atmosphere, have for various reasons never been allotted to private owners. Thus, societies have relied on both of Hardin's proffered solutions – privatization and regulation – to avert the tragedy of open access. As already noted, most property regimes governing access to and use of natural resources are admixtures of individual private ownership, common property management, and state ownership and management, including regulation. These actually existing systems of property rights on environmental goods hardly resemble the idealized typology presented earlier in this chapter.

One purpose of this book is to explain, beyond facile public choice rhetoric about special interests seeking economic rents in political markets, why this is the case. To what extent, if at all, are mixed property/regulatory regimes economically and environmentally preferable to either private property/nonregulatory regimes or public property/regulatory regimes in many, if not most, circumstances? What leads societies to employ different property-based solutions to the tragedy of the commons in various circumstances? And what normative implications do their choices suggest for policy?

V   Structure of the book

The following four chapters describe the utility and limits of each of the four basic property-based approaches to environmental protection. Chapter 2 addresses the public property/regulatory approach, as represented by outright public ownership of resources and by command-and-control regulation. Chapters 3 and 4 discuss, respectively, the utility and limitations of mixed private and public property/regulatory approaches, as represented by transferable pollution right programs and conservation easements. Chapter 5 deals with the private property/ nonregulatory approach, promoted by self-styled "free market environmentalists." And chapter 6 assesses common property/regulatory systems, as discussed in the work of Elinor Ostrom (1990), Daniel Bromley (1992), and others.

Each approach, I will show, has advantages and disadvantages, which make it suitable – preferable, even – for some circumstances but not others. In other words, no single property regime is preferable to all others across all economic, institutional, technological, and ecological contexts. This finding should not surprise us. It would be far more surprising if we discovered that the opposite were true: that a single property regime constituted the universal, first-best choice for avoiding the tragedy of open access, regardless of the wide variety of circumstances in this decidedly second-best world.

Based on the analyses in chapters 2 through 6, chapter 7 sets out a rudimentary model for property regime choice, based primarily on the relative costs of exclusion and coordination. Those costs are determined not just by characteristics of the resource itself but also by its ecological, technological, institutional, and cultural setting. Because of the almost infinite variety and complexity of settings, however, the model possesses, at best, very limited prescriptive or predictive utility. As J. H. Dales (1968, p. 77) notes, every approach to environmental protection (or averting the tragedy of open access) is "in the nature of a social experiment."

Chapter 8, finally, addresses an ancillary but nonetheless important aspect of the complex relation between pollution and property: the "taking" problem. "Taking" issues tend to arise, in the context of efforts to protect the environment, when incompatible property regimes collide. When that happens, property, which is a necessary institution for effective environmental protection, may become, paradoxically, an impediment to it.

2 Public property/regulatory solutions to the tragedy of open access

This chapter assesses the utility and limitations of public property-based approaches to avoiding the tragedy of open access. There are, generally speaking, two distinct methods of imposing public property rights on environmental goods. One is the explicit assertion of public/state ownership. The other is public regulation, which constitutes an implicit assertion of public property rights sufficient to accomplish the regulation's purpose. The first section of the chapter deals with outright public ownership. The second section addresses regulation as a public property-based approach to environmental protection. The chapter will conclude with a preliminary assessment of some of the problems arising from public ownership of environmental goods, which prompt efforts at partial or complete privatization.

I   Public ownership of environmental goods

In the western world we are accustomed to believing that private ownership of resources is not just efficient but the norm. The first belief – that private ownership is efficient – is correct often enough, but the second belief is dubious. Even today in the United States, where the concept of private ownership is as well entrenched as anywhere, the federal government is by far the country's largest landowner. The United States government owns 33 percent of all lands in the fifty states. Adding the acreage owned by state and local governments, the total amount of publicly owned lands in the United States rises to 42 percent (National Research Council 1992). That is a comparatively high percentage of public landownership for a noncommunist country. In the United Kingdom, by contrast, there is very little publicly owned land. The ten National Parks and other specially designated areas that comprise 20 percent of the UK's total land area are mostly superimposed on privately owned lands (Department of the Environment 1992, p. 57).[1] The percentage of public landownership

---

[1] In effect, the UK National Parks constitute a form of mixed property, with the state and the private titleholder both exercising significant property rights in the resources. Chapters 3

in other (noncommunist) countries typically falls somewhere between the relative extremes of the US and UK.[2] In postcommunist Poland, for example, the percentage of land under public ownership and protection is 29 percent (State Inspectorate for Environmental Protection 1998). In Scotland, the state holds 12 percent of the land as public property (Callander 1998, p. 96).

Public/state ownership of water resources is even more common. Throughout the world, private rights in water resources are distinctly limited. In the United States, individuals can own nonnavigable water bodies such as small ponds, and they can own ground water (though only after extraction).[3] They cannot, however, own waters flowing in navigable water bodies; at most, they can possess limited use rights (*usus* and *usus fructus*). Most rights in water are public/state property, managed by the federal and state governments.

The federal government possesses a "navigation servitude" in the waters of the United States, under the Commerce Clause of the Constitution.[4] This servitude empowers Congress to regulate use of rivers and lakes, including the disposal of effluents, so that waterways remain navigable for purposes of commerce. A servitude is, of course, a well-recognized property right,[5] which arises when one owner's property is made to serve the interest of another's property.[6] But the term "servitude" may understate the federal government's interest in navigable waters. The Supreme Court has stated that the waters of the United States are, for purposes of navigation, the "public property of the nation."[7]

For purposes other than navigation, the states have primary authority over navigable waters within their boundaries. Each state holds as public property, in trust for its citizens, title to the beds and banks of navigable water bodies (except in a few cases where an Indian tribe or the federal government owns the beds and banks). Ownership of the beds and banks gives the state substantial control over the water itself. The state's property

---

and 4, respectively, address the utility and limitations of mixed property/regulatory regimes.

[2] The reason for excluding communist countries should be obvious: in those countries, all land and other resources are owned, at least nominally, by the state.

[3] Prior to extraction, ground waters are open-access resources, reflecting the high costs of imposing any property regime on them, while they are hidden beneath the ground (see Dasgupta 1982, p. 15).

[4] See *Gibbon v. Ogden*, 22 US 1 (1824); *United States v. Chicago, Milwaukee, St. Paul & Pacific Railroad Co.*, 312 US 592 (1941).

[5] See *Boone v. United States*, 944 F. 2d 1489, 1495 n. 9 (9th Cir. 1991), noting, in a case concerning federal navigational servitude, that "[t]he label, 'servitude,' implies a property interest."

[6] On servitudes, see American Law Institute (2001), pp. 259–337.

[7] *Gilman v. Philadelphia*, 70 US 713, 725 (1865).

interest is special in that it is inalienable: it cannot be abandoned or fully privatized.[8] Moreover, the state can enforce its rights against riparian "owners," who attempt to use the water inconsistently with the public interest. For example, in 1908 the US Supreme Court ruled that the State of New Jersey could prevent a company from diverting and transporting New Jersey water for sale in New York.[9]

Similarly in the United Kingdom, navigable water bodies are public property.[10] As one Scottish treatise writer (Bell 1899, p. 289) put it,

[m]any things by law excepted from the ordinary rules of appropriation are reserved for the use of the public. These are called *Res Publicæ* in the books of the Roman law. Under this class are – Seas and Shores; Rivers and Harbours; Roads; Fairs and Markets. These are all necessary for public use and intercourse, and as such are vested in the Crown in trust for the subject.

The predominance of public property rights in the UK's navigable waterways is well illustrated by the late eighteenth-century case of *Grant* v. *Duke of Gordon*.[11] Alex, Duke of Gordon held exclusive rights under a 1684 charter from the king to fish the River Spey. The duke constructed a fishing cruive, which impeded navigation. Sir James Grant and others sued the duke to remove the obstacle so that they might float timber downstream. The court ruled in favor of the plaintiffs, holding that the public's rights in navigability outweighed the duke's private interest in the fishery.

Governments also regularly impose public/state property rights in many resources found on or under land and in water. Fish and wildlife, for example, are for most purposes considered public property, although they may be available for privatization by appropriation, for example by capture.[12] Similarly, valuable mineral deposits underlying publicly owned lands are often deemed public property.[13] Even when governments

---

[8] See *Illinois Central Railroad* v. *Illinois*, 146 US 387 (1892). This is not to say that the state cannot grant *any* private rights in waters, but any such grants must be in the public interest, and if they ever come into conflict with the public interest, the public interest must prevail over the private rights. See *National Audubon Society* v. *Superior Court of Alpine County*, 33 Cal. 3d 419 (1983); *Hudson County Water Co.* v. *McCarter*, 209 US 349 (1908).

[9] ibid.

[10] Navigable lakes in the UK may, however, be privately owned if they lie wholly within the land of one proprietor (Bell 1899, p. 293).

[11] *Grant* v. *Duke of Gordon*, III Paton 679 (1776).

[12] The property rights structure of wildlife law will be discussed further in the next section of this chapter.

[13] In the UK, all gold and most silver mines are owned, but subject to alienation, by the crown (Bell 1899, p. 299). In the US, however, the federal government has only occasionally and inconsistently asserted public property rights in valuable mineral deposits underlying public lands.

privatize public lands, they sometimes reserve public rights in the mineral estate.[14] This enables them to set the ground rules for private acquisition of mineral wealth, and to capture some of that wealth for the public coffers when minerals are extracted.

These examples suggest that public/state ownership of natural resources is not unusual or aberrational but routine. Throughout history – at least since the Institutes of Justinian – public ownership has been normal, not exceptional, for many resources. Under Roman law, not even the emperor himself could claim private ownership of the air or water, for they were public resources to be managed for the benefit of all the empire's citizens.

Over the centuries, public ownership has expanded beyond air and water resources to protect environmental goods that were not considered *res publicoe* under Roman law. In medieval Europe, for example, wildlife populations threatened by overhunting were conserved by the imposition of royal ownership and control.[15] The extension of crown ownership over bison populations in sixteenth-century Poland, for example, partly explains why Poland is the only country left in Europe with free-roaming herds of bison (see Cole 1998, p. 25). Even Adam Smith ([1776] 1994, p. 887), the father of classical economics, supported public ownership of certain lands, such as parks and gardens, where the aim was not to produce revenue but to enjoy nature: "Lands, for the purposes of pleasure and magnificence, parks, gardens, public walks, &c., possessions which are every where considered as causes of expence, not as sources of revenue, seem to be the only lands which, in a great and civilized monarchy, ought to belong to the crown." From an historical perspective, the idea of public rights in natural resources is hardly novel.

II   Prima facie justifications of public/state ownership

Making the case for public/state ownership

Despite the prevalence throughout history of publicly owned property in environmental goods (at least in the western world), Richard Posner (1992, p. 84) summarily dismisses public ownership of natural resources:

---

[14] Prior to the mid-nineteenth century, the US government regularly reserved mineral rights when it privatized public lands (see Laitos 1985, p. 258).

[15] Crown ownership does not fit neatly into the conventional typology of property regimes outlined in chapter 1. On the one hand, crown ownership approximates public ownership in that, throughout much of history, the crown was the state for all practical purposes. On the other hand, the crown itself was the private property of individuals or families, especially in monarchies approaching absolutism, making crown ownership quite similar to private ownership. This illustrates, once again, the general weakness of the conventional typology of property regimes.

"there is no economic case for government ownership." Assuming, momentarily, that Judge Posner's assessment is correct, we are left to explain why a completely unjustifiable institution has prevailed for so long. It seems unlikely that a patently inefficient institution would survive for thousands of years (see Alchian 1950). Economic historians (such as North and Thomas 1973) have noted, however, that inefficient institutions can endure for long periods of time, if they are supported by sufficiently powerful vested interests. Some economists and political scientists explain the persistence of inefficient natural resource ownership and management regimes by the interest group theory of politics: environmental groups and the extractive industries both derive "rents" (excess profits) from public ownership of natural resources, and so have a stake in continuing public ownership (see, for example, Buchanan and Tullock 1975; Yandle 1993).[16] No doubt such economic explanations are legitimate; and several of them will be addressed more extensively in chapter 5. But is it really the case, as Judge Posner argues, that there is no positive economic justification for public ownership of natural resources?

In an effort to rebut Judge Posner's presumption that public property in natural resources is generically unjustifiable, this section offers prima facie justifications for public ownership of *some* natural resources in *some* circumstances. The justifications are prima facie in that they are intended not to prove that public property is preferable to alternative property regimes for environmental protection in any particular case, but only to convince the reader that public ownership should be treated seriously as a plausible alternative. Indeed, for some purposes and in some circumstances – depending particularly on economies of scale and transaction costs – it may actually be preferable to alternative property regimes. But arguments about the occasional preferability of public ownership will be postponed until chapters 4 and 7.

It would be simple enough to refute Judge Posner's claim – that there is no economic justification for public property in natural resources – by referring to an ethical principle Judge Posner himself surely embraces: one rightfully owns what one buys from a prior rightful owner. Most of the public lands in the United States were *purchased* by the federal government from other sovereigns, including France (the Louisiana purchase), Mexico (the Gadsden purchase), Russia (Seward's "Folly"),

---

[16] Similar arguments are made about the prevalence of command-and-control environmental regulations, which, like outright public ownership, constitute public property/regulatory regimes for environmental protection. Robert Stavins (1998, pp. 71–2), for instance, has written that "command-and-control instruments have predominated because all of the main parties involved had reasons to favor them: affected firms, environmental advocacy groups, organized labor, legislators, and bureaucrats."

and Native American tribes.[17] What more justification does the federal government require for its ownership beyond the fact that it bought these lands from previous "owners"?

Judge Posner plainly does not mean, however, to question whether the federal government was justified in acquiring the resources in the first instance; rather, his primary concern is the maintenance of public/state ownership and control over time. He implies that a government committed to efficient resource management would have quickly and completely privatized the lands and other resources it acquired. Throughout most of the nineteenth century the US government did just that. Later in that century, however, it decided to reserve some public lands from privatization, in order to create national parks and forests.[18] If Judge Posner is right in claiming that continued public ownership is unjustified, then the federal government must either be driven by considerations other than efficiency or believe (implicitly) that Judge Posner is mistaken about the economic justifiability of public land ownership.

It is obviously true that governments are not exclusively concerned with efficiency (and it is far from clear that they should be). There is also reason to believe, however, that public ownership of natural resources may *sometimes* be preferable to private ownership for reasons that have to do with economies of scale and the comparative transaction costs of public versus private ownership and management. Public ownership of some resources, in certain circumstances, makes prima facie economic as well as ecological sense.

Scale economies and transaction costs in wildlife management

Consider ownership of wildlife resources. In some countries, such as the United Kingdom, wildlife are mostly privately owned.[19] In others, such as the United States, wildlife are mostly public property (prior to

---

[17] Many public lands were, of course, acquired from Native American tribes by conquest rather than purchase, but the vast majority were purchased (see Cohen 1970 [1944], p. 269). Those purchases were often backed, however, by the explicit or implicit threat of force.

[18] On the history of US public lands law and policy, see, for example, Coggins et al. 1993, ch. 2.

[19] Wildlife in the UK have not always been subject to private/individual ownership, however. During the eighteenth century, game animals were treated, to all intents and purposes, as the common property of the aristocracy; commoners were excluded from taking game animals, even if they suffered losses from predation of their lands and crops (see Kirby 1933). Communal rights in wildlife took precedence over private rights in land, as landowners were required to supply habitat and vegetation for wildlife. Indeed, "[w]here there was insufficient forage for both game and stock, the grantee of the rights for domestic forage had to reduce his herd" (Lund 1975, p. 68).

legal capture by some individual).[20] What accounts for this fundamental discrepancy in wildlife law between the UK and the US? Is it simply the case that the UK has it right and the US has it wrong, as Judge Posner's cursory assessment would lead us to believe? Is the British system of wildlife management manifestly superior, economically or ecologically, to the American system?

According to the economist Dean Lueck (1989) *both* systems may be appropriate – that is to say, efficient – given the differing ecological and institutional circumstances that obtain in the US and UK. Those circumstantial differences affect the costs of contracting, among other transaction costs, which can determine whether public or private ownership is preferable. Contracting costs for private landowners tend to increase with the size of the territory needed to preserve wildlife stocks (Lueck 1989, pp. 302, 308–9). As these contracting costs increase, it becomes more likely that wildlife stocks will be publicly, rather than privately, controlled. Lueck observes that, "[i]n the United States, government agencies with large geographical jurisdiction tend to control wildlife with large territories but not those with small territories; private parties or local governments tend to control wildlife requiring smaller territories."

This may explain state control of wildlife in the United States, but what about in the UK, where wildlife are subject to private ownership? The difference in the UK's ownership regime for wildlife reflects differing ecological and institutional circumstances. By the nineteenth century, when property rights in wildlife were first being established in the US,[21] most British wildlife species requiring large territories were already extinct (Lueck 1989, p. 315). Existing British wildlife – with the exception of a few species like the red deer – did not require particularly large tracts of land. This reduced the contracting costs for private owners, which were lower to begin with because individual landholdings in England, Scotland, and Wales were larger and more concentrated than in the US.

---

[20] Wildlife are, in fact, subject to multiple property regimes (see Lueck 1989), but public/state property rights predominate. Whether the government "owns" wildlife remains unclear, however. The Supreme Court has contradicted itself on this point. In the 1948 case of *Toomer* v. *Witsell*, 334 US 385, 399 (1948), the Supreme Court observed that "fish and game are the common property of all citizens of the governmental unit and that the government, as a sort of trustee, exercises this 'ownership' for the benefit of its citizens." Thirty years later, the Supreme Court declared that "[i]t is pure fantasy to talk of 'owning' wild fish, birds, or animals. Neither the States nor the Federal Government... has title to these creatures until they are reduced to possession by skillful capture." *Douglas* v. *Seacoast Products, Inc.*, 431 US 265, 284 (1977). The public/state can, of course, possess substantial property rights in wildlife without being "owners," just as individuals can possess property rights in things they do not "own." A mortgagee, for example, holds substantial property rights in a mortgaged house, but is not its "owner."

[21] See *Geer* v. *Connecticut*, 161 US 519, 529 (1896), holding that the states own, control, and regulate wildlife in "trust for the benefit of the people."

In the middle of the nineteenth century nearly one-tenth of all land in England, Scotland, and Wales – roughly 7.5 million acres – was owned by thirty-five individuals, each of whom possessed estates of 100,000 or more acres (Sutherland 1988, p. 123). Just 400 families owned 20–25 percent of the land. As of 1873, more than half of all the land in England and Wales was owned by 2,250 individuals, each of whom controlled estates ranging from 1,000 to 7,300 acres (Heaton 1948, p. 418). In the United States, the distribution of landownership was far broader, and the average private landholding was much smaller. In 1899, the size of the average farm in the US was 134 acres – one-third the size of the average farm in the UK (Lueck 1989, p. 312). In all likelihood, the transaction – primarily contracting – costs of amassing sufficient wildlife habitat in the US would have been much higher than in the UK.

Lueck's arguments about the differences between wildlife management in the United States and Great Britain provide a prima facie justification for public ownership of wildlife in at least some ecological and institutional circumstances. There are, however, circumstances in which contracting costs to acquire large territories for successful wildlife management may not be too high. In the United States, a consortium of private landowners – the North Maine Woods – managed to amass a land area of 2.8 million acres, to be managed primarily for commercial timber (Anderson and Leal 1991, p. 69). Their investments were financially motivated. The individual landowners were willing to bear the contracting and other transaction costs in view of the expected financial returns from timber sales. It remains to be seen whether individuals would willingly bear substantial contracting costs to amass sizeable contiguous land masses for species preservation or other ecological purposes, where the expected financial returns on investment are minimal or nonexistent. In many cases, species preservation would not constitute a lucrative investment opportunity on any conventional time horizon and discount rate.[22] This is a large part of what makes species preservation – or, more generally, biodiversity – a public good: a good that must be provided by the public because it will be undersupplied by private markets, given existing technologies and conventional time horizons and discount rates.[23]

Still, private landowners might be willing to bear the costs of species preservation *if* species preservation were consistent with other land uses, such as timber harvesting or mining, that *do* offer sufficient profit

---

[22] The time horizon is the period over which individuals seek to recoup investments. The discount rate is the subjective rate of interest at which decision-makers determine the present dollar value of future costs and benefits. For more on discount rates and time horizons, see chapter 5.

[23] On the theory of public goods, see generally Oakland (1987).

potential. Unfortunately, species preservation is often incompatible with such financially lucrative activities. Logging and mining, for example, have been found to interfere with grizzly bear breeding and denning activities, which must be facilitated in critical habitat to ensure species survival.[24]

Not all private landowners are driven to maximize profits, of course. Nonprofit groups purchase tracts of land specifically for preservation purposes. But the largest of these groups – including the Nature Conservancy in the US and the National Trust in the UK – have insufficient resources to purchase the vast reaches of contiguous lands needed to ensure the survival of far-roaming mammals, such as grizzly bears, grey wolves, and bighorn sheep. The US Fish and Wildlife Service (66 Fed. Reg. 8650) has ruled that the "critical habitat" of the endangered Peninsular bighorn sheep encompasses nearly 845,000 acres of contiguous land in southern California. The greatest single parcel of Nature Conservancy property, however, comprises just 56,000 acres. For a private owner this is a vast territory,[25] but it is only one-fifteenth the size of the designated critical habitat for the Peninuslar bighorn sheep, and nearly one-fortieth the size of Yellowstone National Park. The fifty-three National Parks of the United States together comprise more than 149 million acres of land. The largest – Wrangell-St. Elias in Alaska – contains more than 7.66 million acres.

It is worth noting, in this context, that the Nature Conservancy frequently conveys lands it acquires to state or federal governments.[26] In other words, it voluntarily converts private lands to public ownership. Were private ownership always and everywhere preferable to public ownership, as Judge Posner (1992, p. 84) claims, the Nature Conservancy's practice would be irrational, violating an important precept of neoclassical economic theory. The governors of the Nature Conservancy evidently feel, however, that public ownership and management is at least sometimes preferable to its own private ownership and management, given the Conservancy's budget constraints as well as tax and other institutionally created incentives.

[24] See *Cabinet Mountains Wilderness* v. *Peterson*, 685 F. 2d 678 (DC Cir. 1982).

[25] According to the Natural Resources Inventory (2000, table 15), the national median diameter of wildlife habitat on rural, privately owned croplands, pasturelands, and forest lands is less than 800 feet. The estimated median diameter of wildlife habitat on private rangelands, however, exceeds 1,000 feet.

[26] For example, on Oct. 20, 1969 the Nature Conservancy purchased in fee simple part of Wassaw Island in the State of Georgia for $1 million. The very same day, it conveyed all its interest in the Island to the United States for $1. See *McMaster* v. *United States*, 177 F. 3d 936, 938 (8th Cir. 1999), *cert. denied* 528 US 1118 (2000). According to its Annual Report for Fiscal Year 2000, the Nature Conservancy sold or donated nearly $100,000 worth of land to "government and other conservation agencies."

Judge Posner (1992, p. 84) argues that the issues of scale and ownership should be disentangled because a government can, instead of asserting public/state ownership, subsidize private ownership. Rather than claiming ownership of grizzly bear habitat, for example, the government might provide private landowners with the resources needed to acquire and manage the habitat themselves. However, Judge Posner offers no positive economic argument as to why public subsidization of private ownership would necessarily be preferable to state ownership; he merely asserts that government management of publicly owned resources "has been perverse" (Posner 1992, p. 84). He does not assess the comparative transaction costs of a subsidy regime, including the cost of determining the appropriate level of subsidization and the cost of government monitoring to ensure that subsidy recipients manage the resource in accordance with the purpose(s) for which the subsidies are provided. This is not to argue that public ownership is necessarily preferable to publicly subsidized private ownership, but only to point out that Posner's analysis is incomplete. Surely we would not accept that government should subsidize private armed forces, instead of providing public armies and navies, merely because it can; nor would we expect, let alone desire, the state to subsidize private courts of justice to supplant the public judicial system. These are public responsibilities that the state itself typically carries out, notwithstanding the fact that subsidization is a technically feasible alternative. Whether protection of certain environmental amenities is also within the provenance of the state is debatable. As a matter of fact, however, no modern state chooses either to defend itself, allocate justice, or protect its environment exclusively, or even primarily, through public subsidization of private firms.

Aside from Judge Posner's rather casual treatment, public ownership of natural resources has been subject to several more substantial critiques, which challenge the prima facie justifications offered above. Those critiques will be outlined in the last section of this chapter, and reviewed in greater detail in chapter 5.

III   State regulation as an implied imposition of public property rights

It is a fundamental thesis of this book that environmental regulations constitute tacit assertions of public/state property rights in natural resources. The nature and extent of the public rights imposed depends on the nature and breadth of the regulation in question. In many cases, environmental regulations assert only limited public property rights in some resource. Consider, for instance, a regulation requiring transporters of hazardous wastes to notify federal, state, and local officials if a spill occurs in transit (see CFR §171.15). Such a regulation obviously does not assert or imply a government claim of outright ownership but a far more limited public interest in land and water resources potentially affected by hazardous waste spills. In effect, the regulation creates a mixed property regime, comprised of both public and private property rights in the resources potentially affected by toxic releases. Such mixed property regimes will be addressed in chapters 3 and 4. The present concern is with regulations that are so broad as to constitute implicit assertions of public resource ownership.

Early efforts to assert public rights in environmental goods by regulation

For centuries, governments have sought to protect public health and natural resources not only by explicitly asserting public ownership but also by regulating private resource uses that endanger public health and the environment. In the fourteenth century, Polish Law (*Statut Kazimierza Wielkiego*) restricted timber harvesting in order to preserve forest resources, which may explain why postcommunist Poland is home to the last remnants of the primeval European forest (Cole 1998, pp. 12, 25). Throughout medieval Europe, cities enacted pollution control ordinances to protect public health. In Italy, cities regulated waste disposal because "[t]he capacity of any private sector to handle the problem of waste removal was quickly exceeded" (Zupko and Laures 1996, p. 102). French cities, meanwhile, forced environmentally harmful activities to relocate beyond city limits (see Le Goff 1997, p. 40). The City of London went so far as to impose the death penalty for violators of its 1306 ban on the burning of sea-coal (see Brimblecombe 1987, p. 9; Nef 1977).

Regulatory controls proliferated during the nineteenth century, in the wake of the industrial revolution, which led to massive increases in the amounts and types of environmental pollutants. In 1843, a select British parliamentary committee recommended the adoption of legislation to control smoke emissions from furnaces and steam engines. The Railway Clauses Consolidated Act of 1845 required engines to consume their own smoke. Two years later, the Town Improvement Clauses Act imposed limits on factory smoke emissions. The 1875 Public Health Act contained smoke abatement provisions that were still in force in the 1980s (National Society for Clean Air 1983). The Act (as amended in 1891) required industrial and commercial fires and furnaces to consume, as far as practicable, all the smoke they produced (Brimblecombe 1987, p. 163).[27]

Similarly, in the United States, long before the federal government began to regulate air pollution in the 1970s, state and local governments were treating the atmosphere as a publicly owned, rather than open-access, resource. Large cities, which bore the brunt of air pollution problems, took the lead. Chicago enacted one of the country's first smoke prevention ordinances in 1880.[28] Section 1650 of that ordinance provided: "The emission of dense smoke from the smoke-stack of any boat or locomotive, or from any chimney, anywhere within the city, shall be deemed and is hereby declared to be a public nuisance." Residential chimneys were exempted from the provision, which also did not specify a penalty for noncompliance. Another section of the Chicago ordinance (§ 1651) did, however, specify a penalty, in declaring that:

The owner or owners of any boat or locomotive engine, and the person or persons employed, as engineer or otherwise, in the working of the engine or engines in said boat, or in operating such locomotive, and the proprietor, lessee and occupant of any building, who shall permit or allow dense smoke to issue or be emitted from the smoke-stack of any such boat or locomotive, or the chimney of any building, within the corporate limits, shall be deemed and held guilty of creating a nuisance, and shall, for every such offence, be fined in a sum not less than five dollars nor more than fifty dollars.

According to Jan Laitos (1975, p. 434), there were three categories of air pollution regulation in the late nineteenth century. The Chicago ordinance was of the first type, which included regulations treating smoke as a public nuisance and imposing fines (usually not exceeding $100) on smoke emitters.

A second type of ordinance did not merely declare the escape of smoke illegal; these more sophisticated laws placed an affirmative duty on polluters, requiring them not only to remove all ashes and cinders from their shops, but also to construct their furnaces "so as to consume smoke arising therefrom." The third type of ordinance struck at the apparent cause of the city's smoke problem – extensive use of soft, high sulphur, bituminous coal. These ordinances flatly prohibited the importation, sale, use or consumption of any coal containing more than 12 percent ash or 2 percent sulphur.[29]

By the turn of the twentieth century "many smoke nuisance ordinances specified the density and opacity limits of smoke emissions by making

---

[27] England also enacted significant water pollution legislation in the mid-nineteenth century. See generally Luckin (1986).
[28] Chicago, Ill., Gen. Ordinances, §§ 1650, 1651 (1880).
[29] Citations omitted.

reference to the Ringlemann Scale," which "showed six blocks of graduated grey going from near white to near black; most laws specified that any shade of smoke darker than a third block on the scale was a violation" (Laitos 1975, p. 435 n. 28).[30] Any doubts about the constitutionality of these smoke ordinances were settled in 1916, when the US Supreme Court declared: "So far as the Federal Constitution is concerned, we have no doubt the state may by itself, or through authorized municipalities, declare the emission of dense smoke ... a nuisance ... and that the harshness of such legislation, or its effect on business interests, short of a merely arbitrary enactment, are not valid constitutional objections."[31]

Early regulatory efforts in Great Britain and the United States were predicated on the assertion or assumption that smoke pollution constituted a public nuisance, that is, an interference with public "rights." In imposing private duties, Chicago's City Council and Britain's Parliament were implicitly asserting public rights in the environmental amenities – from air quality to fruit trees – their ordinances were designed to protect.

Public nuisance regulation as an assertion of public property rights

The concept of *pollution regulation as an assertion of public property in environmental goods* becomes intuitive once one understands the basis of pollution control in the common-law public nuisance action. At common law, a public nuisance is an unreasonable interference with a right common to the general public (Restatement (2d) Torts § 821B). Nuisance suits, as Coase (1960) famously has described them, allocate previously uncertain rights and duties between property disputants. Calabresi and Melamed (1972) explain further how judicial determinations of liability and remedy affect the allocation of property rights between disputants. If the court rules that Smith is liable for nuisance for contaminating Jones's land and enjoins Smith's activity, it in effect allocates to Jones the property right to be free of Smith's contamination, *and* allocates to Smith the corresponding duty not to interfere with Jones's right to be free of contamination. If, however, the court rules that Smith is not liable, then Smith has the right to continue his activity unabated, and Jones has a corresponding duty to suffer any negative externalities. Finally, if the court holds Smith liable, but requires only compensation (the court does not enjoin the nuisance), the allocation of rights is a bit more complicated. By holding Smith liable, the court recognizes that Jones possesses the

---

[30] Laitos (1975, p. 435 n. 28) goes on to note that the Ringlemann method "measured only density, not volume. Nor could it be used at night, during times of rain, humidity, or high winds."

[31] *Northwestern Laundry* v. *City of Des Moines*, 239 US 486, 491–2 (1916).

property right; by requiring only compensation, however, the court in effect allows Smith to purchase the right from Jones at a court-ordered price. In the case of a *public nuisance*, the public stands in the position of Jones. So, if the court holds Smith liable for a public nuisance, the court is recognizing the public's right to be free of his pollution.

This distinctly Coasean approach to nuisances as bilateral conflicts over property rights is well illustrated by a California appeals court ruling, in which the court forthrightly viewed public regulation of polluting activities as an assertion of public property rights in environmental goods: "Here it appears the Oil Companies are asking us to determine they have a fundamental vested right to release gasoline vapors while dispensing fuel to their customers. How are we to answer the public, on the other hand, who assert a fundamental vested right to breathe clean air? If either exists, it must be the latter."[32]

In the regulatory system it is a city council, state legislature, or administrative agency, rather than a court, allocating the rights and duties as between disputing property claimants. Most local and state pollution control regulations explicitly rest, however, on the foundation of common-law public nuisance. Whether legislative and regulatory bodies are better suited than common-law courts to allocate public rights and private duties with respect to environmental goods is debatable but immaterial at present. The point, for now, is that conceiving of government regulation as a mechanism for assigning and enforcing public property rights is neither novel nor radical. It has a traditional basis in the common law of public nuisance.

One English court, in particular, expressly embraced the notion of pollution as a public nuisance precisely because it interferes with public property rights. In *Attorney General* v. *Sheffield Gas Consumers Co.*,[33] Lord Justice Turner wrote that "[i]t is on the ground of injury to property that the jurisdiction of this court must rest; and taking it to rest upon that ground, the only distinction which seems to me to exist between cases of public nuisance and private nuisance is this – that in cases of private nuisance the injury is to individual property, and in cases of public nuisance the injury is to the property of mankind."

English common lawyers even developed a special cause of action, called *purpresture*, for nuisances involving interferences with public rights of access and enjoyment. The "crime" of purpresture has been expressly

---

[32] *Mobil Oil Corp.* v. *Superior Court of San Diego City*, 69 Cal. App. 3d 293, 305 (1976).

[33] 3 De G.M. & G. 304, 320 (1853). The case involved an alleged public nuisance resulting from the defendant's activity of tearing up streets to lay down gas pipes. The court ruled, however, that the harm stemming from the defendant's activity did not give rise to a public nuisance.

recognized by American courts as well.[34] According to Justice Story ([1884] 1988, § 921), purpresture is "an encroachment upon the king, either upon part of his demesne lands, or upon rights and easements held by the crown of the public, such as open highways, public rivers, forts, streets, etc., and other public accommodations . . . Where one takes that to himself, which ought to be common to many." In *The People* v. *Vanderbilt*,[35] for example, the New York Court of Appeals ruled that the unauthorized erection of a private pier in New York Harbor unlawfully interfered with public rights of navigation and therefore constituted a purpresture.

The salient difference between the ordinary public nuisance action and the special action in purpresture concerns the need to prove damages. Purpresture is more like trespass than nuisance in that damages need not be proved but are presumed from the interference with existing property rights. To succeed with a public nuisance claim, by contrast, "damage to the public right of navigation or other public right must be shown to exist" (Kerr 1927, p. 395). Both causes of action, however, vindicate public "rights." Historically, purpresture actions have protected only well-established public rights in lands, such as easements and rights of way. The courts have not ruled that air polluters, for example, can be sued for purpresture of the publicly owned atmosphere. In theory, however, there is no reason why the purpresture action could not be extended to cases of environmental pollution.

Whether or not public rights in environmental goods can be vindicated through purpresture actions, there is no doubt that the ordinary public nuisance action serves the purpose. The US Supreme Court has declared, for example, that air pollution is "one of the most notorious types of public nuisance in modern experience."[36] Innumerable public nuisance cases hold polluters liable for the harm they cause to the public and resources in which the public has an interest. Most importantly for the present purposes, courts in many cases refer either expressly or by implication to the existence of public property rights in environmental goods. A Michigan appellate court ruled in 1988, for example, that "there exists no right to pollute. Since no such right exists, a polluter has not been deprived of any protected property or liberty interest when the state halts the pollution."[37] In that case, the court upheld a state order requiring an electric power

---

[34] See, e.g., *Union Trust Co.* v. *Atchison T. & S.F.R. Co.*, 64 F. 724, 740 (ND Ill. 1894). A cursory LEXIS search turned up more than 500 references to purpresture in American court decisions, including more than a dozen by the Supreme Court of the United States.

[35] 28 NY 396 (1863).

[36] *Washington et al.* v. *General Motors et al.*, 46 US 109, 114 (1972).

[37] *Detroit Edison Co.* v. *Michigan Air Pollution Control Commission*, 167 Mich. App. 651 (1988).

company to bring its air pollution emissions into compliance with the state's 1965 Air Pollution Act (as amended).[38] Both the trial court and the appellate court agreed that state's legislative intent in that Act was clear: "'the Act read as a whole evince[s] a clear legislative intent to give the Commission broad authority to carry out its task of protecting the quality of Michigan's air.'"[39] The phrase "Michigan's air" would seem to imply a state assertion of public property rights in the atmosphere above the State of Michigan. It is possible that the court did not specifically intend that implication; it might, instead, have intended to make a mere jurisdictional point. However, the implication of state property rights is also consistent with the appellate court's determination that "there exists no right to pollute." In the absence of either public, private, or common rights in the atmosphere, the air would necessarily be open-access – free for use by anyone. In that circumstance, the state has no right to exclude the polluter from the nonproperty atmosphere.[40] It is only the implicit assertion of property rights within the state's Air Pollution Act (or pursuant to earlier common-law public nuisance doctrine), that provides a basis for the state to prevent the polluter's misuse of "Michigan's air."

Michigan is not the only state whose courts have explicitly or implicitly recognized public property rights in environmental goods such as clean air. In *City of Chicago* v. *Commonwealth Edison Co.*,[41] the Illinois Court of Appeals absolved the defendant of public nuisance but in language that expressly referenced a public right to clean air as the touchstone of the public nuisance claim: "As a result of industrial expansion, the courts have utilized several factors in determining whether an industrial operation is an unreasonable interference with the *right to clean air*." A Georgia federal court used similar language to describe an earlier public nuisance ruling by a Georgia state court: "the court found that odors from a plant that processed animal material constituted a public nuisance because they affected a common right of all persons in the area, i.e., *the right to clean air*."[42] The State of Pennsylvania has even declared a public right to clean air and clean water in its state constitution.[43]

---

[38] MCL 336.11 et seq.; MSA 14.58(1) et seq. This Act was repealed and reenacted in substantially the same form in 1994, as part of the Natural Resources and Environmental Protection Act, §§ 13A.101 et seq.

[39] 167 Mich. App. at 659.

[40] In Hohfeldian terms, the polluter might be said to have a "liberty," "privilege," or "nonduty" with respect to the open-access atmosphere (see Hohfeld 1913 and 1917; Cole and Grossman, forthcoming a).

[41] 24 Ill. App. 3d 624, 632 (1974) (emphasis added).

[42] *Briggs & Stratton Corp.* v. *Concrete Sales & Servs.*, 29 F. Supp. 2d 1372, 1375 (MD Geo. 1998), citing *Atlanta Processing Co.* v. *Brown*, 227 Ga. 203 (1971) (emphasis added).

[43] Const. (Penn.), article 1, section 27: "The people have a right to clean air, pure water, and to the preservation of the natural, scenic, historic and esthetic values of the environment."

What are these rights and what is their relevance for public nuisance cases, in which conflicting property rights are central to the dispute, if they are not in the nature of property? If they *are* property, as I claim, a host of other interesting questions arises. When, if ever, is public/state ownership preferable to other property regimes for environmental protection? Assuming that public/state ownership is sometimes preferable, when is it better for the state to declare ownership on behalf of the public, as opposed to implicitly asserting public property rights via regulation? These questions will be addressed, if only tentatively, in chapter 7.

Modern environmental regulation

In the modern era environmental regulation has become ubiquitous. Since the "environmental decade" of the 1970s, governments throughout the world have sought to improve public health and conserve natural resources by regulating harmful private activities, including most industrial processes.[44] These regulations are premised on a conception of the welfare state, according to which government has an obligation to provide certain goods – in this instance, environmental goods – that markets are either unable to provide or fail to provide in sufficient quantities (see Pigou [1920] 1960). This conception of the welfare state is, however, subject to the proviso, emphasized by Coase (1960, 1964, 1988), that governments fail too. If government regulations generate more social costs than benefits, it would be better for society to tolerate the market failure. From a strictly economic point of view, the government should only regulate private economic activities for environmental protection where doing so would improve net social welfare. This normative principle is, however, beside the point of the present chapter, which is not to adjudge the efficiency of environmental regulation but to understand it as a property-based approach to averting the tragedy of open access.

At least two types of regulation qualify as unambiguous assertions of public property rights in environmental goods: outright bans on activities affecting public environmental goods and command-and-control regulations. An example of the former is the ban on the pesticide DDT in the United States in 1972. DDT was among the most common pesticides in use during the 1950s and 1960s. The government banned it as a direct consequence of Rachel Carson's (1962) research into the correlation between DDT use and the decline of songbird populations

Pennsylvania's public natural resources are the common property of all the people, including generations yet to come. As trustee of these resources, the Commonwealth shall conserve and maintain them for the benefit of all the people."

[44] On the emergence of environmental law in the 1970s, see, for example, Andrews (1999).

and contamination of aquatic ecosystems. In banning DDT the federal government imposed on users of DDT an enforceable duty to stop using it in the United States.[45] This enforceable duty necessarily implied corresponding enforceable public property rights in the resources affected by the pesticide.

As Wesley Newcomb Hohfeld (1913, 1917) explained, duties and rights are jural correlates, so that any time one identifies a duty, one should be able to identify a corresponding right, and vice versa. If some person has a duty to perform a certain activity (or to refrain from performing it), at least one other person must have a right to enforce the duty (see also Cole and Grossman forthcoming a). In the case of the DDT ban, the government imposed duties on manufacturers, sellers, and users of the pesticide, and reserved to itself, as agent of the public, the corresponding right to an environment free from DDT contamination. This characterization of the ban entails no necessary implications about the government's purpose in banning DDT. Even if it were motivated by the private agenda of some interest group, the property rights created by the ban, as correlates of the private duties imposed, belong to the state on behalf of the public at large.

In a sense, a product ban is the most extreme form of command-and-control regulation – the government tells regulated industries both what to do and how to do it. A far more common form of command-and-control, however, is the technology-based standard, which is a prevalent feature of air and water pollution control laws in the United States and elsewhere. With technology-based command-and-control, the government sets effluent standards based on what is achievable using the best pollution reduction technologies available at the time. It, in effect, forces regulated industries to install those technologies.[46] In so doing, the government tacitly asserts public property rights in the environmental resource(s) it is protecting. The regulation imposes explicit private duties on polluters that are enforceable by the public, in the same way that the ban on DDT use in the United States imposed a duty on the pesticide's manufacturers, sellers, and users, which the public had a right to enforce.

A prime example of technology-based command-and-control regulation, as an implicit assertion of public/state property rights in environmental amenities, is found in the US Clean Air Act of 1970. That statute

---

[45] It is interesting to note that the government only banned the *sale* of DDT within the United States. It did not ban its manufacture in the US for export and use in other countries.

[46] As a technical legal matter, regulated industries may meet technology-based standards in any way they like (see Driesen 1998, pp. 297–301). As a practical matter, however, regulated industries tend to install the technologies on which standards are based (see Stewart 1981, p. 1269).

requires (among other things) that regulated polluters meet emissions standards, which the Environmental Protection Agency sets on the basis of various technological standards. All major new stationary sources of air pollution emissions must meet emissions standards based on the "best available technology adequately demonstrated" (42 USC § 7411). In areas that have not yet attained national ambient air quality standards, those sources must attain stricter "least achievable emissons rates" (42 USC § 7501(3)). Even in "clean" air regions – areas that have attained national ambient air quality standards – major new stationary sources must comply with emissions standards based on the "best available control technology" (42 USC § 7475(a)(4)). Automobiles must also meet technology-based air pollution control standards. In some cases, they must meet deadlines for complying with technology that does not even exist at the time the regulations are adopted (42 USC § 7541).

In each of these cases, the Clean Air Act imposes on polluting firms industry-wide duties on their use of the atmosphere. If they fail to comply, they are subject to punishment not only by the federal and state governments but also by any individual or group, through so-called "citizen suits" (see 42 USC § 7604). The provision of citizen suits in the Clean Air Act underscores the statute's implicit creation of public rights in the atmosphere. Whether these technology-based command-and-control regulations constitute an efficient form of environmental protection is debatable.[47] The more important point for present purposes is that these regulations constitute an imposition of public/state property rights on the atmosphere.

IV   Problems of public/state property in environmental goods

Problems of explicit public ownership

Just because public/state ownership of natural resources is far more prevalent than most people assume, that does not necessarily mean it is environmentally or economically preferable to alternative property arrangements. Chapter 7 will present arguments that public/state ownership of some environmental goods *is* preferable in limited circumstances. Even in those cases, however, public/state ownership is not without problems, as we should expect in this second-best world. These problems are addressed in detail in chapter 5, where they are central to the private property/non-regulatory program of free-market environmentalism. It is enough, for present purposes, to foreshadow that later discussion.

---

[47] It is a question we will confront directly in the final section of this chapter and in chapter 4.

In large measure, the problems of public/state ownership boil down to the incentives of public resource managers, which all too often lead to the adoption of inefficient and environmentally harmful management policies. Unlike private property owners, the bureaucrats and politicians who manage publicly owned resources are not driven by the profit motive to maximize the discounted net economic value of the assets under their control. This is not a wholly bad thing for environmental protection, as market values rarely, if ever, reflect the total value of environmental amenities. However, the alternative incentive structure under which public resource managers operate does not necessarily lead to superior environmental outcomes.

There are, to be sure, politicians and administrators who are ideologically motivated to preserve and protect publicly owned resources. However, the incentive structure under which they operate may not promote appropriate preservation policies. It may, to the contrary, obstruct environmental protection efforts. Because public resource managers do not personally own the resources under their control, they do not suffer personal financial losses if they make poor management decisions. The losses are, instead, externalized to the public (see Anderson and Leal 1991, p. 4). Consequently, public resource managers are likely to be less concerned than they otherwise would be with maintaining – let alone maximizing – the economic *or* environmental values of the resources they manage.

Some economists (such as Stroup and Goodman 1992) also expect public resource managers to adopt more short-sighted policies than private resource owners, to the detriment of the environmental resources under their control, because of the relatively short election cycles under which democratic governments operate. Elected officials, like other people, tend to want to keep their jobs. Reelection can become an imperative eclipsing other concerns, including environmental protection, even for legislators who believe strongly in taking the long view on matters such as resource conservation. Elected officials are likely to support resource management policies that maximize their prospects for reelection, even if those policies are environmentally inferior, or even harmful.

Unelected bureaucrats are not tied to election cycles, of course, but they are indirectly affected by them to the extent that their budgets and administrative turf depend on the decisions of elected officials. The bureaucrats may, consequently, favor management policies that increase (or protect) their budgets and influence, even if those policies degrade the public resources under their control.

These theoretical problems of public ownership are supported by a good deal of evidence of public resource mismanagement. In the United States, for example, publicly owned rangelands have been subject to overgrazing and desertification because the agency responsible for managing them – the Bureau of Land Management – offers grazing permits to private ranchers at below-market cost (Stroup and Baden 1983, p. 47; Libecap 1981). Similarly, the US Forest Service regularly sells the public's timber at below-market prices, with environmentally harmful consequences for forest resources (see Stroup and Baden 1983, pp. 111–12). The US Bureau of Reclamation sponsors costly and environmentally destructive irrigation projects that appear to serve private, not public, interests (Anderson and Leal 1991, pp. 55–6). These and other horror stories of public mismanagement of publicly owned resources raise a fundamental question: does public ownership merely convert the tragedy of open access into what Thomas Borcherding (1990, p. 99) calls the "tragedy of the political commons"? The implication of this question is that public ownership may not be much of an improvement on open access.

Problems of implicit public ownership by regulation of private access and use

Problems arise not only from the *explicit* assertion of public ownership in environmental goods but also from the *implicit* assertion of public rights through regulation of private access and use. In practice, command-and-control regulation has been among the favored environmental protection devices of government. It is the predominant approach to pollution control in the United States. Command-and-control has also been a favorite among economists and legal scholars – a favorite target, that is. Ever since governments around the world began regulating private access to and use of certain resources in order to reduce the social costs of pollution, critics have complained about the relative (and sometimes absolute) inefficiency and ineffectiveness of command-and-control regulatory instruments.

Consider, once again, the 1970 US Clean Air Act (42 USC § 8651 et seq.), which, on my model, implicitly converts environmental amenities of the atmosphere from open access to public/state ownership by limiting polluters' access to and use of the atmosphere as a place for dumping their waste products. The Act is based predominantly on the kind of technology-based command-and-control regulations discussed in the previous section, and so constitutes a fair example of both the regulatory means of asserting property rights in environmental goods and the problems of such public property/regulatory approaches to environmental protection.

Since its inception, the Clean Air Act has been criticized by economists and legal scholars, who complain that it relies on "blunt," "often wildly inefficient and ... 'irrational'" instruments for achieving its goals (Orts 1995, p. 1236; Krier 1974, pp. 332–5). The statute, which has been described as "one of the more complicated statutes yet produced by the modern industrial state," is characterized by "heavy reliance on administrative expertise and the use of uniform, categorical rules as basic regulatory building blocks" (Meidinger 1985, pp. 451–2) – in other words, command-and-control. "Congress told industry what it could and could not belch from its smokestacks, how clean it would need to make new cars, and the type of pollution-control devices it would have to install" (Hahn 1990, p. 21).

The main goal of the 1970 Clean Air Act (and still its main goal today) is the attainment, 100 percent of the time, of national ambient air quality standards, which are a set of maximum permissible concentrations of air pollutants over various time periods. Congress ordered the newly created Environmental Protection Agency (EPA) to establish National Ambient Air Quality Standards (NAAQS) for pervasive pollutants such as carbon monoxide, sulfur dioxide, and particulate matter, building in an "adequate margin of safety" to protect the health of even the most sensitive human populations *without regard to cost.*[48]

In order to attain the economically oblivious NAAQS, Congress relied on a number of even more dubious (economically speaking) tools. First, legislators ordered the EPA to set technology-based emission standards without regard to differential costs of compliance across or within industries. All firms within a given regulated industry or category of industries had to achieve the same pollution control goal, no matter that it cost one firm $100 million to do so but another only $10 million (see Ackerman and Stewart 1985, p. 1335). Moreover, Congress placed the heaviest emissions reduction burdens on new sources through the imposition of New Source Performance Standards (NSPS), which created perverse incentives. Congress was correct to presume that new factories could design in emissions reduction technologies more cheaply than older factories could retrofit them. But the Clean Air Act's stringent NSPS induced firms to extend the life spans of older, dirtier factories to avoid building newer, cleaner, and, because of NSPS, more expensive plants (see Ackerman and Stewart 1985, pp. 1335–6; Harrison and Portney 1981, p. 27; Keohane et al. 1997, p. 2). Moreover, some critics claim that the technology-based NSPSs created disincentives for regulated industries

---

[48] See *Whitman v. American Trucking Associations*, 531 US 457 (2001).

to innovate new pollution control technologies that might become the basis for revised NSPSs (see Ackerman and Stewart 1985, pp. 1335–6; Stewart 1993, p. 2063).[49]

The Clean Air Act's NSPS were also subject to political manipulation, which compounded their inefficiency. The most famous example may be Congress's vacillation on performance standards for new coal-fired power plants. In the 1970 Clean Air Act, Congress required the EPA to set emissions standards for new sources based on the best available technology that was adequately demonstrated (42 USC § 7411). The EPA interpreted this mandate broadly. Congress did not intend the agency to require specific factories to install specific technologies; rather, the agency was to set emission standards based on available technologies *and* possible process changes and materials substitution. On this interpretation, the agency did not have to set standards that would force all new power plants to install scrubbers on smokestacks; instead, some plants might meet emission standards simply by substituting less polluting but more expensive low-sulfur coal for more polluting but less expensive high-sulfur coal. Economists approved of this more flexible and, therefore, presumably less costly approach to standard-setting. But it generated an intense political controversy that pitted low-sulfur coal producers, located predominantly in the western United States, against high-sulfur coal producers, located primarily in the east. Eastern coal interests won a temporary victory in 1977 when Congress amended the Clean Air Act to, in effect, mandate the use of scrubbers at all power plants, regardless of the type of coal they burned.[50] Since they had to scrub emissions anyway, many utilities that had been burning less polluting low-sulfur (western) coal switched to more polluting but less expensive high-sulfur (eastern) coal. The ironic result may have been a net increase in national sulfur emissions. Meanwhile, the cost of pollution control for the electric power industry rose because end-of-the-pipe solutions like scrubbers tend to be more expensive than process changes and materials substitution.[51]

Besides exacerbating the inherent inefficiencies of the preexisting NSPS program, the 1977 Amendments also added a new program that economists widely condemned. In 1972 a federal district court ruled that

---

[49] Polluting industries are not, of course, the only potential sources of pollution control innovations. The Clean Air Act created positive incentives for independent environmental protection industries to innovate new pollution control technologies, which, if selected as the basis for NSPS, might capture entire markets. The 115,100 companies comprising the US environmental protection industry produced $436 billion in global revenues and employed 1.3 million people in 1996 (Department of Commerce 1997, p. 1; see also Repetto 1983, pp. 276–7).

[50] See *Alliance for Clean Coal* v. *Bayh*, 888 F. Supp. 924, 927 (SD Ind. 1995).

[51] For a thorough treatment of the political conflict between eastern and western coal interests, see Ackerman and Hassler (1981).

the Clean Air Act required the EPA to prevent deterioration of air quality in regions that had already attained the NAAQS.[52] Pursuant to this court order, the agency promulgated Prevention of Significant Deterioration (PSD) regulations that Congress later codified in its 1977 Clean Air Act Amendments. Apparently, Congress agreed that air quality in pristine regions should not be permitted to deteriorate to the level of the NAAQS, which, after all, were merely intended as floors of minimally acceptable air quality. However, assuming the NAAQS had been set properly, they already were protecting the health of the most sensitive segments of the population of clean air regions "with an adequate margin of safety." What legitimate basis was there, then, for curtailing economic development out of concern over marginal, presumptively nonhazardous increases in air pollution?

Regional politics, once again, is a big part of the answer. As Pashigian (1985, p. 553) has explained, "PSD policy was developed to attenuate the locational competition between developed and less developed regions and between urban and rural areas." By the mid-1970s, many dirty air regions, predominantly in the eastern US, were under pressure to reduce emissions in order to attain the NAAQS, which acted as a constraint on economic development. These "nonattainment areas" were fearful of a large-scale shift in economic development to clean air regions, mostly located in the western US. From their perspective, the PSD rules merely leveled the playing field. Clean air regions, of course, viewed the situation rather differently. They saw it as a retilting of the field back in favor of the already heavily developed areas of the north and east. They could not understand why the clean air regions of the west and south should be prevented from developing economically because of the prior development mistakes of the north and east.

These are just some of the components of the Clean Air Act that, according to many economists and policy analysts, have imposed great costs on society. Robert Hahn (1990, p. 21), for example, has estimated that command-and-control air pollution regulations have cost Americans $30 billion per year, in the form of an "invisible tax on users of commodities that are produced by industry." And what has been attained for that price? Eric Orts (1995, p. 1236) notes that "command-and-control often fails to achieve the environmental results hoped for." Indeed, many regions of the United States still fail to meet the NAAQS for one or more regulated pollutants. And the Clean Air Act's special program for controlling "hazardous" air pollutants has been almost completely ineffective (at least prior to the implementation of the 1990 Clean Air Act Amendments).

[52] See *Sierra Club* v. *Ruckelshaus*, 344 F. Supp. 253, 255–6 (DDC 1972).

The net social benefits of the nation's air pollution control efforts would have been far higher, critics claim, if the federal government had adopted less costly and more flexible approaches to regulation than command-and-control. According to some estimates, least-cost approaches would have reduced by a factor of four the total compliance costs of air pollution control (Ackerman and Stewart 1985, p. 1338; Tietenberg 1985, pp. 39–56).

These criticisms of the Clean Air Act are largely, but not wholly, accurate. What is most important about them for present purposes is their implication for the property rights structure of environmental protection. The assault on command-and-control is, in essence, an attack against public property/regulatory approaches, as opposed to some alternative mixed property/regulatory approach or private property/nonregulatory approach. The argument is that instead of asserting only public rights in environmental goods, such as the atmosphere, the government would be better off to create at least some private rights.

Next, in chapter 3, I shall show that a shift (albeit incremental and incomplete) from a public property/regulatory regime to a mixed property/regulatory regime in the 1990 Clean Air Act Amendments has improved the efficiency and possibly the effectiveness of air pollution control. In chapter 4, however, I will revisit the economic history of the Clean Air Act and find that there are, in fact, occasions when command-and-control – the public property/regulatory approach to environmental protection – can be more efficient and effective than mixed property regimes such as transferable pollution permits.

3 Mixed property/regulatory regimes for environmental protection

Although many natural resources around the world are still owned and managed by sovereigns, a great many resources have been completely or incompletely privatized in order to enhance economic efficiency, improve environmental management, or both. This chapter and the next focus, respectively, on the utility and limitations of *partial* privatization and partial *public*ization as environmental protection tools, which result in mixed public and private (common or individual) property regimes. Complete privatization is addressed in chapter 5.

In a real sense, all existing property regimes are mixed. *Pure* public and *pure* private property exist only in the imaginations of economists, legal scholars, and political theorists. Actual property regimes are only more or less public or private. Jim Huffman (1994) has written about the inevitability of "private rights in public lands." By the same token, there are and probably always will be public rights in private lands. Every property regime, then, is an admixture of public and private rights.

This argument can be extended to claim that all property regimes, as admixtures, constitute common property regimes, on an admittedly unconventional definition of "common." Thus, all existing property regimes can be reduced to a single type. But to what benefit? How paradoxical and unilluminating it would be to compress the almost infinite variety of existing property arrangements into a single categorical pigeonhole. That is certainly not the intention of this chapter or the next. The goal, rather, is to assess the utility of certain, specifically defined mixed property regimes for environmental protection.

Mixed property regimes for environmental protection arise from two directions. Starting from a situation of (predominantly) public ownership and control, a government may grant limited pollution and resource-use permits or rights, vesting polluters/resource users with partial legal control over resources, subject however to public rights retained by the government. Examples of this type of partial privatization include the issuance of pollution permits (whether transferable or not) and the granting of private concessions to manage resources on public lands.

Mixed property regimes may also result from conveyances in the opposite direction – from private property to mixed public and private property. Examples of limited *public*ization include the use of *conservation easements*, pursuant to which a private landowner – often for tax reasons, but also perhaps because of a strong desire to keep land undeveloped – conveys to some private, not-for-profit organization, such as the Nature Conservancy, or some authorized government agency the right to prevent future development of the land. I shall discuss this form of partial *public*ization in the final section of the chapter. The first three sections of the chapter focus on partial privatization – specifically, the use of transferable pollution rights to improve environmental performance.

I   Transferable pollution rights in theory

Since the advent of federal pollution control regulation in the late 1960s and early 1970s, economists (such as Dales 1968) have advocated the allocation of limited but transferable private property rights in pollution emissions, as more cost-effective alternatives to pure public property/ regulatory approaches, such as technology-based command-and-control regulations. The idea is that by privatizing *some* public property rights in environmental goods, such as the atmosphere (or bads such as pollution emissions), the government can enlist the market to reduce the costs of achieving its pollution reduction and resource conservation targets.

The great advantage of a system of transferable pollution rights over command-and-control regulation is that it takes account of the different cost structures individual firms have for controlling pollution. As the end of the last chapter showed, command-and-control regulations disregard differential compliance costs, forcing all regulated firms to reduce emissions by the same amount. A system of transferable pollution rights, by contrast, allocates the bulk of the pollution reduction burden to those firms with lower costs of control. Firms that cannot reduce emissions so cheaply are allowed to pollute more, though they must pay for the privilege by purchasing pollution rights from sellers – the lower-cost controllers – on the free market.

In theory, a system of transferable pollution rights is simple to establish. The government sets a pollution control goal, and determines the extent of emissions reductions needed to attain it. Those necessary reductions are then subtracted from current emissions levels in order to derive total allowable emissions. Next, the government unitizes and allocates those allowable emissions, in the form of transferable pollution rights, among regulated firms. The total number of rights in circulation should match the emissions level the government deems appropriate to achieve its pollution control goal. Assuming the government's calculations of existing emissions and necessary reductions are accurate, its pollution control goal should be achieved, whether or not firms can trade rights to pollute, that is, even if the pollution rights are nontransferable. The primary purpose of allowing trading, therefore, is not to reduce emissions – though transferability may create incentives to reduce emissions below government-mandated levels, depending on market conditions – but to minimize the costs of reducing emissions. According to J. H. Dales (1968, p. 107), the transferability of pollution rights "automatically ensures that the required reduction in waste discharge will be achieved at the smallest possible total cost to society." This is not quite accurate. Transferability ensures the smallest possible aggregate *compliance/abatement* cost. This is not the same as "total" cost, which depends on additional factors, such as administrative – particularly monitoring and enforcement – costs (see Cole and Grossman forthcoming b).

Transferability ensures lower compliance/abatement costs by creating markets that efficiently allocate the costs of pollution control among regulated firms. Firms with low pollution control costs may find it worthwhile to reduce their emissions below mandated levels, leaving them with excess rights to sell to firms with higher pollution control costs. In theory, exchanges of pollution rights should occur at any price below the marginal pollution reduction costs of some firms and above the marginal pollution control costs of others. As a result of these exchanges, firms with the lowest costs of control should end up taking on the biggest emissions reduction burden, thereby minimizing the overall compliance/abatement costs of attaining the government's pollution control goal. There is also evidence that transferable pollution rights regimes encourage the development of new abatement technologies, leading to even greater emissions reductions (see, for example, Jung et al. 1996).

Designing and implementing a transferable pollution rights regime, however, is more easily said than done. Technological and institutional constraints may disable the government from accurately calculating existing waste levels and necessary reductions. If these calculations are inaccurate, then the government's environmental goals may not be met or may be met inefficiently. This is similar to the problem of getting the prices right in a tax-based pollution control regime (see Baumol and Oates 1971). With a tax system, of course, the government can adjust the price up or down until it achieves the desired incentive effects on polluters. Dales (1968, p. 95) recommends something similar for transferable pollution rights: the rights (or quotas) may be limited in duration (one-year, five-year, and so on), so that the government can make occasional adjustments in the quantity of rights to ensure the attainment of existing or newly adopted pollution control goals. Such limitations may appear troublesome from a property rights perspective, but they should not be. What Dales recommends is, in effect, a leasing system rather than an ownership system for pollution rights. Such rights certainly retain significant economic value, even though they amount to less than fee-simple ownership.

From a strictly economic perspective, the legal characterization of property rights is less important than their incentive effects for market participants. The less secure and complete sellers' property rights are, the less likely potential buyers will be to purchase them (all else being equal). Leaseholds are less valuable than freeholds precisely because of their more limited tenure and security.[1] And there is every reason to suspect that defeasible (or limited) pollution rights would have lower market value than absolute pollution rights. If pollution rights are too limited, their market value will fall to zero, and the market will simply disappear. There is, however, a wide range of economically valuable property interests between fee-simple ownership and utterly worthless entitlements.

II   Transferable pollution rights in practice

Early experiments

Since the 1970s mixed property/regulatory regimes for environmental protection have been implemented with varying degrees of success. This section focuses on the American experience with transferable pollution rights, because it has been the most extensive (Opschoor and Vos 1989, p. 99). And most of the American experience with emissions trading has occurred under the Clean Air Act (42 USC §§ 7401–7671q).

The first generation of federal pollution control regulations, adopted in the early 1970s, took a predominantly command-and-control (pure public property/regulatory) approach. Federal regulators not only set environmental goals (or pollution reduction targets), but imposed industry-wide, health-based or technology-based performance standards that applied to all plants, regardless of their differential costs of compliance. The Clean Air Act of 1970 included nothing like the transferable pollution rights system that Dales (1968) had envisioned.[2] As early

---

[1] Grossman (2000, p. 141) suggests that American "[f]armers can often take advantage of economies of scale more profitably by renting, rather than buying, additional land." Perhaps for that reason, almost 43 percent of all US farmland is farmed by tenant farmers.

[2] In chapter 4 I show that this early reliance on the pure public property/regulatory approach to air pollution control made economic sense; indeed, it was likely a more efficient approach at that time than alternative mixed property/regulatory approaches, such as transferable pollution rights.

as 1974, however, the Environmental Protection Agency (EPA) was experimenting with transferable pollution rights programs (Hahn and Hester 1989a, p. 109). By 1980 the agency had approved four distinct emissions trading schemes (see generally Liroff 1986).

First, in 1974 the EPA adopted "netting," a policy that allows firms to avoid the application of expensive standards for new and substantially modified sources by netting increased emissions from modernized or expanded existing sources with emissions decreases from other existing sources at the same facility (Hahn and Hester 1989a, pp. 132–3). So long as the net increase in plant-wide emissions does not equal the minimal requirement for a "major" source, as defined in the Clean Air Act, the modernization or expansion will not be treated as a "new" or substantially modified source for purposes of the Clean Air Act. Netting can occur in all areas of the country, whether or not they have attained national air quality standards. But netting applies only to internal trades, that is, to trades between sources located at the same facility. Nevertheless, according to Hahn and Hester (1989a, p. 133) netting has been "the most commonly used emissions trading activity by a wide margin." Between 1974 and 1984 as many as 12,000 sources used netting to avoid more onerous regulatory burdens under the Clean Air Act, resulting in cost savings of between $525 million and $12 billion (Hahn and Hester 1989b, p. 374).

"Offsets" were the second form of transferable pollution rights created by the EPA. By the mid-1970s the agency had become concerned that many regions of the country would fail to meet air quality standards by the 1977 statutory deadline. If that happened, the question arose, did the Clean Air Act permit the construction of new air pollution sources in these nonattainment areas? A construction ban would have entailed great economic costs for nonattainment areas – including most of the major metropolitan areas in the United States – and, consequently, negative political fallout for state and federal politicians and regulators. To avoid this prospect, the EPA in late 1976 promulgated "offset" regulations that permitted the construction of new stationary sources in nonattainment areas. New sources could be constructed provided that their emissions would be offset by reductions at existing sources. Under this offset rule "[e]xisting sources are, in effect, given pollution rights equal to their existing emissions, which can then be sold to new sources or to existing sources that wish to increase their emissions" (Stewart and Krier 1978, p. 593).

Offsets are different from netting in several respects: they apply only in nonattainment regions (and in certain attainment regions, emissions from which contribute to nonattainment elsewhere); they are mandatory;

and they cannot result in a net increase in emissions. The EPA's original offset rule was codified in § 178 of the 1977 Amendments to the Clean Air Act, which additionally required that all new emissions in nonattainment regions be *more than offset* by reductions from existing sources. The purpose of this additional requirement was to ensure that new economic development in nonattainment regions would contribute to the attainment of the National Ambient Air Quality Standards (NAAQS). Subsequently, the 1990 Clean Air Act Amendments established precise offset ratios, ranging from 1.1:1 to 1.5:1, that apply depending on the region's level of nonattainment. For example, in "extreme" nonattainment areas such as Los Angeles, 1.5 tons of Volatile Organic Compound (VOC) emissions must be retired from existing sources for every ton to be emitted from some new source. As of 1988, approximately 2,000 offset transactions had taken place, though only about 10 percent of these were external, that is, involving more than a single facility (Hahn and Hester 1989b, p. 373). The economic effects of these transactions are difficult to estimate. Offsets are not designed to yield direct regulatory cost savings. The fact that offset transactions occur at all suggests, however, that they must provide some economic benefits both for firms seeking to locate in nonattainment regions and for the nonattainment regions themselves (Hahn and Hester 1989b, p. 375).

Next, in 1979 the EPA permitted regulated firms to use "bubbles" to avoid more burdensome regulations. A single plant may contain many individual sources of pollution. The "bubble" policy allows existing plants (or groups of plants under common management) to place their various smokestacks under a bubble, as it were, with a single opening at the top. By treating the entire plant (or group of plants) as a single source with a single emissions target (for each pollutant), plant managers are free to allocate necessary emissions reductions to those smokestacks with the lowest control costs. Instead of having to reduce emissions by a certain amount at each and every smokestack, the plant can reduce emissions more at some smokestacks and less, or not at all, at others. "In effect, emissions credits are created by some sources within the plant and used by others" (Hahn and Hester 1989b, p. 372). By the mid-1980s the EPA had approved forty-two bubbles for firms and various states with EPA-delegated authority had approved another eighty-nine, though only two of these involved external trades (Hahn and Hester 1989b, p. 373, and 1989a, pp. 123–5). The total cost savings from bubbling have been significant. Federally approved and state-approved bubbles have saved an estimated $435 million in regulatory costs. Although this total is lower than the total cost savings from netting, it reflects a higher average saving per transaction (Hahn and Hester 1989b, p. 374).

Also in 1979, the EPA began allowing regulated firms to bank emissions credits for future use, sale, or lease. This banking system is not really a transferable pollution rights scheme in its own right; it is, rather, a mechanism to facilitate the use of bubbles and offsets. The EPA delegated authority to the states to administer their own emissions credit banks. According to Hahn and Hester (1989b, p. 373), however, banking has not been well received by either state administrators or regulated firms. As of September 1986 firms had withdrawn credits from banks for sale, lease, or use only 100 times. Thus, the cost savings realized through banking were "necessarily small" (Hahn and Hester 1989b, p. 374). One possible reason for the reluctance of firms to use the banking system for emissions reduction credits is the lack of secure property rights in the credits, which can be confiscated by state or federal regulators at any time in order to further environmental protection goals (Hahn and Hester 1989a, p. 130).

None of the four pollution trading programs discussed in this section – netting, offsets, bubbles, and banking – provides complete ownership rights in emissions reduction credits (ERCs). According to the EPA (1980, p. 2), "*an ERC cannot be an absolute property right.*" Because of its continuing statutory obligation to attain NAAQS, the agency reserves the right to impose new emissions controls that could, in effect, confiscate saved or purchased emissions reduction credits (see Hahn and Hester 1989a, p. 117). As noted earlier, the lack of completely secure property rights on ERCs is not necessarily a fatal flaw in the system; the market will discount their economic value based on the perceived risk of confiscation. According to Hahn and Hester (1989b, p. 379), however, the lack of secure property rights on ERCs has served "as a disincentive for engaging in trading in nonattainment areas, and especially for external trading in those areas." The lack of secure property rights raises similar issues with respect to the most ambitious transferable pollution rights experiment to date: the sulfur dioxide emissions allowance trading program under the 1990 Clean Air Act Amendments.

*The Clean Air Act's transferable emissions allowance program
for sulfur dioxide*

In 1970, when the federal government took over primary responsibility from the states for air pollution control, one of its main justifications was the problem of interstate air pollution (see Revesz 1996b, p. 2341). Since then, ironically, interstate air pollution has been among the "thorniest" problems for federal regulators (Squillace 1992, p. 301). Acid rain is a prime example. It is created when sulfur dioxide (SO_2) and nitrogen oxide (NO_x) emissions, coming primarily from Midwestern power plants, combine with constituent elements in the atmosphere to produce sulfuric and nitric acids that precipitate back to earth, acidifying lakes, burning forests, and corroding structures. The significant regulatory problem with acid rain is that most of it falls far from its midwestern emissions sources, in the northeastern United States and in Canada.

In 1990, after more than a decade of political wrangling, Congress enacted an innovative new program to control acid rain. The "acid deposition control" program established in Title IV of the 1990 Clean Air Act Amendments sought to cut SO_2 emissions by 10 million tons and NO_x emissions by 2 million tons by the year 2000 (42 USC § 7651). To reduce NO_x emissions, Congress relied primarily on traditional technology-based standards, that is, command-and-control: regulated utilities were required to retrofit controls on existing boilers. The SO_2 reduction effort, by contrast, relied on a new, two-phase property-based approach utilizing transferable pollution "allowances." The different regulatory approaches may reflect the fact that NO_x controls are significantly cheaper than SO_2 controls. The State Utility Forecasting Group (1991, p. 45) estimates the capital cost for NO_x-control retrofits at less than $100 million, compared to $900 million for SO_2-control retrofits. Consequently, the marginal benefits of an emissions trading program for NO_x would be lower, perhaps so low as to be outweighed by the higher administrative costs of such a program (this issue is addressed in chapter 4).

In phase one of the SO_2 program, Congress issued emissions allowances – with each allowance equaling 1 ton of SO_2 emissions – to the 240 dirtiest generators at 110 power plants in twenty-one states. Sixty-three percent of regulated generators were located in just six states: Illinois (17), Indiana (37), Kentucky (17), Ohio (41), Pennsylvania (21), and Tennessee (19). The total number of allowances issued equaled approximately one-half of the total emissions of all 240 generators, in order to achieve a 3.5 million ton reduction in aggregate SO_2 emissions before the second phase of emissions reductions began in the year 2000. The allowances were allocated to individual generating units based on their average quantity of fossil fuel consumed during the three-year period 1985–87, assuming 2.5 pounds SO_2 per million BTUs of fuel input. In phase two the goal is to reduce SO_2 emissions from all but the smallest generating units by an additional 6.5 million tons, based on a formula of 1.2 pounds per million BTUs of fossil fuel input during the 1985–87 period. Congress's pollution reduction targets are not so stringent as they appear, however, because the Act provides extra allowances for plants in "high growth" states, including the six states that produce the lion's share of the country's SO_2 emissions. The Act also provides deadline extensions for plants that take early steps to reduce emissions beyond the

Act's requirements. However, the Act sets a fast 8.7 million pound cap on utility SO_2 emissions after 2000. Moreover, the Act does not hold in reserve any emissions allowances for new sources entering the market; any new sources must obtain allowances from existing ones.

Most of the pollution reduction realized under the Clean Air Act's acid rain program results from the administratively set quotas. They are "commands," but they have been issued without attendant "controls." The Act does not specify *how* sources are to meet emissions reduction requirements. The law does not even require sources to reduce emissions to the levels set by Congress, but only to possess allowances equal to their actual emissions. Congress designed the Act to utilize market forces by expressly authorizing the nationwide buying and selling of emissions allowances. In other words, the allowances it allocated are freely transferable. Sources that can economically reduce their emissions below required levels can sell their excess allowances. Sources with higher costs of controlling emissions can purchase extra allowances, that is, increase their quota, rather than reduce emissions to phase one or phase two levels. Congress even provided for the creation of a futures market in emissions allowances, authorizing generating units to buy and sell allowances for future years (Mazurek 1994).

The goal of the trading system is primarily to minimize the total costs of achieving the legislatively commanded reductions in SO_2 emissions. According to some estimates, it could reduce the total cost of achieving a 10 million ton reduction in SO_2 emissions by 20 percent, from $5 billion to $4 billion or less (Menell and Stewart 1994, p. 410). Not everything about the program is market-driven, however. The program places a premium on monitoring trades and emissions. When a generating unit buys or sells an allowance, that alters its emissions quota. The EPA has to keep track of the trades so that the agency knows, at any given moment, how much SO_2 each generating unit is permitted to emit. To that end, the agency created a central accounting system to which firms must report all allowance transactions. And to ensure that sources are complying with their emissions quotas, they must install continuous emissions monitoring systems and report their actual emissions to the EPA. Sources that violate their emissions limitations are subject to a penalty of $2,000 per ton. This penalty is significant, amounting approximately to twenty times the price of 1 ton of SO_2 at the March 1997 auction.

The key to the design of the acid rain program is the development of a well-functioning emissions market. But certain aspects of the program's design initially caused some to doubt that a robust market would develop. One major concern was the lack of secure property rights in emissions allowances. Congress expressly provided in § 403(f) of the 1990 Clean

Air Act Amendments (42 USC § 7651(f)) that an "allowance is not a property right." And it expressly authorized the EPA "to terminate or limit" allowances, when necessary to achieve environmental goals, without having to pay just compensation for taking property under the 5th Amendment to the US Constitution (Dennis 1993, pp. 1118–22). This provision may serve to placate environmentalists who are offended by the very notion of a right to pollute, let alone the prospect that firms might profit from trading in pollution (see Percival et al. 1996, pp. 829, 832). However, § 403(f) is premised on a typical confusion between property rights in something and the thing itself. An emissions allowance is not a property right, but there certainly are property rights in emissions allowances. A utility that holds an allowance to emit SO_2 cannot prevent the government from confiscating it but certainly can exclude all others from interfering with it. The rights to possess and exclude certainly are property rights in allowances. Indeed, disputes over property interests in emissions allowances have led to civil litigation.[3] Nevertheless, § 403(f) makes clear that the acid rain program was intended only as a partial, rather than a complete, privatization of rights with respect to the atmosphere. Congress's goal was to create a mixed property/regulatory regime, vesting limited property rights in power plants, but reserving substantial property rights to the public (to be managed by its government agents).

In addition to property rights concerns, some analysts expected allowances to be priced beyond any potential market (see Squillace 1992, p. 302). However, the performance of the SO_2 emissions allowance trading system to date has allayed this concern. By November 1995, 23 million allowances worth $2 billion had been transferred in more than 600 transactions under the acid rain program. In addition to external transfers, many sources reduced their emissions and banked excess allowances for future use after phase two emissions restrictions took effect. The result has been a greater than expected reduction in SO_2 emissions and a 10 to 25 percent reduction in acid precipitation in the northeast (see Swift 1997, p. 17).

Sources have reduced their emissions by various means: thirty power plants have installed scrubbers, which reduce SO_2 emissions by more than 90 percent; many plants have switched from high-sulfur to low-sulfur coal (Energy Information Association 1997). The larger than expected reductions flooded the market with available allowances, which meant far lower prices than many analysts anticipated. The first allowances sold in 1992 for between $250 and $400 per allowance; by 1996, the average

---

[3] See *Ormet Corporation v. Ohio Power Company*, 98 F. 3d 799 (4th Cir. 1996).

price was down to $68 (Percival et al. 1996, pp. 831–2). In 1997 the average price rebounded to $106.75 per allowance (see *BNA Chemical Regulation Daily*, March 28, 1997).

In economic terms, the acid rain trading market has proven to be "a terrific bargain" (Percival et al. 1996, p. 832). Even the lowest estimates of its annual health benefits – $12 billion – are four times higher than the highest estimates of annual program costs – $3 billion. And those benefit estimates do not include difficult to quantify environmental benefits, such as reduced acid rain damage to forests, lakes, rivers, and buildings. One recent assessment of the Clean Air Act's acid rain program concluded that "the benefits . . . exceed the costs by a substantial margin" (Burtraw et al. 1997, p. 26).

Apparently, the lack of completely secure and perpetual property rights in emissions allowances has not greatly impeded trading. As noted earlier, markets compensate for the insecurity of property rights (including the risk of confiscation) by discounting prices. If SO_2 allowances were perceived to be highly insecure, their value would fall, perhaps so low as to completely wipe out the market. But the EPA, to its credit, has paid attention to this potentiality, which it has encountered in earlier emissions trading programs (see EPA 1986, p. 43,847 n. 48). In order to preserve the market the EPA has expressed its intention to treat emissions allowances as if they were absolute property rights, except in exigent circumstances (Dennis 1993, p. 1137). The risk of confiscation should, therefore, be remote (see Rosenberg 1994, p. 508 n. 54).

The Clean Air Act's transferable emissions allowance program is not, however, without its problems. In creating a nationwide market in SO_2 emissions, Congress ignored distributional considerations related to emissions of SO_2 and acid deposition. As noted earlier, the states that suffer the most from acid rain are located in the northeast, while the states that produce most of the SO_2 emissions that cause the acid rain are located in the midwest. The emissions allowance trading program does not guarantee that midwestern power plants will reduce their emissions sufficiently to resolve acid rain problems in northeastern states. Imagine if power plants in Indiana purchased emissions allowances from plants in New York. This would permit Indiana plants to continue emitting high levels of SO_2, creating further acid rain problems for the State of New York, while power plants in New York profited from the transactions. This prospect has led to some political and legal skirmishes between northeastern states and the EPA. The problem has not yet materialized, however. Power plants upwind of New York have reduced their emissions more than required by phase one quotas (see General Accounting Office 1994, p. 56).

The US General Accounting Office (GAO) (1994, pp. 43–58) has identified other impediments to a more vibrant market in SO_2 emissions allowances, including the fact that phase one reductions apply to only about 14 percent of the country's power plants. More trading can be expected in phase two, as the program is broadened to cover another 700 power plants. The GAO also points out that potential traders feel insecure about how state legislatures, public utility commissions and the Federal Energy Regulatory Commission will treat SO_2 allowances. Finally, the GAO suggests that the tax treatment of allowance trading under the Internal Revenue Code may discourage trades because sales of allowances are taxed as ordinary capital gains with zero basis. This last assertion is dubious, however. Utilities incur tax liability only when they sell allowances; meanwhile, utilities that purchase allowances realize equivalent tax savings. The tax treatment of trades, therefore, should be revenue-neutral for the federal government.[4] If taxes on emissions allowance transactions created a disincentive for traders, it would be evidenced on the supply side – fewer allowances would be offered for sale. Yet, the price and availability of SO_2 allowances on the market suggests that supplies have been more than adequate; any lack of trading appears to be more a problem of demand, which cannot be explained by federal tax policy.

Uncertainties about the SO_2 emissions trading program may have complicated the compliance strategies of regulated utilities. But trading volume is neither the only nor the most important measure of the acid rain program's success (Burtraw 1996). Allowance trading is but a means to the end of attaining administratively set emissions reduction targets at the lowest possible cost. On that measure, the program has so far proven to be a great success. According to the EPA, in 1995 100 percent of the 110 power plants regulated in phase one were in compliance with their emissions allowances, and they had reduced aggregate emissions of SO_2 to well below the 8.7 million ton limit established in the 1990 Clean Air Act Amendments. Total emissions in 1995 were 5.3 million tons, 39 percent below the ceiling and more than 50 percent below 1980 emissions levels (see *BNA Daily Environment Report*, Aug. 12, 1996). The total cost savings from using the trading system, rather than direct regulatory controls, to achieve this level of emissions reduction are difficult to estimate, but must be substantial. Consider that just four utilities, Central Illinois Public Service, Illinois Power Company, Duke Power, and Wisconsin Electric Power Company, estimate their aggregate savings from purchasing allowances rather than installing scrubbers at $706 million (US General Accounting Office 1994, pp. 33–4). This figure

---

[4] See Revenue Procedure 91–92, Oct. 29, 1992, 92 Fed. Reg. para. 46,595.

almost matches the total annual costs of compliance with phase one requirements – estimated, through 1995, at $836 million – according to a report prepared by the Massachusetts Institute of Technology (Energy Information Association 1997, p. 12). In sum, the Clean Air Act's acid rain program is achieving both pollution reductions and cost savings beyond all expectations.[5]

Other transferable pollution rights schemes

Although the Clean Air Act's acid rain program constitutes the most extensive use to date of transferable pollution rights, there are several other examples worth mentioning. In the mid-1980s, the EPA introduced a short-lived but fairly successful program for trading rights to use lead in gasoline (see Hahn and Hester 1989b, pp. 380–91). Another largely successful program, described in Tripp and Dudek (1989, pp. 378–82), concerned the use of tradeable development permits to conserve the New Jersey Pinelands, the world's largest pineland forest. These successful programs reflect the potential for mixed property/regulatory approaches to achieve environmental protection goals at lower social cost than pure public property/regulatory approaches. However, transferable pollution rights and other mixed property/regulatory instruments are not invariably as effective and more efficient as command-and-control regulations and other public property/regulatory instruments. Less successful transferable pollution rights programs include experiments on Wisconsin's Fox River and Colorado's Dillon Reservoir (Hahn and Hester 1989b, pp. 391–6).

More recently, in 1993 California's South Coast Air Quality Management District (SCAQMD), the agency responsible for implementing federal and state clean air legislation in Los Angeles, established a new allowance trading model to help the country's most polluted city attain the NAAQS. The goal of its Regional Clean Air Incentives Market (RECLAIM) is to reduce stationary source emissions of nitrogen oxide (NO_x) and sulfur dioxide (SO_2) at average annual rates of 8.3 percent and 6.8 percent, respectively, between 1994 and 2003.[6] It may be too early to judge RECLAIM's success, but signs have been promising. As of the end of 1996, some $20 million worth of emissions credits had been traded, $9.9 million in 1996 alone. The average trading price was $142 per ton for 1996 SO_2 credits and $154 per ton for 1996 NO_x credits. Actual NO_x and SO_2 emissions in 1996 were 70.5 tons per day, 29 percent below the

---

[5] For a similarly positive interim assessment of the Clean Air Act's Acid Rain Trading Program, see Schmalensee et al. (1998).

[6] For a complete description of the RECLAIM program see Polesetsky (1995).

allotted level of 98.4 tons per day. And 92 percent of the 330 facilities participating in RECLAIM were in compliance with their emissions credits (see Utility Environment Report, March 4, 1997).

Other states are also beginning to experiment with pollution trading systems as part of their efforts to attain the national air quality standards. Michigan, for example, has a new trading program that applies to all "criteria" pollutants (see Schroder and Johnson 1997). And beyond US borders, several countries have undertaken their own experiments with transferable pollution rights programs. Denmark's 1991 Environmental Protection Act, for example, relies heavily on contractual agreements be-tween polluting industries and the government. Polluters receive permits that embody the contract terms. As with emissions allowances under the American acid rain program, however, Danish pollution contracts only partially privatize rights to pollute (or use natural resources); the government can, if necessary to attain environmental goals, amend permits without expropriating property (see Ercmann 1996, pp. 1226–7).

III   Assessing pollution rights trading schemes as a method of environmental regulation

From these various early experiences with transferable pollution rights analysts have derived certain lessons for designing and implementing successful programs. James Tripp and Daniel Dudek (1989), for example, identify eight "institutional guidelines." The responsible administrative agency must have (1) "clear legal authority" and (2) the "technical capability" to design, implement and enforce the program; (3) the program must be "evasion proof," meaning that regulated sources have no way (through loopholes, waivers, etc.) to avoid either reducing emissions or purchasing additional allowances; (4) the program should have "clearly specified objectives" based on sound science and with strong political backing; (5) trading programs work best when applied to pollution problems with "regional significance," as opposed to those with only local impacts; (6) the tradeable "rights must have economic value"; (7) the program should provide an "equitable and administratively simple method for allocating" tradeable rights, although there may be "trade-offs be-tween fairness and administrative simplicity"; and (8) the institutional structure for buying and selling rights should be designed so as to minimize transaction costs. This last guideline ties in with the sixth: the higher the transaction costs involved in trading – "[t]he greater the administrative or public hassle confronting a prospective buyer or seller of rights" – the less economic value rights will have.

Interestingly, Tripp and Dudek do not list security of property rights as a distinct guideline for a successful transferable pollution rights program, although it implicitly factors into their sixth guideline, concerning the economic value of the rights to be traded. Their decision not to focus on the lack of secure property rights is supported by the success of trading schemes, such as the Clean Air Act's acid rain program and the EPA's earlier lead trading program, both of which involved property rights that were less than fully secure.

Other analysts, however, consider the lack of completely secure property rights in pollution as a potentially major hindrance to trading. Robert Hahn and Gordon Hester (1989a, p. 149) maintain that trading systems would operate more efficiently, creating greater cost savings, if "uncertainties over the definition of property rights" in pollution were eliminated. But even they would not go so far as to recommend absolutely secure property rights in pollution emissions, in recognition that the government might need to reduce emissions further in order to meet environmental quality goals (p. 150).

The few successful experiments with pollution trading have encouraged scholars to innovate new applications for conserving ocean resources (Tipton 1995), endangered species habitat (Sohn and Cohen 1996), and wetlands (Sapp 1995). Although these schemes could all work, it is doubtful that pollution rights trading would be both effective and efficient for all environmental goods in every ecological and institutional context. Kathleen Miller (1996) and Barton H. Thompson (1993) have each identified institutional impediments to successful trading programs in water pollution rights, for example. Indeed, in the next chapter I shall show that the utility of transferable pollution rights programs for achieving environmental protection goals at relatively low cost is distinctly limited. There are institutional and technological circumstances in which command-and-control turns out to be as (or more) efficient and effective than transferable pollution rights. More generally, in some circumstances pure public property/regulatory solutions to the tragedy of the commons are likely to be economically and environmentally preferable to mixed property/regulatory regimes.

IV   Partial *publicization* through conservation easements and land trusts

Mixed property regimes arise not only from partial privatization of public, common, or open-access goods but also from partial publicization of privately owned resources. One increasingly common method of publicization for protecting wild and agricultural lands is for the private owner of undeveloped land to convey a conservation easement – a right to prevent development[7] – to a public or private land trust. This section describes how conservation easements and land trusts operate to preserve wild lands, and explains their status as mixed property regimes for averting the tragedy of open access.

Preserving resources with conservation easements and land trusts

The use of land trusts to preserve private lands with valuable environmental amenities is not a recent innovation.[8] In the late nineteenth century American states began to establish agencies to receive gifts of private lands on behalf of the public. The State of Massachusetts, for example, created "a Trustee of Reservations" in 1891 to "preserve for the public, places of natural beauty and historic interest within the Commonwealth" (Fenner 1980, p. 1042 n. 20). Today, the Massachusetts land trust owns more than 17,000 acres, and possesses easements preventing development on another 7,000 acres (Daniels and Bowers 1997, p. 195). Nearly all American states now have authorized agencies to accept and administer land trusts. In addition, there are more than 1,100 private, not-for-profit organizations, including the Nature Conservancy, that facilitate and participate in land trust transactions.

A land trust is created when a private property owner conveys her development rights either to a public agency authorized to hold land in trust for the public or to a private not-for-profit conservation organization.[9] The property interest conveyed is, typically, a "conservation easement."[10] An easement is, of course, a well-recognized interest in property, created when a "nonowner" possesses positive rights (to do something) or

---

[7] "Simply put, a conservation easement is a legally binding agreement that permanently restricts the development and future use of the land to ensure protection of its conservation values" (Gustanski 2000, p. 9).

[8] The phrase "land trust" is used in two distinct but related ways: to designate the legal institution created by conservation easements and to describe the organization that administers or manages those easements.

[9] Land trusts are not limited to purchasing development rights; they can purchase fee simple interests. When they do, they convert private (individual) property into common property. If, then, they transfer title to some state agency, as in fact they often do, that would constitute complete publicization of the property.

[10] Section 1 of the Uniform Conservation Easement Act (Supp. 1995) defines a "conservation easement" as "a nonpossessory interest of a holder in real property imposing limitations or affirmative obligations the purposes of which include retaining or protecting nature, scenic, or open-space values of real property, assuring its availability for agricultural, forest, recreational, or open-space use, protecting natural resources, maintaining or enhancing air or water quality, or preserving historical, architectural, archaeological, or cultural aspects of real property."

negative rights (to prevent something being done) over another's land. As with other easements, the grantor of the conservation easement remains the title holder – the nominal owner of the land. This is consistent with the "bundle of rights" conception of property. The owner conveys only a part of her total interest in the land – specifically her right to develop it; she retains several other important rights, including the right to possess, the right to use (in ways consistent with conditions specified in the trust), and the right to exclude others.[11] Conservation easements differ from other easements, however, in two important respects. First, the subject of the easement is the right to develop – specifically, the grantee holds the right to prevent development of the servient estate. Second, most conservation easements are perpetual;[12] once the conveyance takes place, neither the private landowner nor any subsequent owner can develop the land. Pursuant to the terms of the trust, the land must remain perpetually (at least in theory[13]) undeveloped. The trustee possesses an enforceable property right to prevent anyone, at any time in the future,

[11] However, the typical land trust agreement obliges the landowner to allow the trustee regular access to the land to ensure compliance with the terms of the trust.

[12] The donation of the easement *must* be perpetual in order to qualify as a deductible gift for federal tax purposes (Daniels and Bower 1997, p. 202). However, perpetuity is not required under the Uniform Conservation Easement Act, nor under most state laws authorizing conservation easements (see Mayo 2000, pp. 40–2). Most states presume, absent express terms to the contrary, that conservation easements are perpetual.

[13] It is possible that a court could, at some later date, find that conditions have changed so substantially that the trust conditions should be amended or waived (see Blackie 1989). If that occurs, then the land may once again become open to development. Section 3(b) of the Uniform Conservation Easement Act reserves "the power of a court to terminate a conservation easement in accordance with the principles of law and equity." In addition, some state laws authorizing conservation easements specifically provide that the easement can be terminated, extinguished, or abandoned by merger with the fee interest (see, for example, Colorado Revised Statutes § 38-30.5-107). Moreover, most states specifically authorize limited duration conservation easements, so that once the easement expires, the land can be put to some other use. A few states (including Alabama, Kansas, and West Virginia) presume the duration of the conservation easement is limited, unless the easement is expressly made in perpetuity (see Mayo 2000, p. 40).
Gerald Korngold (1984, pp. 441–2) argues cogently against *perpetual* conservation easements: "Although it may be difficult today to imagine a more important land-use priority than conservation, a number of cases and events indicate that other uses sometimes may be more critical than conservation. It is not entirely clear, for example, that preservation of land is and always will be preferable to its use as a hospital or church providing services to the community, a lower income housing project, a condominium containing recreational facilities and natural settings for its residents, a public recreation area for picnicking, swimming, and sports, or a commercial or industrial area providing jobs for an economically depressed region. The choice of the best current use of a parcel of land is difficult enough; more difficult still is the decision today regarding future use, because future needs are more speculative. Rigid choices today may defeat the right of future generations to make critical decisions affecting their lives."

from developing the land.[14] Moreover, the trustee has an enforceable legal *duty* to monitor and enforce the trust's terms (Daniels and Bowers 1997, p. 203).[15]

The conservation purpose and effect of the land trust are obvious. But what incentive might a private landowner have to convey highly valuable development rights to some public or private not-for-profit trustee? The answer is money – in the form of cash payments or tax benefits – and a strong preference for resource conservation (along, perhaps, with a strong desire to control future generations from the grave by creating a legal perpetuity). Some – perhaps many – landowners, who appreciate the values of undeveloped land, espouse preservation. But maintaining wild lands is not a cost-free proposition. First and foremost there are the opportunity costs associated with preservation, prominently including the lost value of foregone development. The owner of a small cabin surrounded by 300 acres of pristine forest and meadows bordering on Lake Tahoe – call her Emma – may truly love her undeveloped piece of heaven. The very thought of despoiling it with yet another resort hotel and golf course makes her feel sick. Suppose Emma's land is worth $500,000 in its current state, but would be worth ten times more if developed as a resort with a golf course.[16] What will Emma do when some resort developer offers her $5 million for her land? Will she give a thought to the passing years, her income level, her concerns about providing for herself and her loved ones? And what if, after she's gone, the next owner – perhaps her own child – could reverse her conservation decision and take an offer to sell for development or, worse yet (from Emma's point of view), develop the land himself?

In addition to the opportunity costs of preserving the land, there are also maintenance costs. These costs include excluding trespassers – especially adverse possessors – from the land and paying property taxes, which in most states, for most (nonagricultural) purposes are based on the highest valued *use* of the land. Even though Emma's Lake Tahoe frontage is undeveloped, the state may tax her as if she had built a profitable resort

---

[14] It is important to recognize that the right the trustee possesses is the right to prevent development, *not* the right to develop. The trustee has no authority to undertake or permit development activities, with or without the landowner's approval.

[15] The conservation easement differs from other easements in one further respect, which is legally significant but immaterial to our discussion: the conservation easement is an enforceable "negative easement in gross" (see Cheever 1996, p. 1081). The common law generally refuses to enforce negative easements in gross, but almost all states have adopted statutes specifically authorizing conservation easements and requiring their judicial enforcement (see Garrett 1984, p. 258).

[16] The $500,000 figure may or may not be realistic, but the difference between the undeveloped land's value and its value for development *is* certainly realistic (see Baldwin 1997, p. 108).

on it. Similarly, under federal inheritance tax law, when Emma passes away, leaving her entire estate to her only son, the federal government will tax her undeveloped land based not on its existing nonuse but on its fair market value: what a buyer would pay for the land for any potential *use*.[17] Assuming the estate (in total) is worth more than $600,000 (IRC §§ 2001(c), 2010), it will be taxed at a minimum rate of 37 percent (IRC § 2001(e)). The inheritance tax bill may be so large that the estate cannot pay it off except by selling the land for development, which is precisely what Emma spent her life avoiding. In this way state property taxes and federal inheritance taxes in the United States promote land development, and discourage landowners from keeping land undeveloped.

Conservation easements and land trusts, however, can reduce both the opportunity costs and the maintenance costs of preserving land in its undeveloped state. Reduced costs are, of course, a benefit for the landowner. If that benefit is big enough, the landowner may have a substantial incentive to sell or donate their development rights to authorized state agencies or to private, not-for-profit organizations. At least for landowners who are predisposed to keep their lands undeveloped, the benefits of conservation easements and land trusts minimize the *dis*incentives.

Conservation easements can reduce the opportunity costs of preservation by allowing landowners to profit from their rights to develop without actually developing the land. Landowners with high taxable incomes may gain valuable tax deductions from donating conservation easements to a land trust. The federal income tax code offers a charitable deduction from taxable income for the donation of "important natural habitat" as well as "open space, scenic areas, ... [and] forestlands" (IRC § 170(h)). Landowners can offset up to 30 percent of their adjusted gross income in a year, and the donation can be spread over six years (IRC § 170(b)(1)(B), (C), and (D)). Those with lower annual incomes may not be able to take advantage of these tax deductions, and so will not have the incentive to donate their development rights. They may, however, be able to sell those rights to some private not-for-profit organization, such as the Nature Conservancy, which will subsequently donate the development rights to an authorized state management agency. The sale will, of course, generate capital gains subject to taxation. For this reason, and because private, not-for-profit organizations do not possess enough funds to purchase more than a few conservation easements each year,[18] most conservation easement deals are structured as "bargain sales," which constitute partial sales and partial donations (Daniels and Bowers 1997, p. 202). Landowners

---

[17] See Treasury Department Regulation 1.170A-14(h)(3)(ii).

[18] According to Daniels and Bowers (1997, p. 197), "[n]early half of all land trusts operate with a volunteer staff and an annual budget of under $10,000."

sell their development rights to land trusts for less than market value; the difference between the sale price and the market value constitutes a tax-deductible charitable donation. By donating development rights for significant income tax deductions or selling them for cash, landowners are able to realize at least some of the value of their development rights without exercising them.

Once created, land trusts reduce landowners' costs of maintaining undeveloped lands by lowering state property tax and federal inheritance tax assessments. As noted earlier, these taxes typically are based on the land's highest valued use;[19] so undeveloped lands may be taxed as if they were developed. High tax bills can create a strong disincentive to preserve undeveloped land. That disincentive is effectively negated, however, by the land trust. Because the owner no longer possesses the right to develop the land, federal and state tax codes will not value the land in terms of its development potential; the highest valued use of the land will be its present, undeveloped or only partially developed state (see Diehl and Barrett 1988, p. 8).[20] This can result in substantial cost savings for landowners. If, for example, the tax assessment of a tract of undeveloped land falls from $100,000 to $10,000 because of a conservation easement which prohibits development, at a tax rate of 10 percent the landowner will save more than $270,000 over a thirty-year period (assuming the value of the land and the tax rate remain constant over that period). And when the landowner passes away, her estate may be entitled to exclude up to 40 percent of the value of the land from estate taxes, depending on the land's location and the terms of the conservation easement (see Mayo 2000, p. 61). For a landowner who prefers to keep her land undeveloped, these tax reductions substantially reduce the total costs of preservation. At the very least, they reduce the counterincentives, created by the tax code, that favor land development.

The increasing popularity of conservation easements and land trusts

The use of conservation easements and land trusts has been increasing steadily over the past few decades. Between 1950 and 1994 the number

---

[19] Indiana's conservation easement law, for example, provides that "real property subject to a conservation easement shall be assessed and taxed on a basis that reflects the easement" (Ind. Code § 32-5-2.6-7).

[20] Colorado's property tax code (Colorado Revised Statutes § 38-30.5-109 [1990]), for example, specifically provides that "Conservation easements shall be assessed . . . with due regard to the restricted uses to which the property may be devoted." In New Jersey, the Supreme Court has upheld the principle that granting a conservation easement to a land trust entitles a taxpayer to a reduced property tax assessment. *Village of Ridgewood* v. *The Bolger Foundation*, 517 A. 2d 135 (NJ 1986). Both the Colorado property tax code and the *Village of Ridgewood* case are discussed in Cheever (1996, p. 1090 n. 82).

of land trusts in the United States increased from about 50 to almost 1,100. By the mid-1990s they preserved more than 4 million acres of undeveloped land – "an area larger than the size of Connecticut" (Land Trust Alliance 1994; Baldwin 1997, p. 99). According to a 1994 Land Trust Alliance survey, approximately one-quarter (900,000 acres) of that 4 million acres is managed by state agencies; private land trusts own 535,000 acres in fee simple; and 740,000 acres are maintained in private ownership but subject to conservation easements held by land trusts.[21] The Nature Conservancy alone protects more than 8 million acres in the United States and Canada (Nature Conservancy 1994). Its holdings constitute "the largest private system of sanctuaries in the world" (Baldwin 1997, p. 99).[22]

Admittedly, these land trusts do not preserve much undeveloped land compared to the federal and state governments. The US National Forest System alone comprises 187 million acres (Forest Service 1996, p. 1) – more than forty-six times the amount of undeveloped land held in trust. But, then, the use of land trusts for preservation purposes has only become a popular mechanism for environmental protection in the last few years. Based on recent trends, Frederico Cheever (1996, p. 1087) predicts that the acreage of undeveloped land protected in trust "will multiply in years to come."

The land trust as a mixed property regime

The partial *public*ization of private lands through land trusts creates a mixed property regime. The landowner who conveys their development rights to the trust retains several conventional private property rights, including the right to exclusive possession. Once the trust *res* is conveyed to some public agency, it becomes public/state property. The land is now, in effect, co-owned as partially private, partially public property. In cases where a private land trust retains the interest, the land is co-owned as partially private/individual, partially common property.

Using this form of mixed property arrangement for environmental protection purposes has substantial advantages over traditional forms of environmental protection. First and foremost, it imposes no involuntary regulatory burden on existing property rights. Instead, conservation easements and land trusts create "property rights in conservation." The

---

[21] The survey did not account for the remaining 2 million acres of property in land trusts.

[22] In addition to preserving wildlands, conservation easements and land trusts are also being used to preserve agricultural lands against conversion to residential or commercial uses. According to Daniels and Bowers (1997, pp. 193, 194 table 11.1) just seven of the more than 1,100 local land trusts in the United States protect nearly 200,000 acres of farmland against nonagricultural development.

trustee, who holds both the right and the duty to prevent development, may achieve results similar to a regulatory agency seeking to prevent destruction of wetlands and preservation of endangered species habitat, but without imposing on someone else's property rights (Cheever 1996, p. 1086). There is no imposition because the conservation easement and land trust are created voluntarily, by contract. Assuming no spillover effects, the deal must be efficient (even on Pareto's strict definition); otherwise the parties would not have consummated the deal.

This is not to say, however, that conservation easements and land trusts are a panacea for environmental protection. Like all other property-based regimes, they have their limitations. As a legal matter, they are heavily dependent on the tax code. In the absence of a tax structure that creates strong positive incentives for development, the offsetting deductions and devaluations provided for conservation easements and land trusts would be minimized, if not negated. In a world where property taxes and inheritance taxes are based in the first instance on existing uses *and nonuses*, rather than market value, our friend Emma would receive no tax benefits from conveying her development rights to a land trust. Another incentive effect would, however, remain: by conveying her development rights to a land trust, Emma could prevent development after her death. She could not accomplish that goal if she retained fee-simple ownership to the end of her life.

A more practical limitation of land trusts is that for every landowner who has a sufficiently strong preference for land preservation to convey their development rights to a land trust, there may be many others who have little or no interest in preservation. Even if conveyances – in fee-simple as well as conservation easements – to land trusts are on the increase, how much wild land can we realistically expect them to preserve? Privately preserved wild lands are likely to resemble small and isolated islands in a sea of development. And to what overall environmental benefit? Preserving five acres of wetlands here and twenty acres of timberlands there, amidst hundreds of square miles of development, may bring discrete environmental benefits: a small undeveloped area may be useful for migratory waterfowl or isolated endangered species. Small islands of preservation are unlikely, however, to be of much ecological value to species requiring large contiguous land masses.

In sum, although the conservation easement is a useful mixed property-based approach for environmental protection, its utility is, as we should by now expect, limited.

4   Institutional and technological limits of mixed property/regulatory regimes

The success of the Clean Air Act's emissions trading "experiment" for sulfur dioxide has led many policy analysts to recommend that Congress summarily abandon command-and-control in favor of the "next generation" of efficiency-enhancing controls (Enterprise for the Environment 1998; Chertow and Esty 1997).[1] Their recommendations typically assert or imply that command-and-control regimes are not only *less* efficient than tradeable permit systems (as well as effluent taxes) but inherently *in*efficient, producing more social costs than benefits (see Tietenberg 1985, p. 38; Stewart 1996, p. 587).[2] But this is not always the case.

This chapter shows that pure public property/regulatory regimes, such as technology-based command-and-control measures, can be (and have been) efficient. Indeed, depending on institutional and technological circumstances, they can be *more* efficient than tradeable permit programs and other mixed property/regulatory regimes. Consequently, there is reason to be skeptical of – even to oppose – recommendations to scrap all command-and-control programs in favor of tradeable permits or effluent taxes.

I   Institutional and technological determinants of instrument choice for environmental protection

The Clean Air Act's "experiment" with emissions trading confirms the potential environmental and economic benefits of tradeable permitting

---

[1] Not all scholars have jumped on the bandwagon, however. Rena Steinzor (1998, p. 10362) has cautioned that a radical transformation of environmental policy could result in "severe degradation of environmental quality," if it is not accompanied by new, more stringent duties imposed on polluters. See also Driesen (1998).

[2] The distinction between "inefficient" and "less efficient" is important, though often overlooked. It is quite possible for a certain regime or transaction to be *nominally* efficient – if it produces more benefits than costs for society – but *relatively* inefficient (or *less* efficient) compared to some alternative regime or transaction that would yield greater net social benefits. In economists' terms, a given regime or transaction may be efficiency improving but not optimally efficient (under Pareto or Kaldor-Hicks criteria).

(mixed property/regulatory regimes) over traditional command-and-control (public property/regulatory regimes). Although the volume of trading under the acid rain program has been lower than expected (see Bohi 1994), the program has produced greater than expected emissions reductions at lower than expected cost – certainly at far lower cost than some alternative regulatory regime of command-and-control.[3] Several other studies allegedly demonstrate similar cost differentials between command-and-control regulations and alternative trading or taxing regimes (see Tietenberg 1991).

On closer inspection, however, neither the acid rain program nor other cases prove that tradeable permitting or other mixed property/regulatory regimes are invariably superior to traditional command-and-control. At best they show that this mixed property/regulatory regime would, in many circumstances, outperform command-and-control both economically and perhaps environmentally, *assuming important institutional and technological circumstances.* Indeed, in other institutional and technological circumstances, public property/regulatory regimes can be expected to outperform tradeable permit schemes (or effluent taxes, for that matter) (see Cole and Grossman 1999).

II   "Empirical" studies of environmental instrument choice

The economist T. H. Tietenberg (1991) discusses a number of "empirical" studies that, he claims, demonstrate the efficiency advantages of tradeable permitting and effluent taxation over traditional command-and-control regulations. These studies prove rather less, however, than Tietenberg suggests. In the first place, only one of them (Spofford 1984) is actually "empirical" (comparing the operation of alternative regulatory regimes in a real-world situation); the others (including Palmer et al. 1980; Roach et al. 1981; Krupnick 1986; Seskin et al. 1983; and Maloney and Yandle 1984) are simulations or predictive studies based on models. Moreover, the one truly empirical study does not conclude that "economic" instruments are inevitably more efficient than command-and-control regulation. Its "most striking" finding is that "[i]n regions with nonuniform atmospheric mixing, such as the Lower Delaware Valley, there is no unique ordering of policy alternatives based on efficiency and independent of the details of the particular situation." Although tradeable permitting was found to be the most efficient approach and command-and-control the least efficient overall, "there were enough exceptions to these findings

---

[3] Menell and Stewart (1994, p. 410) estimate the cost savings from emissions trading at 20 percent or more. A more recent estimate finds far smaller, though still significant, cost savings (Carlson et al. 2000).

to be cautious about making generalizations." Indeed, the study found the operation of tradeable permits and effluent taxes to be "surprisingly erratic" from an efficiency perspective (Spofford 1984, pp. 110–11). It is also worth noting that this study (among many others, such as Mendelsohn 1980) ignores the differential implementation and monitoring costs associated with alternative emissions reduction approaches. This necessarily skews the balance in favor of tradeable permits and effluent taxes over technology-based standards, which, as I will show, typically entail lower monitoring costs.

Among studies that do consider administrative costs, the findings are decidedly mixed. Palmer et al. (1980, p. 255) find that "economic incentives impose lower costs on the economy as a whole and offer far greater flexibility in both the timing and extent of emissions reduction." They conclude, however, that "no policy ranks first among all the dimensions of policy comparison." Consequently, they do not "recommend a particular choice among the policy strategies." Roach et al. (1981, pp. 52, 56) conclude that although certain market-based approaches may in theory be more efficient, one must account for the institutional (legal and political) context in which they operate. Hahn and Noll (1982, pp. 143–4) go a step further, concluding that "economic" instruments are not invariably more efficient than command-and-control for institutional (mainly political) reasons, as well as for reasons pertaining to the nature of specific pollution problems. Similarly, Seskin et al. (1983, p. 119) note that

[i]t would be premature to conclude that the less costly [market-based] strategies ... would necessarily be superior *in practice* to more traditional regulatory approaches. This follows from the fact that the policy instruments needed to implement the less-costly strategies may be unavailable because of legal or political constraints, or may be so costly to administer as to offset the potential cost savings in emissions control costs.

In other words, the "less-costly" strategies may not be less costly after all. Most interesting of all, Maloney and Yandle's (1984, p. 247) study of air pollution control regulation suggests that "when information costs are considered, one might argue that the development of clean air regulation since 1970 has actually been the best possible approach" because of

practical problems associated with both plant standards and regionally marketable permits. The monitoring question is most dominant. The technological basis of the uniform percentage source standards has been itself the monitoring device. If the approved technology was in place, and its working order documented, emission control was being accomplished. With transferability, more direct measurement of emissions might be required.

Far from demonstrating the inevitable superiority of market-based approaches to pollution control, as Tietenberg (1991) suggests, these various "empirical" studies show at best that conceivable market-based approaches would *in many cases* perform more efficiently than command-and-control regulations, *assuming certain institutional circumstances.*

Institutional context

The comparative efficiency of alternative environmental instruments cannot be determined in isolation from the institutional and technological circumstances in which they operate.[4] Consider the case of effluent taxes, which in theory are more efficient than command-and-control regulations because the government does not tell polluters how much pollution they can emit, but only requires them to pay a tax for each unit (e.g., ton) of pollution emitted. This allows polluters to individually select levels of emissions, and emissions reductions, based on their differential costs of control. A polluter with relatively low costs of pollution control will, all other things being equal, reduce emissions more and pay less tax than a polluter with higher costs of control. The only real difficulty is getting the price right, that is, setting the tax at the efficient level. If it is set too low, polluters will choose not to reduce their emissions, in which case the program would fail to provide environmental improvements. Conversely, if the tax is set too high, all polluters may choose to reduce emissions rather than pay taxes, which would provide a great boon for the environment, but be highly inefficient from an economic perspective. Either way, the government may adjust the tax level to achieve greater or lesser emissions reductions among polluters.

Although effluent taxes may appear eminently sensible as a matter of economic theory, in the real world their efficiency and effectiveness depend on institutional and technological preconditions. Poland's communist government discovered this in the early 1980s, when it attempted to implement what was at the time the world's most extensive system of environmental taxes (emission fees and fines) within its nonmarket economic system. Simply put, the Poles found that market mechanisms, such as effluent taxes, require effective market institutions to function at all, let alone efficiently. The lack of competitive market institutions in Poland made it practically impossible for the government to rationally set tax levels. And the endemically soft budget constraints under which polluters – virtually all state-owned enterprises – operated, rendered them insensitive to price signals. Central planners regularly compensated enterprises that met production quotas for any environmental penalties incurred. Because

---

[4] Exceptions include Russell and Powell (1996).

economic survival depended on maximizing output rather than profits, Poland's state-owned enterprises had no incentive to participate in activities, including pollution control, that would have enhanced efficiency but reduced total output (see Cole 1998, p. 283).

The case of effluent taxes in communist Poland presents in stark relief the problem of institutional context: a regulatory regime that is effective and efficient in one institutional setting may be neither in another. Under circumstances of weak or nonexistent market institutions and soft budget constraints, effluent taxes, no matter how efficient as a matter of economic theory, were a poor policy choice.[5]

The Polish case is, of course, an extreme one. Institutional constraints on policy choices are always going to be the greatest where the necessary institutions are entirely absent. But, as the third section of this chapter shows, even subtle institutional constraints can affect the relative efficiency and efficacy of economic instruments for pollution control.

Technological context

Technological constraints can similarly affect environmental policy choice. This is particularly relevant to the choice between traditional command-and-control regulations and economic instruments, such as tradeable permits or effluent taxes. To see why, consider a situation in which the government lacks the technological capability to monitor point-source pollution emissions. The government senses that existing emission levels are causing public health problems, but it cannot tell how much any particular emissions source is contributing to the problem. In this circumstance, a technology-based command-and-control regime may well be more effective and efficient than either a tradeable permit scheme or an effluent tax.

If the government simply orders all potential polluters to install available pollution reduction technology (such as scrubbers), it can be confident of achieving at least *some* amount of emissions reduction, even if it cannot precisely measure how much. The installation and operation of the technology itself evidences the attainment of the desired level of abatement (see Maloney and Yandle 1984, p. 247).[6] The government

---

[5] Of course, this leaves the question of whether command-and-control regulations would have worked any better. Poland (and other former Soviet bloc countries) suffered from soft law, as well as soft budget, constraints. On the concept of soft law constraints, see Kamiński and Sołtan (1989). However, to the extent there was any meaningful environmental protection in Poland at all, it was by direct regulation rather than taxation (see Cole 1998, pp. 88–9).

[6] Also see Maloney and McCormick (1982, p. 106); Office of Technology Assessment (1995, pp. 146–7); Arnold (1995, p. 229); Magat (1982, p. 5); Shapiro and McGarity (1991, p. 749).

must, of course, be able to ensure that the technology is actually installed and operating, but these monitoring costs should at least be finite, which may not be the case for the costs of monitoring actual emissions. As will be shown later, this was roughly the circumstance when Congress enacted the Clean Air Act in 1970.

With a tradeable permit system, by contrast, the cost of monitoring for compliance is necessarily higher. In order to implement a success-ful tradeable permit program the authorities must (1) measure current emission levels, (2) determine a desired level of reductions, (3) subtract desired reductions from current emissions, (4) allocate the remainder among regulated polluters, and (5) continuously monitor emissions to ensure that polluters do not exceed their quotas. In the absence of tech-nology that would permit individual point-source monitoring, the govern-ment could not possibly complete steps (1) or (5), which would prevent a tradeable permit program from ever getting off the ground. In the ab-sence of point-source monitoring technologies, under either an effluent tax or tradeable permit scheme, polluters would have scarce incentive to either abate emissions or trade pollution rights (Russell et al. 1986, p. 3). If the government could not keep track of their actual emissions for pur-poses of assessing taxes or ensuring compliance with quota limits, what rational polluter would choose to reduce emissions or purchase rights to pollute?

Under the assumed technological constraint of no point-source emis-sions monitoring, it seems clear that a command-and-control approach, because it does not depend on point-source emissions monitoring, would likely be more effective and efficient than a transferable pollution rights program or an effluent tax. This does not mean that technology-based standards would be either optimally efficient or very effective, but would be the better alternative under the circumstances.

The institutional and technological constraints discussed in this section may seem extreme, but they are not unrealistic. Even subtle institutional and technological constraints can affect the choice of environmental policy, as the next section demonstrates.

III   Instrument choice for the US Clean Air Act, 1970–1990: institutional and technological perspectives

Consider, once again, the case of the US Clean Air Act (CAA), which despite the innovative 1990 SO_2 emissions trading program continues to be heavily dominated by command-and-control regulations. As the final section of chapter 3 showed, many economists and legal scholars de-plore the CAA's heavy reliance on what they consider to be "blunt" and "often wildly inefficient and 'irrational'" regulatory instruments, such as NAAQS and technology-based emissions limitations (Orts 1995, p. 1236, quoting Krier 1974, pp. 323–5). Those instruments do not appear so "irrational," however, once one considers the institutional and technological constraints under which Congress was operating in 1970, when it established the Act.[7]

The 1970 Clean Air Act: instituting command-and-control

In 1970 Congress possessed precious little information about the economic costs of pollution and the economic benefits of pollution control; existing estimates were very rough and subject to great uncertainties. What is worse, no one knew how bad the country's air pollution problem really was. Ambient concentration levels, the rate of pollution emissions, and the extent of emissions reductions needed to ensure safe ambient concentration levels (however "safe" was defined) were hardly known.

The lack of air pollution information reflected existing technological constraints. In 1970 the National Air Pollution Control Administration reported that existing air pollution monitoring equipment and "analytical techniques" were "not adequate to meet current and anticipated future needs in air monitoring, source testing, measurement of meteorological parameters, and laboratory research" (Environmental Policy Division 1974, pp. 1306–7). Equipment for monitoring ambient concentration levels of various pollutants was lacking. Nationwide in 1970 there were 245 particulate matter (dust) monitors, 86 sulfur dioxide monitors, 82 carbon monoxide monitors, 43 nitrogen oxide monitors, and just 1 monitor for ozone (Environmental Protection Agency 1997, p. D-3, table D-1). These monitors and other available analytical equipment "lack[ed] accuracy, sufficient sensitivity to reflect progress in controlling air pollution, or the specificity needed to satisfy air quality criteria requirements" (Environmental Policy Division 1974, pp. 1306–7).[8]

Individual point-source emissions monitoring was in an even more primitive state than ambient concentration monitoring. For the most part, the government had only one option: to rely on industry self-monitoring (to the extent possible) and reporting on emissions rates. Some industries

---

[7] Actually, the 1970 Act was enacted as a series of amendments to three earlier enacted laws: the 1963 Clean Air Act, the 1965 Motor Vehicle Air Pollution Control Act, and the 1967 Air Quality Act. Consistent with the theory of "path dependence" – according to which institutional change tends to be incremental and based on preexisting models, rather than large-scale and path-breaking – the 1970 Act built on foundations established in those earlier laws. On the theory of path dependence, see, for example, Arthur (1989).

[8] For descriptions of the technologies available *circa* 1970 for monitoring air pollution, see Lieberman and Schipma (1969).

were simply unwilling to provide the government with information on their emissions; others said, perhaps truthfully, that the information simply was not available (see Environmental Policy Division 1974, p. 1312). Many sources *did* comply with government requests for information on their emissions. Still, the government had no means of verifying the data it received.

Given the dearth of information about the extent of the nation's air pollution problems and the emissions reductions necessary to attain healthful air quality, Congress in the 1970 CAA rationally focused its attention on rapidly improving air quality, rather than spending more time debating how it should be done or how much. Indeed, in more than 1,500 pages of legislative history that accompanied the Act, there was virtually no discussion of alternative approaches to regulation, beyond a single reference to effluent taxes during a hearing on May 27, 1970 (Environmental Policy Division 1974, pp. 1223–4). Congress never contemplated effluent taxes or tradeable permitting, though economists and environmental policy analysts (for instance Dales 1968) were already advocating their use. This might suggest, on a public choice account, that Congress and the interest groups pressing for federal air pollution control legislation had little interest in efficiency-enhancing economic instruments. But it certainly reflects the real information constraints, particularly relating to emissions levels, Congress faced in 1970.

Beyond information constraints, Congress was deeply concerned with the inadequate staffing of state and federal agencies charged with implementing air pollution regulations. According to a 1970 report to Congress by the Department of Health, Education, and Welfare (the federal agency with primary responsibility for environmental protection before the creation of the Environmental Protection Agency in 1970), "control agencies" were "in general . . . inadequately staffed. Fifty percent of state agencies [had] fewer than 10 positions budgeted, and 50 percent of local agencies [had] fewer than seven positions budgeted." The report estimated that state and local agency staffing would have to increase by 300 percent "to implement the Clean Air Act properly" (Environmental Policy Division 1974, p. 254). Meanwhile, according to Senator Edmund Muskie, who was the chief sponsor of the CAA in the Senate, federal agency staffing needed to be tripled by 1973 to fully implement the Act (Environmental Policy Division 1974, p. 230).

Given the institutional and technological constraints under which it was operating, it made sense for Congress in 1970 to take a public property/regulatory approach to air pollution control. By focusing on technology-based design standards for industrial sources and automobiles, the federal government could minimize its monitoring and staffing deficiencies. So long as pollution control technologies were installed and operating, the government could be assured of *some* emissions reductions, even if it could not precisely measure them. At least it was *possible*, at some finite cost, to monitor the installation and operation of pollution control technology. In the early 1970s, for example, the Los Angeles Country Air Pollution Control District managed to inspect every major source for compliance with technology-based standards once each month (see Willick and Windle 1973).[9] It would not have been possible at that time, however, to monitor point-source emissions for all regulated pollutants at any finite cost.

Several contributors to a volume published a year before the 1970 CAA was enacted recognized this advantage of command-and-control. George Hagevik (1969, p. 178) wrote, "[t]he advantage of [direct regulation] is that it permits the government to take interim steps even though it has almost no idea of relevant measurements." The economist Harold Wolozin (1969, p. 39) noted that "[f]ormidable detection and monitoring problems are implicit in effluent fee schemes, a problem compounded by the primitive state of technology in these areas." Wolozin (p. 40) quoted from a presentation by William Vickrey at the 1967 annual meeting of the Air Pollution Control Association:

The real problem which advocates of effluent charges must face is the problem of metering, or of estimating in some way the amount of effluent actually generated by various emitters. Here the problem of air pollution is seen to be a particularly difficult one in that the number of small emitters and of the emitters difficult to meter effectively is large and their contribution to the problem is too great to be ignored.

Paul Gerhardt (1969, p. 169) concurred that "a fee system could be exceedingly difficult and costly to administer ... [E]mission measurement technology is presently inadequate to meet the requirement that a regulatory agency be able to determine with some precision just how much an individual polluter is contributing to the atmospheric burden."

Because of existing technological constraints, regulatory approaches such as effluent taxes and tradeable permits that depend on regular and precise point-source monitoring of emissions were impracticable in 1970. They may have been efficient in theory – perhaps more efficient than the command-and-control mechanisms that Congress codified in the 1970 CAA – but only if monitoring costs were ignored. Unfortunately, many economists and legal scholars who write about instrument choice in environmental protection do just that: they ignore monitoring costs.

---

[9] Not every state or local government was as diligent in enforcing compliance, however (see Downing and Kimball 1982).

As Russell et al. (1986, p. 3) have noted, most environmental policy analysts tend to assume "perfect (and incidentally, costless) monitoring." This may be convenient analytically, but it is obviously unrealistic, and it skews perceptions of the relative efficiency of effluent taxes and tradeable permits versus command-and-control regulations. Given that regular and precise point-source monitoring is necessary to accurately assess taxes or determine compliance with emissions quotas (pursuant to a tradeable permit scheme), *and* given the infeasibility of monitoring emissions from tens of thousands of individual smokestacks and millions of automobile tailpipes in 1970, it was rational – indeed, efficient – for Congress to rely on technology-based command-and-control standards.

The 1977 Clean Air Act Amendments: retaining the regulatory status quo

Institutional and technological circumstances changed significantly, though not decisively, between 1970 and the first set of major amendments to the Clean Air Act in 1977. On the institutional front, the Environmental Protection Agency, which was created in 1970 to implement the CAA, showed a surprisingly rapid learning curve for a fledgling agency that, at the outset, possessed virtually no economic expertise. Before it was a year old, the agency's first administrator, Russell Train, testified before Congress in favor of President Nixon's proposals for effluent taxes on sulfur dioxide emissions and lead additives in gasoline (Environmental Policy Division 1978, p. 2541). Congress did not enact either tax proposal, but it is interesting to note that President Nixon did not propose the tax on sulfur dioxide emissions as a preferable alternative to technology-based standards; rather, he proposed it as a second-best option because no technologies were then "available" for controlling sulfur dioxide emissions (see Council on Environmental Quality 1971, pp. 27, 30).[10]

By the mid-1970s the EPA was implementing its own policies designed to introduce some much needed flexibility into the regulatory system, and thereby reduce compliance costs for regulated industries (see Liroff 1986; Hahn and Hester 1989).[11] These innovations demonstrated the agency's increasing competence on economic issues in environmental regulation, and reflected, in part, a substantial alleviation of agency staffing deficiencies. In 1979 the federal EPA had more than 500 employees nationwide working exclusively on clean air programs. State and local governments,

---

[10] Subsequently, both sulfur dioxide emissions (in 1990) and lead additives in gasoline (in 1982) were subject to tradeable permitting.

[11] These administrative innovations – netting, offsets, bubbles, and banking – were discussed above, in chapter 3.

meanwhile, devoted more than 6,500 personnel to air pollution control (National Commission in Air Quality 1981, p. 94, table 4). Whether this level of staffing was sufficient to meet the increased monitoring, data collection, and record-keeping needs of effluent tax or tradeable permit regimes is, however, unclear.

Technological constraints on effluent taxes and tradeable permits were also marginally reduced by the time Congress amended the CAA in 1977. The total number of ambient concentration monitors for "criteria" pollutants had increased by more than a factor of six;[12] the number of particulate matter monitors rose from 245 (in 1970) to 1,120 (in 1975); ozone monitors increased from 1 to 321; and so on (Environmental Protection Agency 1997, p. D-3, table D-1). Moreover, the quality and reliability of the monitoring equipment and analytical techniques for data interpretation had improved, though evidently not enough to make tradeable permitting or effluent taxes feasible alternatives to command-and-control. A 1977 report by the National Research Council "identified the lack of statistical rigor in the design and analysis of most environmental monitoring networks" (Council on Environmental Quality 1990, p. 56, citing National Academy of Sciences, National Research Council 1977). The first continuous emissions monitoring system (CEMS) became available in 1975 (see Jahnke 1993, p. 2). This marked an important step toward making effluent tax schemes and tradeable permit programs feasible. But in 1977 monitoring technologies still were not sufficient to permit the cost-effective replacement of command-and-control regulations with "economic" instruments. As Marc Roberts wrote in 1982 (p. 99):

[w]hen economists discuss such matters [as emissions trading] they sometimes talk as if monitoring devices were widely available to cheaply and reliably record the amount of all pollution emissions. If that were the case decisions about whether a source had curtailed its pollution by the promised amount and whether a new source was emitting no more than the tradeoff transaction implied could be left to straightforward data gathering by an enforcement agent. Unfortunately, such monitoring devices typically are not available.

Given the continuing infeasibility of tradeable permitting and effluent taxation, stemming primarily from technology constraints, Congress in the 1977 CAA Amendments rationally left the existing command-and-control system in place. And the two major new programs Congress added to the Act in 1977 – the nonattainment area rules and the Prevention of Significant Deterioration program – were based on the same old

---

[12] A "criteria" pollutant is one for which the EPA has established national ambient air quality standards under the Clean Air Act. Today, there are six such criteria air pollutants: particulate matter, sulfur dioxide, carbon monoxide, nitrogen oxides, and lead.

command-and-control model. The 3,400 pages of legislative history accompanying the amendments reveal that Congress was only marginally more interested in effluent taxes and tradeable permits in 1977 than it had been in 1970, although it had a great deal more information about pollution levels, necessary reductions, and regulatory alternatives. At least the information was available to any legislator who chose to be informed.[13]

The continuation of command-and-control in the 1977 CAA Amendments is usually explained from a public choice perspective: neither Congress, the EPA, the regulated industries, nor environmental groups favored a switch to alternative and less costly regulatory approaches (see, for example, Keohane et al. 1997). But Congress's decision to stick with command-and-control in 1977 was rational given the continuing infeasibility of effluent taxes and tradeable permits, due to persistent technological constraints. There was also a sense in Congress that the existing program was not overly expensive. National expenditures for air pollution control in 1975 were $15.7 billion, amounting to only about 1 percent of the economy's total output of goods and services. Meanwhile, air pollution was "conservatively estimated" to cost the economy (in health and material damage) more than $25 billion annually (Environmental Policy Division 1978, pp. 3050–1).

What Congress did not know in 1977, but we know now, was that the existing command-and-control system was actually producing sizeable net social benefits. A 1982 study determined that the Clean Air Act produced net social benefits of more than $26.3 billion between 1970 and 1981 (Freeman 1982).[14] A more recent study by the EPA estimates that the CAA produced (inflation adjusted) net benefits of $909 billion between 1970 and 1980 (Environmental Protection Agency 1997, p. 56, table 18). This cannot be overemphasized: the presumptively costly command-and-control system of the Clean Air Act was, and still is, producing huge net social benefits. Again, Congress did not know this when it enacted the 1977 Amendments, but there was a sense that the Act was not imposing excessive costs on society.

So, what impetus was there for Congress to make a costly switch to new and as yet untested regulatory approaches? No studies available to Congress in 1977 (and no studies completed since then) support the proposition that replacing the existing command-and-control system with alternative approaches would have produced larger net social benefits in

[13] The legislative history included studies that suggested large cost advantages of effluent taxes over command-and-control regulations (see Environmental Policy Division 1978, pp. 1192–205).

[14] Freeman's assessment was subsequently confirmed by Portney (1990).

1977, after accounting for the costs of transition to the new system, including increased monitoring costs.

The 1990 CAA Amendments: an incremental shift toward a mixed property/regulatory approach

As the last chapter showed, the adoption of an emissions trading program in the acid rain provisions of the 1990 Clean Air Act Amendments represented a new direction in environmental policy. It was not, however, a simple matter of Congress finally realizing what economists had known for decades: that tradeable permits are more efficient and effective than technology-based standards. The move to tradeable permits was facilitated by institutional, technological, and economic developments between 1977 and 1990, including: the rising marginal costs of air pollution control; the emerging perception that those costs were overtaking the social benefits of the Act; the EPA's increasing economic expertise; and, most importantly, the development of reliable and cost-effective CEMS.

Between 1977 and 1990 emissions of all criteria pollutants fell. The average decline in emissions was 24 percent (though only 11.2 percent if reductions in lead emissions are excluded).[15] As a consequence, ambient air quality improved significantly. National ambient concentrations of criteria pollutants fell between 1981 and 1988 by an average of 22.6 percent (but only 10.6 percent if ambient lead concentrations are excluded).[16] These substantial improvements in air quality came at a higher cost to society, however, as the total annualized costs of air pollution control increased (in constant 1990 dollars) by 63.5 percent, from $15.9 billion in 1977 to $26 billion in 1990 (Environmental Protection Agency 1997, p. A-16, table A-9).[17]

This did not mean that the CAA was producing net social losses. To the contrary, it was still yielding substantial – indeed, growing – net social benefits. Between 1970 and 1975 the Act produced estimated net, inflation adjusted benefits – defined as the "mean monetized benefits less annualized costs for each year" – of $341 billion (Environmental Protection Agency 1997, pp. 55, 56, table 18). From 1975 to 1980 estimated net benefits nearly tripled to $909 billion; they rose to $1.13 trillion by 1985,

---

[15] Calculated from figures presented in Council on Environmental Quality (1990, pp. 320–2, table 39).

[16] Calculated from figures presented in Council on Environmental Quality (1990, p. 323, table 40). Five of the six criteria pollutants experienced drops in ambient concentration levels. The exception was ozone, ambient concentrations of which increased by 7 percent.

[17] On emissions rates in 1977 and 1990, see Council on Environmental Quality (1990, pp. 320–3, tables 39 and 40).

and stood at \$1.22 trillion in 1990. The agency's benefit and cost figures, as well as its discount rates, are, of course, debatable. Independent sources agree, however, that the benefits of the Clean Air Act clearly exceeded its costs between 1970 and 1990 (see Davies and Mazurek 1998, p. 278; *BNA National Environment Daily*, Dec. 16, 1998).

Congress, when it enacted the 1990 CAA Amendments, was unaware that the CAA was continuing to produce net social benefits. Many in Congress perceived, inaccurately, that the Act was becoming too costly. The 10,000 pages of legislative history that accompanied the 1990 Amendments are replete with expressions of concern and debates over the respective costs and benefits of new and existing air pollution control programs (Environment and Natural Resources Policy Division 1993, pp. 731, 1058, 1091, 1179, 1193, 4829, 7187, 9736–55, 9826, 9867). And, because perception is at least as important as fact in the legislative process, congressional interest in efficiency-enhancing policies may have increased as legislators and others *perceived* that additional increments of air pollution control could be obtained under the existing program only at a net cost to society.

There is more to the story of the 1990 CAA Amendments, however, than congressional perceptions of costs and benefits. Important institutional developments since 1977 provided reason to believe that federal and state agencies could successfully implement and enforce tradeable permits and other alternatives to traditional regulatory approaches. Certainly, by 1990 the federal EPA was more open to the use of alternative regulatory mechanisms, such as tradeable permits. The agency had been preparing economic analyses (regulatory impact analyses or RIAs) of its major regulations virtually since its inception.[18] And it had grown comfortable with cost-benefit analysis as a tool of environmental policy. As the EPA noted in a 1987 report, "[e]nvironmentalists often fear that economic analysis will lead to less strict environmental regulations in an effort to save costs, but our study reveals that the opposite is just as often the case" (Environmental Protection Agency, 1987, p. 2). In order to meet its obligations to perform economic analyses, the agency by 1990 was employing more than 100 economists, which gave it greater economic expertise than any other federal health and safety agency (Davies and Mazurek, 1998, p. 32).

In part, the EPA's increased economic expertise and comfort with economic instruments was due to a small-scale and temporary but largely

---

[18] The EPA's rules were first subject to "Quality of Life" reviews by President Nixon's Office of Management and Budget (see Environmental Protection Agency 1987, p. S-2). Subsequently, the agency was required to perform economic analyses of its major rules under executive orders issued by Presidents Carter, Reagan, and Clinton (see Davies and Mazurek 1998, p. 32).

successful experiment in tradeable rights to lead content in gasoline. As part of its phase-out of leaded gasoline, from 1982 to 1987 the EPA allowed trading in "rights" to add lead to gasoline. Refiners that produced gasoline with lower lead content than mandated by federal standards could sell or bank their excess lead content. Smaller refiners that could not afford to meet the federal lead content standards were able to reduce their compliance costs by purchasing "lead rights" instead of reducing lead content. The lead content market proved to be "very active," and produced "hundreds of millions of dollars" in cost savings (Hahn and Hester, 1989b, pp. 380–91).

It is important to understand just why this program was successful. Lead content trading was technologically feasible when emissions trading was not because lead content, unlike fugitive emissions, is easily measured *at all times*; the amount of lead in gasoline remains relatively constant at all fuel levels. Undoubtedly, the EPA's successful experiment with trading in gasoline lead content increased the agency's confidence that tradeable permitting was a useful policy tool.

Just as the EPA was becoming more familiar with, and expert in, dealing with economic approaches to environmental protection, state environmental agencies were becoming better staffed and equipped. Between 1974 and 1992 state air quality expenditures more than doubled from $249 million to $516 million (in constant 1992 dollars) (Davies and Mazurek 1998, p. 32). This may have alleviated federal concern about the states' abilities to monitor and enforce federal air pollution control programs.

Even more important for the 1990 Amendments than institutional developments were technological changes that made tradeable permitting (as well as effluent taxes) administratively feasible. Continuous emissions monitoring systems, the first of which appeared two years before Congress enacted the 1977 CAA Amendments, were widely available and affordable in 1990. As James A. Jahnke wrote in 1993 (p. 8), "CEM systems . . . advanced considerably over the past 15 years, with improved sampling techniques, analyzers, and data processing systems being integrated to meet the challenges posed by new requirements." By 1991 the US government was requiring continuous monitoring at twenty-four categories of sources subject to New Source Performance Standards under the CAA. In addition, CEMS were required for all electric power generators regulated under the CAA's acid rain program (Jahnke 1993, p. 12–3, table 2-1). CEMS were not yet available for all air pollutants or for all categories of sources,[19] but they made tradeable permitting feasible – that

---

[19] For instance, in 1998 the EPA was still working out the bugs in a CEMS for particulate matter emissions from hazardous waste incinerators (see BNA *National Environment Daily*, June 29, 1998).

is, cost-effective – and, in some cases, preferable – that is, more efficient – for certain combinations of pollutants and sources.

To sum up, when Congress enacted the 1990 CAA Amendments: it had increased information about market mechanisms for environmental protection; new technologies – particularly CEMS – were available to adequately monitor point-source emissions; state agencies were better funded; the EPA had developed superior economic expertise; and there was rising concern about the costs of air pollution control. These factors combine to explain why Congress decided to begin experimenting on a larger scale with alternative regulatory approaches, such as emissions trading. Whether or not the CAA was still producing net social benefits (which it was, as I shall show), the reasons for preferring command-and-control – particularly concerns over monitoring and enforcement – were waning. At least with respect to certain air pollution problems, the theoretical efficiency advantages of tradeable permits and effluent taxes could finally be realized.

Chapter 3 already addressed the success of Congress's 1990 experiment with tradeable "allowances" for sulfur dioxide emissions. One oft-neglected point, central to that program's success, is Congress's insistence, in the text of the statute itself, on continuous monitoring of sulfur dioxide emissions, "to preserve the orderly functioning of the allowance system, and . . . ensure the emissions reductions contemplated by this [program]" (42 USC § 4651k(a) (1977)). This statutory language reflects two critical perceptions. First, "[u]nlike other control requirements of the Clean Air Act, utility emissions of SO_2 and NO_x are capable of verification in a cost-effective manner through the use of continuous emission monitors." Second, "[t]he requirement for CEMS is the linchpin in this title for without good emissions data, a problem that has hampered enforcement of the Act to date, no allowance or emissions trading scheme can affectively [sic] operate" (Environment and Natural Resources Policy Division 1993, p. 1040). The clear implication is that absent the technical capability to precisely monitor emissions "in a cost-effective manner," tradeable permitting cannot be said to be feasible, let alone preferable to direct regulation. It is the existence of cost-effective technologies for measuring SO_2 emissions that has made the emissions trading program workable.

Despite the success of the acid rain program's emissions trading program, it is important to bear in mind (as Congress apparently did) that reliable and cost-effective CEMS are still not available for all combinations of pollutants and sources regulated under the CAA. This may explain why Congress did not make wholesale changes in the 1990 Amendments, but restricted its use of emissions trading to only one program. As the

New Institutional Economics might predict (see North 1990), Congress's policy shift away from the pure public property/regulatory approach of command-and-control toward the mixed property/regulatory approach of tradeable permitting was deliberate, incremental, and inconsistent. However, the real lesson of the Clean Air Act's history, for present purposes, is that mixed property/regulatory regimes, such as tradeable permits, are not invariably more effective or efficient than pure public property/regulatory approaches, such as technology-based standards. A great deal depends on the institutional and technological context.

IV   Institutional and environmental policy implications

In some cases, it makes sense for the state to retain full control over resources, rather than allocating limited property "rights" in environmental goods to private owners. This is particularly true when privatization would raise monitoring and enforcement costs so much as to offset likely compliance cost savings.

This conclusion seems at odds, however, with what we think we know about the inefficiencies of public resource ownership generally. Especially since the fall of communism in Eastern Europe, the expectation is that privately owned property will always be used more efficiently and conserved more effectively. This is an issue we will meet head-on in the next chapter. For present purposes, however, it is important to note that public ownership of environmental goods, such as the atmosphere, can have efficiency advantages over mixed ownership, when private property owners can successfully externalize their pollution costs, and the government does not possess the technological or institutional capacity to monitor compliance with rules designed to internalize those costs. In that circumstance, it may make more sense for the government to retain ownership and control over the resources. Although public ownership does not reduce the incentives of private resource users to externalize their pollution costs, it allows the government to impose enforceable duties on those users, which can effectively internalize their externalities to some, albeit uncertain, extent, without having to rely as heavily on costly monitoring of private behavior. Thus, the structure of property rights, or choice of property regime, is itself a variable of environmental policy that depends substantially on institutional and technological circumstances (see Samuels 1999).

This last point carries obvious implications for international, as well as domestic, environmental policy. Consider, for example, the Kyoto Protocol to the United Nations Climate Change Convention (art. 3, 1, 3–4, 10–13, art. 4, 1, art. 6, 1–4, reprinted in *BNA Environment Report*,

Dec. 12, 1997), which requires signatory countries to reduce their green-house gas emissions by 6 percent, and institutes a global emissions trading regime to minimize the costs of attaining those reductions. Negotiators simply presumed that a trading system would provide a lower cost mechanism than traditional command-and-control for meeting the Protocol's goal. They may be right, but the analysis in this chapter provides some reason for doubt. Many countries – and not just "less developed" ones – lack the institutional and technological capabilities to regularly and precisely monitor quotas and actual emissions, which is necessary "to preserve the orderly functioning" of the trading system. Fraschini and Cassone (1994, p. 102), for example, contend that the "quite backward" state of emissions monitoring and enforcement technology in Italy "explain[s] why economic instruments . . . are virtually absent" from Italian water pollution control policy. There is no reason to expect that countries will reduce their greenhouse gas emissions to comply with quotas that cannot be effectively monitored and enforced. At least with technology-based command-and-control standards, the international regime would be assured of achieving some level of emissions reduction, simply by enforcing the installation and operation of mandated technology. Again, this is not to say that mixed property/regulatory approaches, such as tradeable permitting and effluent taxes, are never more efficient instruments for environmental protection. They often are. But contrary to what seems to be the prevailing wisdom among economists and legal scholars, they are not policy panaceas for efficient environmental protection. On a total cost approach, which accounts for monitoring and enforcement costs as well as compliance costs, no single environmental instrument achieves the lowest net social costs, or produces the greatest net social benefits, in every institutional and technological circumstance (see Cole and Grossman, forthcoming b).

5 The theory and limits of free-market environmentalism (a private property/nonregulatory regime)

A small but highly productive group of economists and libertarian legal scholars reject both the public property/regulatory approach and the mixed property/regulatory approach to environmental protection. The former they consider a form of "feudalism," with government "lords" imposing Byzantine and irrational obligations on regulated "tenants" (Yandle 1992); the later a form of "market socialism," with the government creating, overseeing, and limiting market transactions (Anderson and Leal 1991, pp. 158–9; McGee and Block 1994). Just as society has rejected both feudalism and market socialism as forms of economic organization, so they claim society should reject them as approaches to environmental protection. These self-styled "free-market environmentalists" deny the need for *any* form of government-sponsored environmental regulation. Instead, they promote a nonregulatory, complete private property "solution." This chapter assesses their claims.

I The worldwide trend toward privatization

Privatization has been sweeping the globe. Since the Reagan–Thatcher revolution of the 1980s, governments throughout the world have been selling off public assets to private owners in order to improve efficiency and increase production.[1] Between 1985 and 1994, $468 billion worth of state-owned enterprises were sold off to private investors (Poole 1996, p. 1). But privatization so far has been limited to economic enterprises. Governments have not, with a few notable and highly controversial exceptions,[2]

---

[1] The presumption that privatization of economic enterprises always enhances economic efficiency is questionable, however. A growing body of empirical research indicates that privatization, in the absence of well-functioning market institutions, does not enhance efficiency (see Nellis 2000; Antal-Mokos 1998; Black et al. 2000).

[2] In 1990 New Zealand's government offered for sale more than a million acres of plantation forests, in order to raise money to pay off the national debt (see Wijewardana 1990). But this sale was exceptional. In Great Britain in 1994 the Conservative government of British Prime Minister John Major was forced to abandon plans to privatize national forests in the wake of massive public opposition (see *Economist*, Feb. 5, 1994; *Scotland on Sunday*,

begun selling off their vast natural resource holdings, including forests, parks, waterways, wildlife, and the atmosphere.

This is a mistake, according to free-market environmentalists, who claim that the same economic arguments favoring private ownership of economic producers – the polluters and resource users – also support private ownership of environmental goods (that is, natural resources). As Richard Stroup and Sandra Goodman (1992, p. 427) have expressed it, "government ownership and control works just as badly with environmental resources as with all other resources." In their view, privately owned natural resources would be better managed not just economically but environmentally.

II   What constitutes privatization

The term "privatization" is ambiguous. As used in the law and economics literature, it encompasses a wide variety of mechanisms by which a public entity conveys property rights to a private entity or entities – everything from outright giveaways or sales of public lands to licenses or concessions under which private individuals, groups, or firms finance, construct, or manage hotels, airports, wastewater treatment plants, highways, prisons, and schools (Poole 1996, p. 1). In this broad definition, "privatization" can, but need not, be total. As discussed in chapters 3 and 4, the allocation of marketable pollution permits constitutes a form of limited privatization, as the government conveys to private parties limited entitlements to use the public's atmosphere. But free-market environmentalists typically (though often implicitly) reject this broad understanding of "privatization." What they mean by the term is something quite narrow and unambiguous: the *complete* transfer of public rights in natural resources to private individuals, groups, or firms through outright sale or gift (Anderson and Leal 1991).

III   The theory of free-market environmentalism

Conventional welfare economics explains environmental problems as symptoms of market failures, caused by externalities, which justify corrective government intervention in the marketplace (see Samuelson 1980, pp. 450; Royal Commission on Environmental Pollution 1971, pp. 4–6). Government intervention can, of course, take various forms, including subsidies or payments, financial penalities or fees (taxes), and coercive commands such as prohibitions, regulations, and directives.

May 29, 1994; *Guardian*, May 19, 1994). Similarly in America, during the 1980s, public opposition forced the Reagan administration to hastily rescind plans to privatize public lands (see Leman 1984).

Free-market environmentalists do not deny that environmental problems arise from market failures; nor do they take issue with the need for responsive government action (though they often sound as if they do). However, they challenge the conventional welfare economics story of the causes of environmental problems and appropriate governmental responses. It is true that environmental problems are caused by market failures, as welfare economics suggests, but free-market environmentalists extend the analysis to ask what causes the market failures. Their answer: environmental market failures stem from the incomplete specification of property rights in environmental goods. Government-sponsored remedies that ignore that root cause are palliatives at best. They may treat the symptoms of environmental externalities, but they do not correct the underlying cause of the market failure. The only way to do that – and, thus, the only truly appropriate and effective remedy for environmental problems – is to completely specify private property rights in environmental goods; that is to say, privatize them. Free-market environmentalists claim that a system of completely specified and protected property rights should prevent inefficient externalities and, therefore, market failures. In the absence of market failures, government regulatory intervention is neither necessary nor justified.

It is important to recognize that the theory of free-market environmentalism cannot be explained solely by reference to the tragedy-of-open-access model (introduced in chapter 1), which merely recognizes the need to establish *some* property regime – public, common, or private – to limit access to, and use of, scarce resources. The free-marketeers argue, in addition, that *public* property regimes are insufficient for effective and efficient conservation. The complete privatization of environmental goods is, by contrast, a sufficient and necessary condition for optimal environmental protection. Thus, the important distinction for free-market environmentalists is public property (*res publicae*) versus private property (*res privatae*), where private property is defined to include both individual property (*res individuales*) and (private) common property (*res communes*) (Anderson and Leal 1991, p. 3).

IV Public ownership, bureaucratic mismanagement, and government failure

The theory of government failure

Free-market environmentalists contend that there should be no public property rights in environmental goods for reasons that derive largely from the public choice literature (see Downs 1957; Buchanan and Tullock 1962; Olson 1965; Niskanen 1971). Put briefly and too simplistically, public choice theory applies market theory to political actions. Political and legislative processes are treated as economic markets, in which the participants act to maximize their own individual welfare rather than some more broadly conceived social welfare. In this view, the results of political and legislative processes are best described not as the deliberative decisions of bodies dedicated to improving the public weal, but as the outcomes of contests for political largess between groups of self-interested individuals (see Mercuro and Medema 1997, ch. 3). The theory of free-market environmentalism, for the most part, extends this analysis to the management of publicly owned resources.[3]

In essence, free-market environmentalists deny the very possibility of "public" property, claiming that private interests – whether those of politicians, bureaucrats, or favored interest groups – inevitably assert what amounts to *dominium* over nominally public assets (see Huffman 1994). Like ordinary private owners, the politicians and bureaucrats who are *de facto* owners of *de jure* public property will manage resources so as to maximize their private, self-interested utility (Anderson and Leal 1991, p. 4; Stroup and Baden 1983, p. 43). But the incentives of public resource managers are quite different from those of private owners for two main reasons (which I briefly outlined in the final section of chapter 2).

First, bureaucrats and politicians are not personally invested in the resources under their control. Consequently, if they manage resources poorly, they do not bear the economic losses. That does not mean, however, that no one bears those losses. As Terry Anderson and Donald Leal (1991, p. 4) explain, the "political sector operates by externalizing costs" to the public. Private property owners may also externalize the costs of poor *private* resource management decisions in some circumstances, but they can only do so because property rights are incompletely specified (p. 20). Were property rights completely specified in all environmental goods and thoroughly protected, private resource owners would be unable to inefficiently externalize costs to other property owners. Affected property owners would be able to force the internalization of externalities merely by enforcing their property rights through private litigation.[4]

The most important difference between the incentives of public resource managers and private owners, according to free-market environmentalists, is the relative short-sightedness of the former. Environmental issues often have significant time preference aspects. For example, an old

---

[3] On the application of public choice theory to environmental regulation, see generally Svendsen (1998).

[4] An important caveat: complete private ownership would not necessarily result in the complete internalization of costs because some externalities may be efficient; that is, the cost of internalizing them might exceed the benefits to be gained. On the concept of efficient externality, see, for example, Demsetz (1968).

growth forest harvested today will not be available to future generations of users or viewers. The decision to presently harvest or conserve the forest will depend significantly on whether the owners/managers focus on short-run or long-term net benefits. All resource users explicitly or implicitly weigh present use values against expected future benefits, if current use is foregone. This comparison is complicated by the fact that a dollar spent or saved today is worth more than the same dollar spent or saved, say, nine years in the future, because today's dollar can be invested at some positive rate of interest, so that it will be worth more than a dollar nine years from now. If invested at an interest rate of 8 percent, compounded annually, it will be worth precisely 2 dollars. Viewed from the future, a dollar spent or saved nine years from now is worth only one-half of the same dollar spent or saved today, using an 8 percent *discount* rate. When making resource management decisions, private resource owners and public resource managers *always* (implicitly or explicitly) discount future expected costs and benefits, reducing them to present-day dollars, which can then be compared directly to current use values. If the discounted expected future value is greater than the present use value, the resource will be conserved, that is, invested for future use; otherwise, it will be presently used or consumed.

The comparison of present and expected future values depends predominantly on two variables: the estimation of future value and the owner/manager's subjective discount rate, which measures the rate with which they reduce future values to present dollars. A low discount rate favors longer-term investments or conservation; a higher discount rate tends to favor current use or consumption. To take a simple example, suppose a new environmental policy requires some industry to install scrubbers on smokestacks to reduce air pollution emissions; and that policy is expected to yield net social benefits of $1.5 million per year over an eight-year period. The total value of the policy is $12 million ($1.5 million per year × 8 years), but the total *present* value of the policy (the total expected value of the policy in present-day dollars) is only $9.77 million, utilizing a 5 percent discount rate. With a higher discount rate, the total expected net present value of the policy would be lower; with a lower discount rate, it would be higher. If most of the costs of the environmental policy accrue in early years, but most of the benefits are deferred to later years, a high discount rate may render the policy unattractive, even if the policy is expected to ultimately produce net social benefits (defined as total expected benefits in excess of total expected costs).

Government intervention for environmental protection is commonly premised on claims that the discount rates of individual resource owners exceed the social rate of discount (assuming there is such a thing), resulting in too rapid resource use and depletion (Hotelling 1931; Howe 1979). But free-market environmentalists counter that private resource owners can be expected to have lower discount rates and longer time horizons than the politicians and bureaucrats who manage publicly owned resources (Stroup and Goodman 1992). As Richard Stroup and John Baden (1983, p. 24) put it, "there is no 'voice of the future' in government equivalent to the rising market price of an increasingly valuable resource. The wise public resource manager who forgoes current benefits cannot personally profit from doing so." For politicians facing reelection in two-, four-, or six-year cycles, the choice between preserving natural resources for unborn generations or developing them for living generations of voters is obvious. Politicians do not make resource management decisions based on abstract principles of intergenerational justice, but on their estimates of the expected costs and benefits to living constituents (see Pashigian 1985).

Bureaucrats do not face reelection, of course, but they are dependent on the legislative authorizations and annual budget decisions of politicians who do. While private resource owners seek to maximize the discounted net present value of their assets, public resource managers are often motivated to maximize budget allocations and administrative turf (Orzechowski 1977). Their actions respond to political rather than market conditions, even if doing so "reduces the total value of production" (Libecap 1981, p. 9). Given their incentive structure, bureaucrats are likely to favor, and therefore to subsidize, resource uses that increase (or protect) their budgets and influence, regardless of economic waste or environmental degradation. Even if this were not true – even if public agencies could be depended on to maximize economic and environmental values in resource management – it remains doubtful that any government agency could "accurately measure, simulate, predict, and plan for both ecological and economic outcomes" (Rasker 1994, p. 392).

The usual result of bureaucratic management, according to free-market environmentalists, is *government failure* to allocate environmental goods efficiently. In many, if not all, cases "public" ownership does not protect the environment from market failure, but itself becomes "the cause of environmental problems" (Baden and Stroup 1990, p. 132). And because governments fail too, market failure cannot automatically justify government intervention in the marketplace (Castle 1965, p. 552).

Evidence of government failure in natural resources management

The free-market environmentalist literature is replete with stories of government mismanagement of publicly owned resources, where "mismanagement" is defined, if only implicitly, as economically inefficient and/or environmentally harmful management (see Anderson and Leal 1991; Stroup and Baden 1983; Nelson 1995; Klyza 1996). Richard L. Stroup and John A. Baden have explained, for example, how government ownership and control of rangelands has led, for more than a century, to overgrazing and desertification:

overgrazing on the western Great Plains by cattlemen on public lands destroyed the fragile ecological balance of the grasslands, preparing the way for the dust bowl. Without the extension of private property rights into this area, each stockman was driven by economic incentives to overgraze before someone else did, to run more stock than the land could sustain through time, and to graze too early in the year before the young grasses matured and seeded. Nor was there any incentive for any user to reseed overgrazed areas or to attempt any form of irrigation. Similar conditions still prevail on BLM [Bureau of Land Management] lands where cattlemen and sheepmen can graze their animals on land they do not own (and may not be able to use the next year) at fees below what they would pay on private land. Under these conditions, they have an incentive to overgraze. (Stroup and Baden 1983, p. 47)[5]

Why does the BLM charge ranchers below-market rates for grazing their cattle on the public lands? Gary Libecap (1981, pp. 100–1) explains, "bureaucrats do not bear the costs nor receive the benefits of their actions and, hence, can ignore market signals and engage in socially wasteful land management practices." So, it costs the agency little to implement a policy that pleases an important constituency – ranchers who use the public lands for grazing cattle – thereby reducing the likelihood of political battles that could prove costly to the agency in terms of both budget and power.

Stroup and Baden (1983, pp. 111–12) also note how US Forest Service management of publicly owned timber stands has resulted in both economic inefficiency and environmental degradation:

There are two major problems with public timber management. First, the US Forest Service systematically supports inefficient timber production. Instead of investing the nation's resources where the marginal returns are the highest, the Forest Service is influenced by political considerations only haphazardly related to site productivity. The agency engages in accounting practices, such as the allowable cut effect, that distort and inflate reported returns on investments. By maximizing the volume of extractions from a site rather than seeking the efficiency potential of that site, the Forest Service has deprived the nation of billions of board feet of timber each year.

The second problem involves environmental quality. In essence, the Forest Service has forced taxpayers to underwrite the costs of logging uneconomical sites. For years, citizens have paid the difference between the costs of logging and the value of the products hauled from the woods. Every time this occurs, the public quite literally subsidizes the reduction of environmental quality.[6]

[5] See also Libecap (1981).
[6] See also Stroup and Baden (1973); Hyde (1981).

Terry Anderson and Donald Leal (1991, pp. 55–6) describe economically and environmentally costly irrigation projects sponsored by the federal Bureau of Reclamation:

Even though federal dam construction practically ground to a halt during the 1980s, costs are still being exacted on the treasury and the environment. One example of the environmental cost was revealed when contaminated drainage water forced the closing of California's Kesterson Wildlife Refuge, an important stopover for millions of migrating waterfowl. The culprit was an unusually high level of selenium, a naturally occurring chemical, that is benign at low levels but lethal at high levels. Biologists found that as a result of the selenium poisoning, wild duck eggs often did not hatch and when they did grotesque deformities were common. The source of the selenium-laced water that found its way to Kesterson was California's Central Valley Project, an irrigation project that provides subsidized water to farmers in the San Joaquin Valley...

The fiscal and environmental problems inherent in federal water projects are not the fault of bad managers. They result from an institutional framework that does not discipline federal managers to be either fiscally or environmentally responsible. Moreover, the system builds an iron triangle among politicians, water users, and bureaucrats that is difficult to dismantle. If the discipline of free market environmentalism was at work, massive, subsidized projects would not be built, higher water prices would encourage efficiency, and polluters would be liable for the damage they produce.[7]

Richard Epstein (1995, pp. 293–4), among others (including Anderson and Leal 1991, pp. 306–8), decries the "perverse incentives" created by well-meaning but misguided federal wildlife preservation policies.

Where government officials can designate certain wildlife habitats as protected, they have no incentive to determine whether the public gains are worth the private losses. Worse still, that grant of state power creates perverse incentives for the landowner who discovers a valuable habitat on her property. Her immediate reaction is one of gloom, even though the social value of the land is higher with the habitat than without it, for her ordinary private uses of that land may now be restricted without compensation. The greater the social value of the land, the less value it has to her, at least under the current law. Owing to the aggressive intervention of the state, her response is likely to be socially counterproductive. The well-advised landowner is *better off* destroying the habitat before it becomes public knowledge. "Shoot, shovel, and shut up" becomes the order of the day.

A recent empirical study supports Epstein's argument. Dean Lueck and Jeffrey Michael (2000) found a strong correlation between the forest management practices of 400 private landowners and the proximity of their forests to populations of endangered red-cockaded woodpeckers. The closer a forest plot was to the woodpecker populations, the more likely that plot was to be harvested, and the younger the age at which

---

[7] Also see Shanks (1981).

it was harvested. These correlations suggest that forest owners may have been taking preemptive action to avoid having their forest lands regulated as endangered species habitat. Lueck and Michael (2000, p. 30) conclude that regulations designed to protect endangered species actually reduce their habitat.

The entire history of public resource ownership and management, Thomas Borcherding (1990, p. 99) laments, is an immense tragedy of the "political commons," the only solution to which is complete privatization. As Terry Anderson (1994, p. 38) sees it, privatization is a matter of "getting the law out of the way," so that markets can work their magic for environmental protection, just as they have for economic production.

V   The complete privatization "solution"

Free-market environmentalists claim that privatization – the specification of complete private property rights in environmental goods – would avert both market failures and misguided government efforts to correct them, resolving problems ranging from the mismanagement of timber resources to global warming (Anderson and Leal 1991). Their argument is a logical, but not necessarily warranted, extension from Harold Demsetz's classic article, "Toward a Theory of Property Rights" (1967), which established that private property rights in land evolve in virtually all cultures at some stage of socioeconomic development – specifically, when resource scarcity rises to a certain level relative to the rate of demand, creating a threat to the continued existence of the resource – in order to reduce the externalities and transaction costs that impede efficient resource conservation. If property rights reduce externalities, the logic goes, then more completely specified property rights should more completely reduce externalities.[8]

Privatization replaces the decision-making of bureaucrats and politicians with the decision-making of private owners whose incentive structures, according to free-market environmentalists, conduce to economically and environmentally sound resource management. Unlike "public" resource owners, who make management decisions – present use versus conservation – without the benefit of market prices to guide their valuations, private owners operate within the marketplace where prices can accurately measure an asset's value. Stroup and Goodman (1992, pp. 431–2) explain how the information provided by market prices induces private resource owners to take a longer-term perspective in resource management decision-making.

---

[8] In contrast to free-market environmentalists, other economists, such as Demsetz (1968) and Coase (1960), believe that efficiency is at least sometimes maximized through government action rather than market transactions.

The current market price reflects the present, discounted value of all future revenue flows that are expected to stem from the asset.

The ability to capitalize future value into an asset's present value induces property owners to consider the long-term implications of their asset-use decisions. It creates a strong incentive for owners to consider fully the effects of deferring consumption of their asset returns. Furthermore, it implies that property owners will be responsible to future users. Any activity that reduces the future benefits or increases the future costs stemming from an asset results in a reduction of that asset's current value. As soon as an appraiser or potential buyer anticipates future problems, his assessment of a property's value falls, and the owner's wealth declines immediately.

Thus, "[p]otential buyers interact with owners to maximize asset value over time." And this logic holds for common and corporate, as well as individual, resource owners. But as the stories of public mismanagement suggest, it does not hold for public resource managers, who make their management decisions outside the marketplace, without the benefit of the information market prices provide. Free-market environmentalists conclude, therefore, that the privatization of publicly owned resources would promote better-informed and longer-view management of environmental goods.

Some publicly owned environmental goods are, of course, easier and, therefore, less costly to privatize than others. Most public lands, such as national parks and forests, would be fairly easy to parcelize and allot to private owners. But other environmental goods, such as the atmosphere, would be notoriously difficult and, therefore, very costly to privatize. Clean air is a subtractible public good – a good from which no one can be excluded, but which can be depleted by use (see Goetze 1987, pp. 188–9). Free-market environmentalists point out, however, that neither clean air nor any other resource is inevitably a *public* good. It is not strictly impossible to impose private property rights on the atmosphere, only too costly so long as the supply of clean air remains plentiful relative to the rate of demand. Under these circumstances, the costs of developing the technologies necessary to create enforceable boundaries and, hence, property rights, are not economically justifiable; the transaction costs would outweigh the benefits to be gained from privatization. This situation is not immutable, however. It is quite possible for clean air to become scarce enough relative to the rate of demand to justify the costs of privatization. Alternatively, the supply of clean air might remain constant relative to the rate of demand, but the costs of imposing property rights could drop because of technological innovations (Anderson and Leal 1991, pp. 165–7). The innovation of barbed wire in the 1870s, for example, greatly reduced the cost of enclosing land, which facilitated settlement and private ownership of formerly public lands (Anderson and Hill 1975, p. 172). What counts as a "public good," then, is determined economically by reference to the rates of supply and demand and the costs of privatization, given the technological capabilities of the time. Under the right circumstances, property rights can be imposed on all environmental goods.

Free-market environmentalists point to many cases where private property rights and markets have combined to conserve or produce environmental goods. Private environmental organizations, such as the Nature Conservancy, pay market prices for lands they dedicate for conservation (Anderson and Leal 1991, pp. 70–1).[9] The Nature Conservancy is, of course, a nonprofit organization, but many for-profit companies also find that good resource stewardship enhances profits. The International Paper Company, for example, finds it profitable to manage its forest resources for wildlife as well as for timber (Anderson and Leal 1991, p. 68). This and other examples, free-market environmentalists contend, prove the power of private property to protect and promote environmental values.

There is no doubt that private property is often an effective and efficient means of protecting certain environmental values. Most private home owners would not knowingly degrade their own back yards. But are free-market environmentalists right that private property is the universal, first-best solution to the tragedy of open access *and* the tragedy of the "political commons"?

VI   The limits of free-market environmentalism

Searching for first-best solutions in a second-best world

The first problem worth noting about the theory of free-market environmentalism is its reliance on the fallacy, exposed at the start of chapter 1, that environmental problems are due ultimately to the lack of well-defined property rights in environmental goods. Where free-market environmentalists go wrong is in failing to ask the next logical question: why are property rights often so ill-defined? The answer is, of course, that property rights are expensive – sometimes too expensive – to define (see Dahlman 1980, p. 83). In other words, the costs of creating, delineating, and enforcing property rights can be prohibitive. This is not to say that the absence of property rights is immaterial to environmental protection but only that the absence of property rights cannot be the ultimate cause of environmental problems, because *both* are consequences of other factors, notably transaction costs, which free-market environmentalists too often

---

[9] Anderson and Leal (1991, pp. 70–1) do not, however, offer an explanation for the Nature Conservancy's frequent practice (described in chapter 2) of turning lands it acquires into public/state property by conveyance to government agencies.

neglect. Paradoxically, if we inhabited a world in which property rights could be established at zero cost, then property rights would not even be necessary to ensure optimal environmental protection, for reasons explained in section 4 of chapter 1.

Once we move to the real world and bring transaction costs into play, it becomes apparent that the free-market environmentalists have assumed a tremendous – almost insurmountable – burden of persuasion. In this second-best world, in which transaction costs are always positive and usually quite significant, their claim that a single institution – private property – constitutes the first-best solution for all environmental problems, is inherently implausible. It is almost inconceivable that *any* single institution would constitute a universal, first-best solution to the tragedy of open access (see generally Coase 1960; Komesar 1994).

Free-market environmentalists surely are right about the environmental inadequacies and economic inefficiencies of bureaucratic resource management. Private resource ownership is economically and environmentally preferable to public ownership and regulation in many circumstances. That hardly proves, however, that the complete privatization of all environmental goods is both necessary and sufficient for effective and efficient environmental protection in *all* circumstances. To prove that, advocates must show that privately owned resources are inevitably better conserved and protected from pollution than publicly owned and managed resources. At the very least, they need to show that the benefits of privatization would always outweigh the costs, including the transaction costs.[10] This would require a systematic study of the costs and benefits of privatization, for which their numerous anecdotes are no substitute.

Private discount rates and time horizons

Among the empirical and theoretical studies that do exist, several suggest that private ownership is *not* the best solution to every environmental problem. Colin Clark's (1973a) studies of the economics of whaling, for example, demonstrate that the "extermination of an entire [whale] population may appear as the most attractive policy, even to an individual resource owner," when "(a) the discount (or time preference) rate sufficiently exceeds the maximum reproductive potential of the population, and (b) an immediate profit can be made from harvesting the last remaining animals."[11] Private resource owners are, indeed, often short-sighted,

---

[10] Transaction costs are the key to understanding institutional choice (see Coase 1937 and 1960; Komesar 1994).
[11] Also see Clark (1973b); Larson and Bromley (1990); and Schlager and Ostrom (1992).

and they discount future costs and benefits quite heavily, as the following empirical examples illustrate.

In Botswana, pasture lands were privatized beginning in the mid-1970s, in order to reduce overexploitation. As President Sir Seretse Khama explained when introducing the privatization policy in 1975, "[u]nder our communal grazing system it is in no one individual's interest to limit the number of his animals. If one man takes his cattle off, someone else moves in. Unless livestock numbers are somehow tied to specific grazing areas, no one has an incentive to control grazing" (quoted in Fidzani 2000, p. 21). A subsequent comparison of grazing rates and environmental impacts before and after privatization revealed, however, that privatization did not improve the economic or environmental management of the grazing lands. Output per head of cattle remained constant; cost per head was higher for privatized ranches than for ranches remaining under tribal governance; margins per head were lower on privatized ranches; and the return on capital was 61 percent lower for privatized ranches (Carl Bro International 1984). Based on this and other studies of Botswana's privatization policy, N. H. Fidzani (2000, p. 29) draws the stark (perhaps too stark) conclusion that privatization is not "the answer to range degradation."

Botswana's experience with privatization of grazing lands is not unique, as Stephen Toulmin (2001, pp. 104–5) explains:

In much of Africa, as in Indonesia, the introduction of European methods of cultivation and systems of landholding is now seen to reduce, not increase, the productivity of local agriculture. For example, the long-term carrying capacity of rangelands in sub-Saharan Africa – the number of cattle that can in the long term be raised and put to work in those areas – was (it seems) under-estimated by European onlookers, and even reduced, by imposing property boundaries of kinds customary in Europe itself. Older traditions, by which cattle from many communities and owners were free to range together across larger territories, finding food and water where the current year's weather allowed, have turned out to be more productive than the imported practice of fencing off farms and confining grazing herds to limited pastures.

In Great Britain during the nineteenth century private timberland owners virtually denuded the countryside. As of 1919 the UK had the smallest percentage of forested land – just 3 percent or 700,000 acres – of any country in Europe (Evans 1992, p. 57). This deforestation occurred almost entirely on privately owned lands (as noted in chapter 2, there is very little publicly owned land in England and Wales). To remedy this problem, Parliament in 1919 created a new *public* organization, the Forestry Commission, to purchase and reforest land. In its first year of operation, the commission purchased 19,000 hectares of land and planted trees on 700 hectares. Within twenty years (that is, by 1939), the commission had planted 172,000 hectares, increasing the total acreage of forest lands in Great Britain by nearly 25 percent (Evans 1992, p. 57).

In the United States, government bureaucrats did not create the dust bowls of the 1930s; supposedly "'omniscient' private entrepreneurs" plowed up the prairies against the advice of agricultural experts (see Bromley 1991, p. 171). Similarly, private landowners (timber companies) denuded the timberlands of northern Wisconsin during the nineteenth century. As James Willard Hurst (1984, pp. 105, 127, 435) has written, the companies that owned the timberlands

acted as lessees or licensees to cut without limitation of waste, and by tax default or sale at junk prices to farmland speculators they resigned responsibility for the productive forest within a few years of the time when they ostensibly assumed it...

... the industry's behavior made plain that lumbermen had no interest in buying the "land." What they wanted was the timber. In practice, what they bought was an unconditional license to cut, since after they cut they either let the land default to government for unpaid taxes or sold it cheaply, not as timber-productive land – which, indeed, it scarcely was, in the condition in which they left it – but as land wishfully assigned to agriculture.

The overshadowing capital loss, of course, was in the timberland itself. At the end of the nineteenth century lumber boom a scant 10 percent of the original northern Wisconsin forest remained capable of producing merchantable saw logs. By the late 1920s it was plain that the bulk of the cut-over lands was wholly unsuitable to farming; after fifty years' effort, less than 7 percent of the cut-over had been "improved" for farming, and much of this land was not capable of supporting its owners.

More recently, during the energy crisis of the 1970s, American consumers purchased energy-*inefficient* but lower-priced appliances, rather than energy-efficient but higher-priced models, despite being provided with information about the long-term cost-savings of the energy-efficient appliances. In their actual buying decisions, American consumers displayed implicit discount rates ranging between 17 percent for air conditioners and 243 percent for water heaters (Ruderman et al. 1987).[12] In the 1980s, private timberland owners displayed similarly high discount rates when they accelerated harvests beyond sustainable levels in order to avert or pay for junk-bond-financed hostile takeovers (Power 1996,

---

[12] Even recognizing the budget and credit constraints under which consumers make purchasing decisions, a 17 percent discount rate is extraordinarily high (see Thompson 2000, p. 30). Frank Arnold (1995, p. 192) asserts that "[a]nalysts in practice use 2 percent and 3 percent quite frequently, although it is not unusual to see rates in the 5- to 7-percent range." Government agencies historically set the social discount rate by reference to the rate of interest on long-term government bonds (Young and Haveman 1985, p. 488).

p. 138). In none of these cases did private ownership and markets guarantee the low discount rates and long time horizons needed for resource conservation.

Market values, information, and economies of scale in environmental ownership and management

Free-market environmentalists have also been criticized for their background assumptions, including the assumption that market prices capture all relevant values (see, for example, Power 1997, pp. 241–3). They ridicule government management agencies for assigning values to environmental goods without prices, but the free-marketeers themselves simply presume that market prices incorporate all values worth considering (Menell 1992, pp. 493–4). Such a presumption is unwarranted. Writing about endangered species preservation, Jason Shogren and Patricia Hayward (1998, p. 48) note that "[p]rices either understate the full range of services provided by a species, or do not exist to send a signal to the marketplace about the social value of the asset."

Free-market environmentalists also presume that private resource owners would possess environmental information superior to that possessed by public resource managers (Anderson and Leal 1991, pp. 4–6, 170–2). Critics point out, however, that environmental regulation itself was largely a response to inadequate environmental information provided by the market (Blumm 1992, p. 379; Hines 1966, pp. 197–201). Peter Menell (1992, p. 502) argues that "[e]conomies of scale in research and difficulties in appropriating returns to innovation may enable even highly imperfect public institutions to outperform private entrepreneurs in some technological fields." There is little reason, therefore, to presume that private owners would possess superior environmental information with which to manage environmental goods. Partly for this reason, Alan Randall and Emery Castle (1985, pp. 613–14) caution that we ought "to be suspicious of normative uses of land market theory in support of privatization proposals."

Economies of scale are important not only for the provision of environmental information but also, in many cases, for the provision of environmental goods themselves. For example, a recent study found that "farms with larger acreage have a higher probability of making [soil] conservation expenditures" (Featherstone and Goodwin 1993, p. 76). And the scale economies involved in soil conservation are minuscule compared with those involved in the provision of many other environmental goods, such as wilderness or species habitat, which can require contiguous land masses larger than entire states. Anderson and Leal (1991, p. 69) provide a lone anecdote about a group of private landowners who contracted with one another to provide a 2.8-million-acre recreation area in the North Maine Woods in upper New England. But this may be the exception that proves the rule. As noted in chapter 2, there was a financial motivation for the North Maine Woods that may not exist in many cases concerning wildlife preservation. According to economist Dean Lueck (1991, pp. 250, 251), in many, if not most, cases "the contracting costs among landowners may eliminate the potential gains" from the private provision of wildlife habitat. Individual landholdings, meanwhile, tend to be "small compared to the territories of most valued species." Thus, private landowners suffer from a comparative disadvantage in wildlife regulation, which may explain why wildlife are mostly publicly owned and regulated.[13] Some free-market environmentalists (for example, Nelson 1995) implicitly concede that scale economies sometimes favor public (state or federal) ownership of environmental goods, when they distinguish between public resources that should and should not be sold off to private owners.

The transaction costs of common-law solutions to environmental problems

Another criticism of free-market environmentalists is that their "[s]anguine view of markets and legal institutions contrasts sharply with their deeply cynical perception of public institutions" (Menell 1992, p. 505). They provide no reason to expect that common-law courts should be immune from the political and economic pressures that influence legislative decisions. Beerman (1991, pp. 187–8), for example, notes the failure of public choice theorists to confront the "economic influences on judicial behavior." Nor do free-market environmentalists provide any reason to believe that traditional common-law remedies, such as nuisance and trespass, would efficiently internalize pollution costs. As many legal scholars (including Brunet 1992) and economists (including Menell 1991) have explained, common-law remedies are highly imperfect and costly mechanisms for resolving complex environmental disputes, which involve large numbers of parties and causation proof problems. Ronald Coase (1959, p. 29) has, characteristically, presented the argument most concisely:

if many people are harmed and there are several sources of pollution, it is more difficult to reach a satisfactory solution through the market. When the transfer of rights has to come about as a result of market transactions carried out between large numbers of people or organizations acting jointly, the process of negotiation

---

[13] See chapter 2. Also see Lueck (1989); Rasker et al. (1992).

may be so difficult and time-consuming as to make such transfers a practical impossibility. *Even the enforcement of rights through the courts may not be easy. It may be costly to discover who it is that is causing the trouble. And, when it is not in the interest of any single person or organization to bring suit, the problems involved in arranging joint actions represent a further obstacle.* As a practical matter, the market may become too costly to operate.

In these circumstances it may be preferable to impose special regulations (whether embodied in a statute or brought about as a result of the rulings of an administrative agency).[14]

Consider a stylized case involving the hypothetical air pollutant, pol lutox.[15] Pollutox is a byproduct of many industrial activities and internal combustion engines. It is a pervasive pollutant known to harm human health and the environment. Virtually every medium-sized city in the country of Freeland has several sources of pollutox emissions. Plants that emit pollutox, in order to be good neighbors, build tall smokestacks to place their pollutox emissions high into the prevailing winds, which carry them far away from the source. This avoids creating local air pollution problems. The winds carry the pollutox emissions hundreds of miles away. It is very difficult (and, therefore, expensive) to determine where the pollutox emissions from any given source ultimately fall from the sky. But where and when they do, they cause health and environmental problems. Automobiles are another major source of pollutox emissions. Every single car emits a very small amount of pollutox – too little by itself to cause any significant harm. But tens of thousands of cars within a thirty-mile or so radius can cumulatively produce enough pollutox to create a local public health threat.

One day, several residents of Urbania, a large city in the State of Caladonia in the country of Freeland, were working in their gardens, when they began to suffer acute respiratory problems and were hospitalized – some for a few hours, others for several days. The doctors determined the cause of their respiratory problems was pollutox inhalation. Assuming for the sake of the argument that this constitutes a social problem – indeed, a market failure – requiring *some* government solution,[16] what is the best approach? Statutory regulation of pollutox emissions or common-law adjudication of claims arising from pollutox damage?

The common-law approach suffers from several inherent problems. First, what is the cause of action? Does the common law provide some

---

[14] Emphasis added.   [15] This example is adapted from Cole (2000, pp. 931–2).

[16] This is a crucial assumption because, in some cases at least, the costs of correcting the market failure by any government action would exceed the benefits to be gained. See Coase (1960, p. 118). A truly thorough comparative institutional analysis would have to include an assessment of the "no action" alternative.

mechanism by which victims can sue to recover their hospital bills and lost wages? Well, if the gardeners in our hypothetical city were property owners, they could sue for nuisance. As a practical matter, however, they would encounter great difficulties in pursuing a nuisance claim. First and foremost, they must identify some defendant to sue, which means they have to determine the source or sources of the pollutox emissions that harmed them. We know that it was not a local factory because their high smokestacks ensure that *their* pollutox emissions fall far outside of the local area. We might suspect that the source of the pollutox emissions was local automobile traffic, but then, who do you sue? You cannot sue every motorist in the city of Urbania. Anyway, what if the pollutox that caused the harm *didn't* come from cars? You have to locate some source or sources, perhaps hundreds of miles away, and prove to the satisfaction of the court that *their* pollutox emissions *caused* the harm. Even if that were possible, and often it is not, it would be a very costly proposition. To prove pollution harm may require testimony from a battery of expensive expert witnesses to inform the court about the chemistry and meteorology of airborne pollutox emissions, including pollution dispersal and diffusion rates, and the harm caused to humans by pollutox inhalation. If the plaintiffs pooled their resources, they might be able to cover all the necessary litigation expenses, but how likely is it that all of them would be willing to ante up?[17]

Let us suppose for the moment that the plaintiffs *could* prove their claim and prevail in court. Suppose they identify a plant in the small town of Ruralville, in the neighboring State of Orezona, as the source of the particular pollutox emissions that harmed them. But that plant, it turns out, is Ruralville's only significant employer, and it is barely solvent. The plant simply cannot afford either to abate its pollutox emissions or pay compensation for the harm caused. Any remedy would likely put the plant out of business, with significant repercussions for employment and general social welfare in Ruralville and its surrounding areas. Is a common-law court institutionally well suited to acquire the information and make the kinds of judgments necessary to render a sound *public policy* decision in this case?

This stylized case highlights just a few of the many problems associated with common-law solutions to large-scale pollution problems, where: large distances and time lags exacerbate causation proof problems; large numbers of parties make efficient bargaining and negotiation unlikely; and the social repercussions of any solution extend well beyond the

---

[17] This question raises the issues of "hold-outs" and "free-riders," two forms of "strategic behavior" familiar to economists engaged in transaction cost analysis. On these forms of strategic behavior, see, for example, Menell and Stewart (1994, pp. 60–3).

nominal parties to the dispute. In short, the transaction costs associated with common-law resolution of the pollutox problem are enormous.

It is precisely *because* common-law remedies are perceived to be relatively inefficient mechanisms for resolving environmental problems that the field of environmental law has been dominated by statutory regulation over the past three decades. By the 1970s there was a sense that proactive regulation of pollution would be more effective, and possibly more efficient, than the case-by-case adjudication of individual common-law claims brought after the fact of harm, especially considering the sizeable causation proof and other problems inherent to common-law adjudication (see Krier 1970; Brenner 1974; Laitos 1975, p. 444).[18] The implication was that the transaction costs of dealing with environmental problems through statutory and regulatory means would be lower than the transaction costs of using the common law as the exclusive mechanism for correcting environmental market failures.

Despite the costliness of common-law adjudication, some free-market environmentalists, including Meiners and Yandle (1988) and Yandle (1997), maintain that common-law remedies are both sufficient to protect the natural environment and generally preferable to the existing regulatory system. They may be right in specific cases, particularly those involving small numbers of parties and no significant causation proof problems – that is, cases involving low transaction costs. All of the cases discussed by Meiners and Yandle (1988) and Yandle (1997) are of this type. They do not cite a single nuisance or trespass case involving many parties and large distances. To their credit, Meiners and Yandle (1988) expressly recognize that such cases create problems for common-law remedies. For example, they attribute the dearth of common-law air pollution cases to the transaction costs associated with identifying defendants over large distances. Nevertheless, they conclude that "the common law, bolstered by local regulation, can protect the environment more effectively and fairly than can congressional statutes and bureaucratic regulations." This conclusion is hardly supported by their own analysis.

It is far from self-evident that the "local regulation," with which Meiners and Yandle would "bolster" common-law remedies, would avert the problems they attribute to federal and state "bureaucratic regulations." There are, of course, legitimate arguments to be made about the appropriate level of government for environmental regulation in varying circumstances (see, e.g., Libecap 1996; Revesz 1996a; Engel 1997), but Meiner and Yandle (1988) do not make them. More to the point, the fact that common-law remedies are *sometimes* effective, combined with the fact

---

[18] On the evolution of environmental law from judicially enforced torts to complex regulatory system, see Reitze (1999).

that government environmental regulation is cumbersome and often inefficient, does not prove that the common law is either sufficient or preferable to government regulation over the run of cases. Proving that would require more than a few references to successful environmental lawsuits and blanket complaints about "flawed" government regulations. What is needed is a comparative institutional and transaction-cost analysis showing that the common law is sufficient and preferable to regulation across the broad spectrum of environmental conflicts.

It is worth noting in this context that many modern environmental problems do not involve a discrete number of neighbors living in close proximity, who can easily identify one another, but: large numbers of parties, who cannot easily identify one another; pollutants that cover large distances and have long life-spans in the environment, making identification of sources difficult and costly; and harms with potentially very long latency periods. In these complex circumstances, it remains extremely doubtful – almost inconceivable – that common-law nuisance and trespass actions could, by themselves, supply sufficient environmental protection, making them preferable to the existing combined system of regulation *and* common-law remedies.

Free-market environmentalists have, on occasion, acknowledged the need for transaction-cost analyses for their policy prescriptions. In their 1991 book, *Free Market Environmentalism*, Terry Anderson and Donald Leal (p. 167) concede that "[p]roperty rights are costly to define and enforce." In an earlier work, Anderson and coauthor Peter Hill (1983, p. 438) explicitly recognized that "the definition and enforcement process may preclude whatever gains might have been realized by the establishment of [property] rights."[19] Yet one is hard pressed to locate in the free-market environmentalist literature efforts to systematically assess the transaction costs of privatization. Gary Libecap's book, *Contracting for Property Rights* (1989), is exceptional in providing historical and empirical transaction-cost analyses. But his findings hardly support the complete privatization of all environmental goods. Rather, his analyses explain why some open-access resources have been privatized, while others have been subjected to public ownership/regulatory control or remain open access.

Are environmental goods just like other economic goods?

Finally, it is not at all clear that environmental amenities are best treated like any other economic goods, as free-market environmentalists maintain. Natural resource amenities are not quite like economic producers, and the differences may justify treating those amenities differently at law.

---

[19] Others, who are not free-market environmentalists (such as Hanna et al. 1995, p. 18; Noll 1989, p. 1253), have made the same point.

Private ownership of resource-using and polluting firms is critical because it averts the *regulatory conflict of interest* that arises whenever the state is responsible for enforcing environmental regulations against economic enterprises in which it has a direct financial stake. The Hungarian economist János Kornai (1986) has famously explained how governments invariably soften budget constraints for state-owned enterprises, relieving them of the competitive pressures of the marketplace. The French jurist Laurent Cohen-Tanugi (1985) has noted a similar softening of law constraints: the state relaxes regulatory standards and enforcement against enterprises in which it has a direct financial stake. Softened budget and law constraints pose a great – perhaps the greatest – threat to effective and efficient environmental protection and resource conservation. More than any other institutional factor, they explain the environmental and economic failings of communism in Europe (see Cole 1998, pp. 146–53).[20]

Communist states were unwilling to enforce strict environmental regulations against enterprises in which they had a significant financial interest. Polluting and resource-using enterprises throughout the former Soviet bloc were systematically insulated from the enforcement and fiscal consequences of environmental laws and regulations. Consequently, the communist countries of Europe suffered from environmental crises unparalleled in human history. Since 1989, when communist institutions were replaced by democratic and market institutions, many former Soviet-bloc countries have experienced remarkable improvements in environmental protection.

In postcommunist Poland, for example, the private sector's share of economic growth has overtaken the residual public sector. Budget and law constraints have hardened for almost all sectors of the economy, leading to improved economic and environmental performance. Poland's economy has been among the fastest growing in Europe for several years running. Meanwhile, pollution emissions have declined dramatically and continuously since 1990 (see Cole 1998, pp. 190–4, 212). Indeed, environmental protection is among the great success stories of Poland's transition to market democracy. This success is due in no small part to the replacement of the former command economy with competitive markets, in which enterprises must profit to survive. As the state's role in the economy has declined, budget and law constraints have hardened

---

[20] The environmental consequences of state ownership of economic enterprises have been just as bad in noncommunist countries. Consider the differential treatment in the United States (and other countries) of privately owned versus publicly owned nuclear power. Privately owned nuclear power plants (overseen by the Nuclear Regulatory Commission) have been policed far more effectively and transparently than federally owned nuclear facilities (overseen by the Departments of Defense and Energy) (see Cole, 1998, pp. 149–50).

significantly. Strict environmental laws are now being enforced against noncomplying polluters, and environmental fees and fines are significantly affecting their incentives for resource use.

A free-market environmentalist might wonder, however, whether environmental protection in post-communist Poland might have improved even more had the state privatized not only its state-owned enterprises, including polluting and resource-using enterprises, but also its environmental goods, such as public lands, forests, and waterways. There is reason for doubt. In Poland's case at least, public ownership of environmental goods did not automatically give rise to the regulatory conflicts of interest that resulted from public ownership of polluting and resource-using enterprises.

As communist Poland became one of the world's most polluted countries, it nevertheless managed to retain approximately 27 percent of its territory in pristine condition (see Organization for Economic Cooperation and Development 1995, p. 88). The economist Tomasz Żylicz (1995, pp. 64–5) explains this apparent paradox:

> because the communist industrialization concentrated in areas of traditionally high intensity of production, vast regions remained largely underdeveloped. These regions and their almost intact natural capital represent an asset which is becoming increasingly scarce in Europe... about 8.5 percent of the area of the country remains relatively unscathed by development. Commercial forests and farms operating within sustainable and ecologically accepted principles include about 19 percent of Polish territory. Hence over a fourth of Poland represents an asset that many areas of Europe no longer have.

Where the state did not provide an opportunity to exploit, develop, or pollute publicly owned resources, those resources, including national parks and forest reserves, remained pristine. As a consequence, post-communist Poland possesses ecological assets no longer found in the rest of Europe, including the last stands of primeval European forest and the last free-roaming herds of European bison. It needs to be stressed that this was not just a fortuitous coincidence of Poland's industrial development, but part of a deliberate state policy of nature conservation (described in Cole 1998, ch. 2). During its forty-five years of existence, People's Poland increased the number of national parks from two to twelve, and the total area of national parks from less than 7,500 hectares to more than 165,000 hectares.

The purpose of this exposition is not to revise the history of failed environmental protection under communism but to challenge a fundamental premise of free-market environmentalism: that public ownership of environmental goods works just as badly for economic efficiency and environmental protection as public ownership of other resources. Public resource management may not be optimal or even preferable to private resource ownership in many cases. Poland's history suggests, however, that the property regime may not always be the key factor. Other factors, such as management policies, budget constraints, discount rates, economies of scale, technological capabilities, even culture and ideology, may play more important roles in specific cases.

This raises an interesting question for free-market environmentalists. Do their anecdotes of "government failure" in environmental resource management carry necessary implications for ownership? Or might they simply reflect curable defects in regulatory policy? Interestingly, virtually all of the free-market environmentalists' horror stories of government mismanagement concern environmental goods subject to multiple-use management, which by its very nature – balancing economic development and environmental preservation values – generates regulatory conflicts of interest. Of the dozens of stories of government mismanagement of environmental goods that Terry Anderson and Donald Leal (1991) recount in *Free Market Environmentalism*, for example, not one concerns resources subject to single- or dominant-use management, such as wilderness areas.

Privatization would itself amount to a conversion from multiple-use to dominant-use management, with the dominant (but not necessarily exclusive) use determined by the interest of the private owner. If such a conversion from multiple-use to dominant-use by privatization is feasible, however, then one wonders whether insuperable obstacles prevent the government from achieving the same end by altering its management regime, without changing the ownership structure. It seems clear, at any rate, that public ownership of environmental goods does not inevitably result in a tragedy of the political commons, even in countries, like Poland, with generally woeful records of environmental protection. Nor, as this chapter has shown, does private ownership ensure proper environmental management.

VII   Realistic privatization

There is a weaker version of free-market environmentalism that is more realistic than that which dominates the literature. The weaker version maintains that: (1) privatization is a legitimate and sometimes preferable option, which should be considered in comparative institutional analyses for policy-making; and (2) the choice of institution – public ownership/ regulation versus private ownership/no regulation – is not a once and for all decision but is contingent on changing institutional and technological circumstances.[21]

Public goods sometimes become private goods

This weaker version of free-market environmentalism appears uncontroversial, although it rightly implies an important consideration that conventional welfare economists sometimes neglect: there is no such thing as a pure "public good." As shown previously, "public goods" are determined economically by reference to the rates of supply and demand and the costs of privatization, given existing technological capabilities. Because technological capabilities and rates of supply and demand are subject to change, some resource that is deemed a "public good" today, such as the atmosphere, may become efficiently *privatize*able at some time in the future. Put simply, what counts as a "public good" can change. It is vital, therefore, that institutional choices do not become reified, but remain subject to revision as ever-changing circumstances alter comparative institutional analyses.

It is important to bear in mind that historical change is not unidirectionally towards private property. Property rights sometimes evolve in the opposite direction, from more sharply defined private rights to more ambiguous correlative rights. This has been the case, for example, with water law. Carol Rose (1990), citing Morton Horwitz (1977), notes the shift in common-law water rights from private to common property. More recently, Joseph Dellapenna (2000, p. 366) argues, there has been a further shift as "about half the states that formerly followed the common property approach of riparian rights have changed to a system of public property now coming to be called 'regulated riparianism.'"

Weak vs. strong free-market environmentalism

The weaker version of free-market environmentalism described above is not consistent with the stronger, orthodox version presented earlier. The weaker version recognizes that the best mix of property rights and regulatory regimes depends on institutional and technological factors, while the orthodox version posits that *all* environmental goods should be completely privatized for optimal efficiency and environmental protection. The orthodox version implicitly rejects the very concept of "public good," so that there is no longer any point in engaging in comparative

---

[21] This weaker version of free-market environmentalism is usually presented implicitly, rather than explicitly. See, for example, Nelson (1995), advocating the privatization of some, but not all, public lands.

institutional analysis for public policy-making. It simply dispenses with the contest, and declares victory on behalf of total and final privatization. The only appropriate public policy for environmental protection, according to proponents of the orthodox version of free-market environmentalism, is no public policy (other than enforcing private property rights and contracts).

In the absence of a detailed assessment of the costs and benefits of privatization, how could Anderson and Leal (1991, p. 165) possibly conclude, for example, that the privatization of roads together with strict liability rules for common-law enforcement would *efficiently* resolve traffic congestion problems? As Bill Funk (1992, p. 512) has asked: "Who is going to sue for damages under this strict liability regime? The class of all persons in the greater metropolitan area? What damages are we talking about? . . . And what about causation?" Robert Ellickson (1993, p. 1385) realistically notes that "[t]he laying out of a major road is a quintessential 'large' event that private landowners and travelers cannot well coordinate on their own."

Examples such as this may explain why some critics consider the orthodox version of free-market environmentalism an "institutional fantasyland" (Menell 1992). The danger is that fantasy lands are designed to appear more attractive than the real world. As Edella Schlager and Elinor Ostrom (1992, p. 260) have written, "[n]o real-world institution can win in a contest against idealized institutions." Yet the sheer lack of realism in much of the free-market environmentalist literature may explain why their privatization prescriptions, though widely disseminated in the academic and popular media, have not garnered broader public, academic, or political support.

6   The limited utility of common property regimes for environmental protection

Discussions of property rights for environmental protection tend to focus on the choice between public and private/individual property regimes, to the exclusion of common property regimes. This neglect may stem from the unfortunate conflation of common property with open access discussed above in chapter 1. Common property regimes have, however, proven capable of averting the tragedy of the commons in various circumstances and over long periods of time. Common ownership may even be preferable in some circumstances to alternative public and private property regimes for environmental protection (see Ostrom et al. 1999, p. 278; Stevenson 1991, p. 70; Dagan and Heller 2001, p. 572).

This chapter assesses the utility and limitations of common property regimes for environmental protection. The first section defines common property regimes, in contradistinction to public/state and private/ individual property regimes. Section 2 explains how common property regimes can, and in some places do, provide a useful solution to the tragedy of open access. The third section probes the limits of common property solutions. Section 4 discusses a theoretical framework for explaining and predicting the success or failure of common property regimes. And section 5 concludes with a caveat about judging the "success" of common property regimes from an environmental point of view.

I   What is common property?

As explained in chapter 1, the "tragedy of the commons" is a misnomer to the extent it implies that the problem of resource conservation and environmental degradation is one of common property. In actuality, the problem is one of nonproperty or open access, for which the imposition of common property rights constitutes, at least in some cases, a viable solution. Common property can be thought of as any set of property rights owned by more than one individual. In this sense, common property incorporates joint tenancies, tenancies in common, tenancies by the entirety and other forms of marital property, partnership property, corporately owned property, and even public/state property. At law, any estate in land less than fee-simple absolute *must* be a common property regime; beyond the holder of the fee, some person or persons must possess a vested or contingent legal interest. Moreover, mixed property regimes such as those discussed in chapters 3 and 4 can legitimately be thought of as common property.

Throughout this book and particularly in this chapter, the label "common property" is restricted to its conventional meaning of property owned and managed by groups of private individuals living in close proximity to the resource, to the exclusion of other groups in society (c.f. Ostrom 1990; Stevenson 1991; Bromley 1992). What distinguishes common property from private property, under this definition, is the number of owners/managers. With private property, as conventionally defined, there is but a single owner who possesses the right to exclude all others from the resource. With common property, by contrast, there are multiple owners who may not exclude one another – although they may collectively regulate one another's access and use – but who may exclude all others from the resource. Common property is distinguished from public property in two important respects: first, the owners comprise a single identifiable group of individuals, rather than the public at large; second, common property systems are not managed by politicians and bureaucrats in some faraway capital but by the the co-owners themselves, collectively.

II   Averting the tragedy of open access with common property regimes

As a matter of theory, common property regimes avoid the tragedy of open access by limiting the number of resource users *and* regulating their use. As Glenn Stevenson (1991, pp. 58–9) explains, "[o]pen access is defined by the lack of constraints on both the number of users and the amount that each user may extract. . . . Under common property, however, both of the problem-causing characteristics of open access are remedied. Group size is limited and rights and duties to limit extraction are defined among the included users." In the "vital areas of having a defined group and having limited individual use rates," common property is like private property. Therefore, "it may stand beside private property as a solution to the open access problem."

As an empirical matter, there have been numerous successful common property regimes, where "success" is defined as the avoidance of resource depletion and degradation through overconsumption over a long period of time.[1] Several examples follow.[2]

The open field system

The open field system persisted in England and across northern Europe to the Ural mountains for at least 1,000 years (see Dahlman 1980, pp. 34, 36).[3] In that system, arable croplands were treated as private/individual property, while nonarable or, in a rotation system, uncultivated lands were treated as commons for grazing livestock. The nature of the open field system thus exemplifies Coase's (1960) point that what is owned is not the resource itself but property rights in the resource. In this case, there is a single resource – land – with multiple uses, including crop production and grazing, subject to dual property systems – private and common. The open field system also falls within this book's definition of mixed property regimes. For present purposes, however, we are concerned only with the common property attributes of the resource.

The nominal owners of individual parcels of land could exclude all others from croplands under cultivation, but could not exclude other members of the community from using their fallow lands as pasturage for livestock:

Both in legal theory and as a historical fact, only the partners in the cultivation of the tillage land were entitled to the pasture rights, which were limited to each individual by the size of his arable holdings. Outside of this close corporation any persons who turned in stock were trespassers; they encroached, not only on the rights of the owner of the soil, but on the rights of those arable farmers to whom the herbage belonged. (Dahlman 1980, p. 23 n. 8, quoting Lord Ernle 1968, p. 297)

---

[1] This definition of "success" is consistent with the sustainable harvest criterion, which is often used to evaluate the success of common property regimes (see, e.g., Berkes 1992, p. 166). Daniel Bromley (1991, p. 3) offers a slightly more complex definition of "success" in common property management: "(1) the natural resource has not been squandered; (2) some level of investment in the natural resource has occurred; and (3) the co-owners of the resource are not in a perpetual state of anarchy."

[2] For additional examples, see Bromley (1992); Ostrom (1990); Ostrom and Gardner (1993); Netting (1976); and McCay and Acheson (1987).

[3] The open field system was also found in America from colonial times to the end of the nineteenth century. In Plymouth, Massachusetts, for example, an Act of 1633 expressly extended public grazing rights over privately owned lands (see Hart 1996, p. 1272). During the nineteenth century, in arid and semi-arid regions of the American West open field grazing was practiced "even when and where ... constraints on the emergence of private property rights were absent" (Sanchez and Nugent 1994, p. 44). In parts of the southern United States, until the end of the nineteenth century, uncultivated fields remained legally open for communal grazing unless actually enclosed (see Kantor 1998).

Clearly then, the commons were not open access but the exclusive property of the villagers themselves. They were "common only to a certain well-defined group of people, and not public property for anyone to use at will" (Dahlman 1980, pp. 100–1).

For the villagers, the pasturage was *common property, not open access*. Individual villagers were not at liberty to graze as many animals as they liked. Governmental or quasi-governmental structures, most notably the village court, regulated and supervised their use "to avoid the overuse and underinvestment problems that are usually associated with communal property" (Dahlman 1980, p. 26). The village court was a meeting of all the villagers at which ploughing and harvesting dates were established, "so that the changeover from [common] grazing to [private] cropping could be accomplished in an orderly manner" (Dahlman 1980, p. 109). The court regulated crop rotations to ensure that each farmer contributed a fair share to the common grazing lands. Most importantly, the village court "stinted" grazing rights – meaning that it allocated use rights among individual village members. The usual stinting rule limited the number of animals a villager could graze on the open field based on the share of arable lands he owned (Dahlman 1980, p. 132); those who contributed the highest percentage of land to the open fields were justly allowed to graze the most animals. The village courts closely supervised the commons to ensure that no one exceeded their stinting rights. Between court sessions, the village beadle or reeve monitored the open fields, and resolved disputes over grazing rights (Dahlman 1980, p. 206). Those who exceeded their stints, or otherwise failed to comply with village by-laws, were fined (Dahlman 1980, p. 134).[4]

To the extent this regulatory system depended on governmental or quasi-governmental organizations such as village court, the open field system shared certain characteristics of public/state property. This is not to say that common property and state property are one and the same thing, however. All property systems – even private property regimes – depend on government organizations, such as courts, to institute rules regarding permissible uses – primarily by defining *im*permissible uses, for example through nuisance law – and resolve disputes over property rights. Moreover, as explained in chapter 1, scholars who write about common property regimes distinguish common ownership from public ownership based on the relation of the decision-making body to the resource users. The greater the role of resource users in management decision-making, the more likely the regime is to be considered common, rather than public/state. Under this description, local government

---

[4] For an extensive review of open field by-laws and other regulations, see Ault (1972).

control of resource management is not inconsistent with common property ownership, *if* the local government is itself part and parcel of the community of common owners, as was generally the case with the village courts that regulated the use of open fields. The courts were composed of the villagers themselves. All villagers were required to attend and participate in the village courts "on pain of a modest fine" (Stevenson 1991, p. 154). The purpose of court meetings varied but, with respect to the open fields, the courts: enacted the by-laws governing use of commons; elected juries to resolve disputes over open field uses; chose "pinders," who impounded stray cattle and released them to their owners upon payment of a fine; and selected enforcement officers to monitor the fields. "No pay accrued to any of the jobs, and duties were rotated regularly" (Stevenson 1991, p. 54). Moreover, all court decisions were rendered "[b]y common consent" of the entire village (Ault 1965, p. 41), although not by simple majority vote. According to Dahlman (1980, p. 26) the village courts employed a collective decision-making rule that "can best be understood as voting in relation to size of the economic interest belonging to each farmer in the village." The village courts that managed the open fields nonetheless constituted organizations of local self-government (see Dahlman 1980, p. 100).

In addition to regulation by the village courts, the feudal legal institution of the frankpledge or tithing helped to ensure that fields were not subject to overuse as a result of population increases. If the population of the village increased significantly, thereby increasing the number of users of the commons, either the stints would have to be reduced or the pasturage would eventually become overburdened. The frankpledge or tithing averted this Hobson's choice by controlling immigration. In order to become a member of the village unit, a newcomer had to be accepted into a frankpledge; that is, some existing member(s) of the village had to agree to assume responsibility for them (Dahlman 1980, p. 101). The village could preserve its rents in the open fields, and prevent them from being overused by refusing to extend the frankpledge, thereby limiting the size of the ownership group. In addition, Smith (2000) suggests that the scattering of privately owned strips – so that each individual landowner possessed several, noncontiguous parcels – also limited entry to, and exit from, the common ownership group by creating a complicated property rights structure.

But was the open field system efficient? The fact that it lasted for more than 1,000 years across Europe should lead to a presumption that it was. That presumption must be rebuttable, however, because, as noted in chapter 2, inefficient institutions can persist for long periods of time, if they are supported by sufficiently powerful vested interests. While a certain property institution may be inefficient for society as a whole, it may operate efficiently for some segment or segments of society that are able to influence institutional policy. This does not appear to have been the case, however, with the open field system. Dahlman (1980, pp. 89–92) argues persuasively that the obstruction of efficient institutional changes by rent-seeking groups is not a plausible explanation for the persistence of the open field system.

[T]here are several reasons why we shall be able to rule out such an interpretation as unreasonable in the context of the open field system. First, there is the historical fact that the open field system existed side by side with enclosed farms for hundreds of years within the same country . . . If the open field system were inefficient from an allocation standpoint but efficient as an instrument for income reallocation for a dominating group, then it becomes inexplicable why the system was never introduced to all agricultural regions. Further, the open field system is confined to northern Europe and was never employed in the Mediterranean basin. This points to the fact that the open field system was most probably dependent upon such geographical conditions as soil quality, climate, erosion, that determined the mix of output suitable for open field farming. Thus, we should look for the keys to an understanding of the system in resource endowments, technology, and markets, rather than in a presumption that the system was designed to be a vehicle for income redistribution.

In addition, Dahlman (1980, p. 90) notes, the adoption of the open field system across northern Europe by diverse cultures with different institutions mitigates against a simplistic rent-seeking interpretation. The system displayed far more stability, adaptability, and resilience over a very long period of time than one would expect of an institution established primarily for income distribution or rent-seeking.

In place of the rent-seeking explanation of the open field system, Dahlman (1980, p. 209) offers a transaction-cost explanation, based predominantly on the theory of the firm:

We may . . . look at the open field village as a firm. It is a collection of decision rights created by a voluntary relinquishing of those rights by their owners. Implied in the relinquishing of those rights is a way of organizing the relative influence of each member of the collective thus created: a voting rule, and a way to share the proceeds, i.e., a profit sharing rule . . . [S]uch rules formed the very foundation of medieval agricultural society.

Later (p. 211), Dahlman writes, "we should describe the open field system as a collection of attenuated decision-making rights established through a process of mutually beneficial exchanges between self-interested economic agents." And he shows that this firm-like organization of the village commons was efficient compared with a private/individual property regime for grazing. Specifically, the open field system saved on the costs of staking out and protecting individual claims, and maximized the returns to scale in grazing at lower cost than would have been possible under individual private ownership (Dahlman 1980, pp. 115–21). "If the grazing groups were owned privately," Dahlman (1980, p. 7) notes, "the large-scale grazing areas desired could only be attained by continual transaction between the farmers involved: collective ownership completely bypasses this problem."

The conclusion Dahlman (1980, p. 121) draws is unambiguous.

[I]f there are private property rights in the arable, if outside non-owners can be kept out, and if each farmer practices mixed husbandry, collective rights in the grazing areas can unambiguously be shown to save on transaction costs as com- pared with private ownership if there are increasing returns to scale in grazing. This conclusion can only be strengthened if the waste has additional uses which every farmer would want a share in, such as digging peat, gathering firewood, cut- ting timber, excavating minerals, irrigating meadows, as long as there are some returns to scale in the production of these services. This explains why the com- mons were commons and were not parcelled out to owners in severalty. It all hinges on the transaction costs of achieving a large grazing area, given the private rights in the arable.

England's open field system did not differ greatly from commonfield agricultural practices that persisted across northern Europe for more than a millennium. Today, however, few commons are left in Europe; most have been enclosed and converted to private property. In England, open field grazing survives at only one location – Laxton – and there only because Parliament has prohibited enclosure (see Chambers 1964). Laxton is, in effect, an agricultural museum, where the open field sys- tem is preserved as an historical artifact. It would be a mistake, however, to suppose that commonfield agriculture is an obsolete institution with no contemporary relevance. Variations on the open field system persist today in many parts of the world, including the mountains of Japan and Switzerland,[5] the Himalayas, Vietnam, and Andean mountain regions of Peru and Bolivia (see Campbell and Godoy 1992, pp. 99–100).

Commonfield agriculture in Andean mountains of Peru and Bolivia

Joan Thirsk (1964) has identified four "core" characteristics of com- monfield agriculture as practiced throughout the world: (1) individuals own separate but unenclosed parcels of arable land for raising crops; (2) these individually owned croplands, when fallow, are treated as common

---

[5] For a comparsion of the Swiss grazing commons with the English open field system, see Stevenson (1991, pp. 85–157).

pasture lands, on which all villagers are entitled to graze their animals; (3) villagers are also entitled to gather peat, timber, firewood, and other resources from the common pastures; and (4) the "assembly of cultivators" regulates and supervises the common property regime. Each of these four characteristics was present in the English open field system. They are also evident in the still-existing commons of South America's central Andean highlands, although ecological and institutional circumstances there are extremely different from those that persisted in England during the long tenure of the open field system.[6]

Andean villagers treat fallow lands as common property for communal grazing, but cultivated croplands remain the private property of individual farmers. There is a fixed crop rotation system, so that lands become fallow at known intervals. Individual farmers decide what crops to sow, but decisions about which fields are to remain fallow, and for how long, are made collectively at the village level. Because the soil at higher altitudes is less fertile, they have to remain fallow longer, which may explain why the institution of commonfield agriculture is more commonly found in the mountains than in the valleys.[7] Where commonfield agriculture is practiced, each household receives an allotment of common grazing rights measured by an *unta* – "that which one can see" (Campbell and Godoy 1992, p. 109).

In the Andes, open fields make "good practical sense" for several reasons: there are substantial returns to scale in grazing; the costs of exclusion – by fencing, for example – are relatively high; and existing village institutions render manageable the transaction costs of collective decision-making (Campbell and Godoy 1992, pp. 110–11). In other words, commonfield agriculture is efficient.

Japanese Iriachi

In Japan, common lands known as *Iriachi* have persisted since at least the thirteenth century.[8] At the end of the Tokugawa period in the mid-nineteenth century these common lands comprised approximately 12.5 million hectares of forested and uncultivated mountain lands. Today, more than 2.5 million hectares of *Iriachi* remain. They are owned by villages, and all villagers share equal rights to use them. Access and use are,

[6] This description of commonfields management in the Andes is based on Campbell and Godoy (1992).

[7] According to Campbell and Godoy (1992, p. 110), commonfields comprise between 20 and 70 percent of landholdings in the Andes regions of Peru and Bolivia. The percentage tends to rise with the altitude.

[8] This description of the *Iriachi* in Japan is based on McKean (1992).

however, strictly controlled through elaborate regulations. Households –
the smallest unit of accounting in Tokugawa Japan – historically were
obliged to contribute to the common supply of winter fodder for grazing. However, this does not mean that they had to open their fields to
livestock owned by others. The villagers were, in fact, forbidden from
grazing their animals on the commons. Instead, they cut grass from the
commons, and took it to their livestock, which remained on their own,
private lands.[9] Villagers could also take wood from the common forests,
but only from certain kinds of trees, of a certain size, using specified
tools. In some cases, for some purposes, individual villagers had to obtain a permit from the village authorities before entering *Iriachi*. These
and other rules governing use of the commons were enforced with social
and legal sanctions. Violators could be fined or, for particularly egregious
or ongoing violations, expelled from the village.

Margaret McKean (1992, pp. 65–6) distinguishes four management
regimes for the *Iriachi*. The "classic type," which prevailed during the
Tokugawa period, limited use of the commons to sustainable harvesting activities that left the *Iriachi* essentially unchanged. Villagers with
access rights could gather thatch, bamboo, charcoal, herbs, and other
products at designated times, according to rules devised by their village.
Another management form, which McKean calls "direct group control,"
prohibited individual access to the commons entirely, in favor of group
cultivation "to supplement village treasuries." The income earned from
the commons was then distributed among the villagers/co-owners or invested for village projects. A third management regime, "divided use,"
constituted partial privatization of the *Iriachi*. The common land was
parcelized and allotted, usually for three-year terms, to individuals, who
could use the land as they wished, but within limits established by the
village. Individual allotments could not be sold, and structures could
not be built on the land. The final management regime was "contracted
use," which developed when villages experienced labor shortages. In that
circumstance, they would contract with outsiders, granting them limited
access and use rights. These four regimes should not be viewed as
mutually exclusive. According to McKean (1992, p. 166), most villages
that maintain *Iriachi* today combine elements of the four, depending on
their management goals and circumstances.

Most importantly for our purposes, McKean's (1986, p. 534) studies
of the Japanese *Iriachi* have "not yet turned up an example of a commons that suffered ecological destruction while it was still a commons."

---

[9] McKean (1992, p. 76) suggests that this rule might have prevented overgrazing by raising
the costs to individual users of the commons of increasing the number of grazing animals.

In other words, the imposition of common property regimes effectively staved off the tragedy of open access over many centuries. This meets our criterion for "success."[10] But whether the *Iriachi* were (and are) an efficient institution is more difficult to judge. We know that the *Iriachi* existed (and still exist) alongside private property regimes. If they were obviously inefficient, it would not have been difficult to convert them to private property. Indeed, over the centuries many commons in Japan *were* converted to private property. But not all. We do not know why some communities privatized grazing lands while others retained commonfield agriculture, or whether privatization actually enhanced efficiency. In the absence of a persuasive economic explanation for the incomplete privatization of *Iriachi*, it would be difficult to conclude that this centuries-old institution was inefficient.

Common rights in Turkish fisheries

Successful common property regimes have not been limited to land resources. They have also proven useful for staving off the tragedy of open access to marine resources. These cases have heightened significance because so much of the empirical research about the tragedy of open access comes from overexploited fisheries (see, for example, Warming 1911; Gordon 1954; Scott 1955).[11]

In Turkey, common property regimes governing fishing rights on the Çamlik lagoon and at Alanya on the Mediterranean Sea have managed to sustain harvests and avoid overcapitalization over a long period of time.[12] At the Çamlik lagoon, the fishing cooperative exercises exclusive control over the fishery. Membership of the cooperative is restricted to residents of certain neighboring villages, excluding large farmers and those who earn wages from employment in other sectors. The members of the cooperative protect their common rights by regularly patrolling their fishing area.

At Alanya, in September of each year a list of eligible fishers is prepared, including those who are not at the time members of the cooperative. All fishing locations traditionally used by Alanya fishers are named and numbered. Eligible fishers draw lots for fishing sites, and each boat is assigned a number corresponding to its draw. The boats begin fishing at locations designated by their draws, and then move each day one location to the east. "This gives each fisherman an equal opportunity at the best sites,"

---

[10] See note 1, above, and accompanying text.
[11] Both Gordon (1954, p. 134) and Scott (1955, p. 116) explicitly recognized, however, that common property regimes might avert depletion of marine resources as well as private/individual property regimes.
[12] The description of common fishing rights in Turkey relies on Berkes (1992).

as the fish migrate east to west from September to January, and back east again from January to May (Berkes 1992, p. 170). As Fikret Berkes (1992, p. 170) stresses, "[t]hese operational rules are formulated by the fishermen themselves." The list of fishing sites is like a contract, which they endorse. The list is then deposited with the mayor of each village. Violators of the agreement are subject to social sanctions, including potential exclusion from the list of eligible fishers.

The Çamlik lagoon and Alanya fisheries have experienced

no decrease in overall catches over the years, no sharp drops in the catch per unit of effort, no obvious overcrowding in the fishing area, and no indication of vessels and fishermen dropping out of the fishery. In these areas, the fishermen indicated that conflicts were for the most part resolved internally and the majority of them expressed general satisfaction with the fishery. (Berkes 1992, p. 167)

It should be noted, however, that the fisheries are also regulated by the Turkish government. Turkey's 1971 Aquatic Resources Act restricts the licensing of commercial fishers, regulates net size, and prohibits trawling within three miles of the coast (see Berkes 1992, p. 168). These regulations tacitly assert public/state rights in the otherwise common property fisheries. Nevertheless, in this case (as in the others described in this section) the imposition of common property regimes has succeeded in staving off the tragedy of open access over a very long period of time.

III   The limits of common property solutions

The success stories recounted in the previous section show that common property regimes are *sometimes* capable of averting the tragedy of open access. But not all common property regimes succeed. Indeed, they seem to fail at least as often. The success stories of the Alanya and Çamlik lagoon fisheries in Turkey are offset by the failures of two other Turkish common property fisheries at Bodrum and the Bay of Izmir. Those fisheries collapsed because the fishers – the common owners – failed to develop effective rules for limiting entry and use (see Berkes 1992; Ostrom 1990, pp. 144–6). Similarly in the Bahia region of Brazil, the once successful "sea tenure" system[13] instituted by coastal villages collapsed in the 1970s, as villagers failed to prevent the introduction of new, more efficient fishing technologies and encroachment by outsiders, which "gravely damaged" the fisheries. "[S]hort-term speculation and overcapitalization ... led to a sudden overfishing of a number of native estuarine and reef species"

---

[13] Sea tenure is a regime of "collectively managed informal territorial use rights in a range of fisheries previously regarded as unownable" (Cordell and McKean 1992, p. 183).

(Cordell and McKean 1992, p. 199). In these and many other cases,[14] common property regimes have failed to prevent the tragedy of open access.

At least in Turkey and Brazil, local fishers *tried* to avoid the tragedy of open access by instituting common property regimes. In many other cases, local communities have not even mustered the effort. Barton Thompson (2000, p. 246) notes that "the people with the most to lose if the commons is destroyed – the resource users themselves – often combine together to oppose proposed solutions." As commercial fisheries around the world have declined, and several have closed completely, fishers have generally been unwilling to cooperate to institute common property solutions. Similarly, farmers and other water users who pump groundwater in the southwestern United States have obstructed efforts to limit the rate of withdrawal, even though the result – rapidly failing acquifers – is plainly against their collective interest (see Thompson 2000, pp. 249–53). Proponents of common property solutions are forced to concede that "[t]he dismal frequency of degraded grazing commons, despoiled forests, overexploited groundwater and depleted fisheries shows only too clearly that collective action cannot be presumed to be always a viable route for common property resource management" (Wade 1987, pp. 95–6).

Even in cases where common property management appears to succeed, they tend to be replaced in the course of time by private property regimes. The open field system no longer exists in England (except in one location, where it is maintained as a historical artifact). It is surely worth asking why such a long-lived and apparently efficient common property institution was ultimately replaced by a private property regime. More generally, we require a theory of common property regimes that can usefully predict, or at least explain, successes and failures (see Ostrom 1990, p. 183).

IV   Elinor Ostrom's theory of common property systems

The challenge confronting anyone attempting to elaborate a coherent theory of common property systems is that "success" or "failure" is often determined by highly specialized circumstances that are difficult to model. A great deal depends on distinctive factors such as local culture, social trust, the magnitude and pace of social and institutional change, local methods of dispute resolution, and unique attributes of the resource

---

[14] For other examples of common property "failures," see, for example, Ostrom (1990, pp. 143–78), Palmer (1993), and Jodha (1985).

itself. It is clear, for example, that elevation was an important factor in property regime choice for livestock grazing in both the Andes mountains of Peru and Bolivia and in mountainous regions of Japan. Glenn Stevenson's (1991, pp. 209–10) empirical study of Swiss commonfield grazing similarly revealed that "natural factors are significant explanatory variables for the determination of rights systems. In particular, better natural soil quality, its accompanying grass condition, and better climatic conditions favor a grazing area's becoming private [rather than common] property."

Despite the specialized factors that make each case highly individual, it should be possible – within a substantial range of variability – to specify a set of design principles for successful common property regimes. Elinor Ostrom (1990) has assessed a wide array of successful, failed, and "fragile" common property regimes in an effort to derive a framework for explaining and predicting the success or failure of other common property regimes. From the successful cases, she discerns seven "design principles" of "robust" common property regimes:

1. the boundaries of the commonly owned and managed resource and the rights of users to access it are clearly defined
2. rules concerning resource use are appropriate to local ecological, economic, and institutional conditions
3. the individuals (or households) subject to common management rules participate in making and changing those rules
4. the users or agents accountable to them effectively monitor resource use to ensure compliance with management rules
5. a graduated system of sanctions, with the severity of the sanction based on the seriousness of the offense, is enforced by the users themselves or agents accountable to them
6. low-cost mechanisms exist for resolving conflicts among resource users or between the users and management officials
7. the common ownership and management regime is recognized and respected by external governmental authorities

For complex cases, where the common property regime is part of some larger resource management system, Ostrom identifies an eighth design principle: the various common property institutions and organizations are "organized in multiple layers of nested enterprises" (Ostrom 1990, pp. 90–102).

All of Ostrom's "design principles" were present in the case of England's open field system (at least for the period covered by Dahlman 1980). Ostrom (1990, p. 180, table 5.2) herself asserts that similarly "robust" commonfield agriculture regimes in the Swiss Alps and the Japanese *Iriachi* met all the conditions. To the extent other common property regimes have failed, it is because one or more of Ostrom's "design principles" were absent or only weakly present. For instance, at the failed common property fisheries at Bodrum and the Bay of Izmir in Turkey the only design principle in evidence was (7) – external recognition and respect for the common property regime – and that principle was only weakly established (Ostrom 1990, p. 180, table 5.2).

The next logical question is what determines the presence or absence of the "design principles." What leads (or fails to lead) resource users to cooperate in order to impose a common property regime to avert the tragedy of open access? Ostrom's response to this question is refreshingly nonidealistic. Rather than positing groups of incredibly altruistic individuals, who willingly sacrifice their individual self-interest in favor of a commonly perceived common good, Ostrom relies, more realistically, on the less than saintly *homo oeconomicus*, including individuals who engage in what Oliver Williamson (1975, p. 47) calls "self-interest seeking with guile." Such individuals, according to Ostrom (1990, p. 186), will make "contingent commitments" to participate in, and abide by the rules of, common property regimes so long as they expect that (1) other similarly situated individuals will do likewise *and* (2) the long-term benefits from participation and compliance exceed the long-term benefits from adopting a deviant, individualistic strategy. If, however, individual members of the ownership group expect that they can maximize their individual net benefits by deviating from group ownership rules, the common property regime will tend to fail.

This framework does not, however, explain how individuals come to develop expectations about their long-term benefits. Specifically, it fails to explain circumstances, identified by Barton Thompson (2000), where individuals steadfastly refuse to participate in common property regimes, even though they recognize that refusal may be against their long-term self-interest. It also fails to explain the opposite circumstance, in which individuals choose to cooperate in a common property regime even though they expect their self-interest would be better served by some other, more individualistic strategy (see Goetze 1987, p. 197). Put in more general terms, the framework does not explain why and how groups of individuals sometimes succeed and sometimes fail in overcoming the collective action problems associated with establishing and maintaining common property regimes. Ostrom (1990, p. 187) acknowledges this problem, and attempts to construct an explanation that is consistent with her case studies.

She begins with conventional theories of collective action, according to which cooperation in common property regimes is more likely when: the total number of resource users/decision makers is small, but not so small as to make agreement between them ineffective for resource management; the individuals apply relatively low (implicit) discount rates in resource management decision-making; the individuals are relatively homogeneous in culture and attitude; and a sufficient number of individuals possess requisite leadership attributes (Ostrom 1990, p. 188). In applying these conditions to her own case studies, however, Ostrom encounters "several anomalies." For example, some successful common property regimes involve relatively large numbers of individuals – more than 13,000 in the case of common property irrigation systems in Spain (Ostrom 1990, p. 188). On the other hand, a failed common property fishery in Sri Lanka involved only 200 individuals, who were culturally homogeneous and exhibited low discount rates. The Sri Lankan fishery satisfied most, if not all, of the conditions specified in conventional theories for overcoming collective action problems, but did not. Consequently, Ostrom is forced to look beyond conventional theories of collective action to explain the ability or inability of resource users to cooperate in establishing and maintaining a common property regime.

She finds assistance in the "New Institutional Economics,"[15] which focuses on the transaction costs associated with institutions and institutional change. Ostrom undertakes a transaction-cost analysis of cooperation (or the lack of cooperation) among resource users attempting to resolve open-access problems. Her analysis yields six conditions which can predict, if only weakly, prospects for successful cooperation to establish and maintain common property regimes. Cooperation is likely to be found when (in Ostrom's order of importance; 1990, p. 211):

1. most individuals in the group share a common perception that they are better off cooperating than not cooperating in resource ownership and management
2. most of them would be similarly affected by common management rules or rule changes
3. most of them employ low discount rates
4. transaction costs are relatively low, that is, the costs associated with gathering information about the resource and those who use it are low, and so are the costs of enforcing or changing ownership/management rules
5. social norms of reciprocity and trust predominate within the group
6. the group of resource users is relatively small and stable

These six conditions could be reduced to just one, which is Ostrom's fourth: the level of transaction costs. At least in theory, if transaction

---

[15] For a general introduction to New Institutional Economics see Furobotn and Richter (1998). For a more concise but still useful introduction, see Mercuro and Medema (1997, ch. 5).

costs are quite low, none of the other factors should matter: the number of parties, their social norms and relative homogeneity seem to be important only insofar as they bear on transaction costs. A small and relatively stable number of resource users, as specified in condition (6), will, all other things being equal, entail lower transaction costs than a larger, more variable group. Similarly, social norms of reciprocity and trust tend to be significant just *because* they reduce transaction costs, especially monitoring and enforcement costs.

Ostrom's transaction-cost explanation is consistent with Dahlman's (1980) history of the English open field system. It is also consistent with Stefano Fenoaltea's (1988) explanation of the eventual replacement of that system by a private property regime. According to Fenoaltea, the open field system was efficient only so long as the interests of villagers remained uniform. That uniformity was slowly destroyed as commercialization of agricultural production spread across Europe. Commercialization engendered different and conflicting opinions about proper resource use. When the interests of resource users diverged, the transaction costs of collective decision-making increased, ultimately to a point where those costs more than offset the benefits from continued common property ownership and management. At that point, Fenoaltea concludes, it became efficient to replace the open field system with a management regime based on individual private property.[16]

Jean Ensminger (1990) offers a similar transaction-cost explanation for the privatization of common grazing lands among the Orma people of northeastern Kenya: widening markets and reduced costs of transporting agricultural products to those markets increased the benefits of private land ownership, above and beyond the costs of enclosure. Ensminger notes, however, that privatization did not benefit all members of the Orma; the tribal elders who approved the regime shift benefitted disproportionately. As Ostrom's (1990, p. 186) theory predicts, the elders' commitment to the preexisting common property regime was contingent; once their expected net benefits from the more individualistic strategy of privatization exceeded their expected net benefits from continuing common management, they acted to replace the common management regime.

Finally, Barry Field's (1989) transaction-cost analysis of common-field agriculture challenges an assumption widely shared among property

---

[16] It is important to recognize that this rather simplistic economic explanation of the transition from common property to private property in English agricultural production presumes the critical technological innovations and changes in sociopolitical dynamics that precipitated or facilitated the enclosure movement; it ignores entirely the complex social consequences that followed.

rights economists: that property rights evolve unidirectionally from more informal, communal systems toward more formal, well-defined systems as development pressures increase (see, for example, Demsetz 1967).[17] Field presents evidence that commonfield agriculture in Europe was antedated by a more individualistic, private property system. He posits that, under some circumstances – specifically, where the value of output is increasing, thereby raising the costs of exclusion to such an extent that the costs of exclusion exceed the costs of coordination – development pressures may encourage a shift from private to common property.[18]

Applying Ostrom's framework to consensus-based resource management regimes

Ostrom's theory (1990) purports only to explain traditional forms of common property regimes, such as the English open field system, the Japanese *Iriachi*, and Turkish fisheries. But it can also explain recent efforts at consensus resource management.

In Thanet, on England's southeast coast, English Nature recently spearheaded an effort to protect local chalk cliffs, wildlife populations, beaches, and unique vegetation.[19] Under European Union law, Thanet's coast was designated a Site of Special Scientific Interest for its geology, marine life, and birds; a Special Protection Area and Wetland of International Importance for wintering and breeding birds; a candidate Special Area of Conservation for marine life associated with its chalk caves and reefs; and a candidate Special Area of Conservation for its dune habitats (Pound draft 1999, p. 3). These various designations obligated the British government to develop a management plan that would protect Thanet's environmental amenities. At the same time, however, the Thanet region has Objective 2 economic funding status under the European Union

[17] It should be noted that Demsetz has never explicitly argued that property rights always evolve toward private/individual property, although this is a plausible implication of his article "Towards a Theory of Property Rights" (1967). However, Demsetz, in stark contrast to "free-market environmentalists" (as noted in chapter 5, above) expressly maintains that efficiency is at least sometimes maximized through government action rather than market transactions (see Demsetz 1968, p. 34).

[18] Other authors have made similar arguments about the occasional evolution of property regimes from more specific to less specific rights in contexts other than commonfield agriculture. Rose (1990) argues, for example, that common-law water rights have evolved from more sharply defined private rights to more ambiguous correlative rights.

[19] English Nature is the British government's lead agency on nature conservation issues. Established by the 1990 Environmental Protection Act, and funded by the government, English Nature is responsible for (among other things) implementing English conservation commitments under EU directives and international law, and designating and managing National Nature Reserves, Marine Nature Reserves, and Sites of Special Scientific Interest.

Regeneration Development Fund because of high unemployment and other symptoms of economic stagnation in the region. English Nature sought to develop an environmental management plan that would not conflict with but promote economic regeneration in the region. In an effort to avoid the imposition of a costly regulatory solution, English Nature brought together 103 individuals, representing 42 different organizations with a stake in the Thanet coast, in order to design a consensus-based, self-regulatory management regime.[20] These stakeholders included commercial fishing fleets, recreational fishing associations, bikers, bait diggers, horseback riders, hoteliers, jet skiers, water skiers, swimmers, local schools, archaeologists, and environmentalists. In a series of four "workshops," led by professionally trained facilitators, Thanet's stakeholders achieved a remarkable breadth and depth of agreement on coastal zone management. They agreed to create a coastal park, which would integrate coastal management, and market the coast for its various extractable and nonextractable amenities. They also agreed that economic regeneration funding (under EU Objective 2 status) should be tied to conservation criteria. User groups, such as jet skiers and fishers, volunteered to impose on their members codes of conduct designed to preserve coastal amenities (Pound draft 1999, p. 18). The process remains incomplete, however. The formal management plan has yet to be finally adopted; and user groups are still preparing detailed codes of conduct for their members. Consequently, it would be premature to declare English Nature's efforts at Thanet a success.

It is not too early, however, to assess consensus management plans generally as a form of common property. As with other commons, Thanet's coastal amenities are treated as if they belong to all the stakeholders, who cooperate in their management and protection. The stakeholders have voluntarily subjected their use of the Thanet coastline to guidelines and conditions. They overcame collective action problems to create a self-imposed regulatory system that effectively converts open-access resources to their common property.

Although Ostrom (1990) was not concerned with this type of common property regime, it fits well within her framework. By bringing all the stakeholders together, providing them with information, and permitting them to exchange ideas and opinions in a nonadversarial setting, English Nature significantly reduced the transaction costs of collective action. The "stakeholders" came to realize that at least some win/win consensus solutions were available.

---

[20] Notice that the concept of "stakeholder" is broader than the concept of "users" in most studies of common property regimes. To be a "stakeholder" one need not "use" the resource or be a member of the local community.

This is not to argue, however, that consensus management efforts are a panacea for the collective action problems of common property regimes. For one thing, consensus management efforts themselves entail substantial transaction costs – including the costs of identifying, contacting, inviting, and securing the attendance of all "stakeholders," as well as the costs of facilities, food, professional facilitators, *etc.* – with no guarantee of success at the end of the process. There is also reason to doubt the long-term sustainability of consensus management regimes, given inherently changeable circumstances. Existing stakeholders may disavow the management regime they agreed to, if the benefits of exit exceed the costs. Also, new "stakeholders," whose interests were not contemplated in the original management agreement, may arrive on the scene. Most importantly, if the consensus management regime is purely voluntary, it may prove unenforceable in the absence of a credible threat of government intervention. In other words, the commitment of the "stakeholders" to the common property regime may be contingent on their expectation that its failure would result in more costly government regulation. Finally, it would be unreasonable to expect that diverse stakeholder groups could find agreement on all issues pertaining to resource management. In fact, that is not even the goal of consensus management efforts. The goal, rather, is to minimize and cabin disagreements. In some cases at least, residual disagreements can be expected to impact on resource conservation.

V   A final caveat: "success" may not be all it's cracked up to be

In reviewing the literature on common property regimes, one is struck by the unwavering focus on resource *use* and output.[21] The ultimate determinant of "success" or "failure" is the sustainability of *production* over time of *commodities* – goods to be consumed at home or sold at market. Studies of common property regimes pay little, if any, attention to *noncommodity* natural resource amenities. If there are examples of common property regimes, as conventionally defined, that have been designed to preserve noncommodity, environmental resources, they simply do not appear in the literature.

There is no reason to presume that a common property regime instituted to govern a fishery, for example, will preserve related, noncommodity amenities. While fish stocks are sustained, other marine resources may be degraded or even intentionally destroyed because they have no

---

[21] This is obviously not true of my discussion of consensus-based environmental management, but that is an atypical common property regime, which is generally not discussed in the literature.

commodity or exchange value *to the users*. A common property regime designed to preserve a local tuna fishery, for example, may be considered a "success," as conventionally defined in the literature, even if it authorizes the use of nets that decimate local dolphin populations, so long as stable tuna populations are maintained. Similarly, a common property irrigation system will be deemed a "success," so long as it effectively and efficiently provides water for member farmers, even if their irrigation activities cause pesticide run-off that harms fish populations and downstream, nonmember farmers. The criterion of success is the long-term sustainable harvest of the commodity resource *for the users*, not the general preservation of environmental amenities. Thus, a common property regime may avert one tragedy of open access while ignoring, or exacerbating, another.

7   The complexities of property regime choice for environmental protection

I have examined four basic property-based approaches to environmental protection (defined in terms of avoiding the tragedy of open access): public/state property, mixed public/state and private/individual property, pure private/individual property, and common property. Each approach has proven useful for resource conservation in some circumstances. None, however, has proven optimal for averting the tragedy of open access in every circumstance. Hence, this book's mantra: there is no universal, first-best property-based solution for environmental protection in this second-best world.

The next task is to assess the myriad factors that explain property regime choice in various ecological, technological, institutional, and economic circumstances. The objective is not to develop a normative theory, or even to generate useful predictions (although that would be a welcome consequence), but to understand and appreciate the complexities of property regime choice.[1] This chapter offers an informal model that is, of necessity, rudimentary. To elaborate a fully fledged model for selecting property-based regimes would require an entire book of its own, if it could be done at all.[2]

Section 1 of the chapter sets out the informal model and compares it with models offered by other authors. Section 2 introduces various complicating factors – everything from resource location and size to historical contingency and ideology – that limit the normative and predictive capability of any theoretical model. In light of the inherent complexity of institutional choice for averting the tragedy of open access, section 3 suggests, finally, that the best means of averting the tragedy of open access lies in the circumstantial application of various property regimes and admixtures of property regimes.

[1] As Coase (1994, p. 17) has asserted: "Faced with a choice between a theory which predicts well but gives us little insight into how the system works and one which gives us this insight but predicts badly, I would choose the latter."

[2] J. H. Dales (1968, p. 42) suggests the effort would prove futile: "even if we had all the scientific data we wanted, we still would not be able to construct a fully reliable benefit-cost table for an actual pollution problem."

I   Modeling property regime choice: what counts as "best"?

Coordination costs + exclusion costs = total costs

The "best" property regime for environmental protection is that which achieves society's exogenously set environmental protection goals at the lowest total cost, defined as the sum of exclusion and coordination costs given the environmental amenities targeted and their ecological circumstances, economies or diseconomies of scale, technological capabilities, and institutional and organizational constraints. Exclusion costs are the costs of drawing and enforcing boundaries to restrict access to and use of the resource to the owner(s) of the property. Coordination costs are those associated with solving the kinds of collective action problems discussed in chapter 6.

Richard Epstein (1994, pp. 20–2) has suggested a similar criterion for selecting between private/individual and common property regimes: "[a]ny responsible search for a sound system of property rights searches for the net social advantage by minimizing the sum of the rival inconveniences." The "inconveniences" to which Esptein refers are the same coordination and exclusion costs that are central to my analysis. "The question," Epstein writes, "is which of the two sets of costs – coordination or exclusion – is likely to prove larger. The question here cannot be answered in the abstract, but depends heavily on the nature of the resource in question and the technology that is available to exploit it."

Epstein follows Coase (1960) in specifying the goal of property regime choice: to maximize social product by minimizing social costs. But society's goal in protecting the environment is not always to maximize the social product but social welfare more broadly conceived. The very existence of the Endangered Species Act demonstrates that decision-makers at least sometimes sacrifice production in favor of preservation. This implies that social welfare is sometimes enhanced by sacrificing production in favor of preservation; in other words, the value of fore-gone production is less than the value of the benefits obtained through preservation.

Moreover, Epstein's formulation of the proper method for determining "net social advantage" is problematic. He suggests that the choice of property regimes should be based on which set of costs – "exclusion" or "coordination" – is lower. If exclusion costs are lower than coordination costs, then a private property regime is preferable to a common property regime. If, however, exclusion costs exceed coordination costs, then a common property regime may be best. This formulation is problematic because it implicitly assumes that the sum of exclusion and coordination costs remains constant across alternative property regimes. It treats coordination and exclusion costs as entirely a function of the nature of the resource itself, without regard to the property institution that society superimposes on that resource. As Coase (1960) has pointed out, however, the choice of legal rule – in this case, the choice of property regime – can itself influence the total of exclusion and coordination costs, that is, total transaction costs.[3]

There is an example of this in chapter 4, which illustrated how pure public/state property-based approaches to air pollution control, such as technology-based command-and-control regulations, can be more efficient in some technological and institutional circumstances than mixed property approaches, such as tradeable emissions allowances. Chapter 4's historical analysis of the 1970 Clean Air Act revealed that the mixed property-based approach entailed higher monitoring costs than the public/state property regime, although the latter entailed higher compliance costs than the former. Whether Epstein would categorize compliance and monitoring costs as "exclusion" or "coordination" costs is not important. What is important is that the choice of property regime significantly affected the overall cost structure of resource management. That is why it is more appropriate to focus on the sum of coordination and exclusion costs, rather than the lesser of coordination and exclusion costs, as Epstein (1994) suggests.

The total cost criterion offered here entails two other implications that require further elucidation. First, the criterion does not dictate what a society's environmental protection goals should be, but attempts only to determine the most efficient property-based regime for attaining them. It is in essence a cost-effectiveness standard. This is consistent with J. H. Dales's (1968, pp. 39–40) admonition about the limited utility of economic analysis for environmental protection:

---

[3] Robert Ellickson (1993, p. 1326) argues that, to maximize social welfare, it is not enough to minimize transaction costs; it is equally important to minimize deadweight losses stemming from failures to exploit potential gains from trade. However, those deadweight losses typically stem from information constraints or asymmetries that are themselves among the costs of transacting.

It might be argued that a property regime that prohibited all transactions would entail zero transaction costs but cause huge deadweight losses: transaction costs would be zero because there would be no costs associated with transacting; but deadweight losses would be high because the lack of alienability impedes welfare-enhancing trades. However, although the costs associated with *actual* transactions would be zero, the costs of *potential* transactions, which are those we are most concerned about in assessing deadweight losses, would be infinite. It should still be possible, therefore, to minimize the deadweight losses associated with unexploited potential gains from trade by minimizing the costs of transacting – in this case by replacing the property regime that prohibits all transactions with a regime of generally transferable property rights. Of course, there are also transaction or transition costs associated with changing institutions.

[T]he economist is quite unable to draw up a table showing all benefits and costs of all anti-pollution policies that are proposed (or that might be proposed); he is therefore quite unable to say that one policy is demonstrably superior to all others.

But this is not to say that economics is altogether useless in dealing with real-world pollution problems. There is one sense in which economic analysis can almost always be very helpful. I have so far been using the word "policy" to mean "what is to be done." But even when we have decided what we will do, we still have to decide how to do it. In resolving this second question of means to achieve some given end of policy, economic analysis is, I think, indispensable; indeed I think it can almost always lead us to the best answer.

Dales (1968, p. 77) goes on to note that

whether we approach pollution problems from the standpoint of economics (benefit-cost analysis) or the standpoint of law (property rights) we can find no best solution to them; . . . any anti-pollution policy is therefore bound to be *in the nature of a social experiment* that is neither right nor wrong, but only more or less successful in leading to wise and socially agreed-upon patterns of use of our air and water resources.[4]

Dales's attitude is consistent with the assertion, repeated throughout this book, that the quest for optimal solutions in the real world is futile. There is no optimal level of environmental protection in the real world, only a de-manded level, reflecting what decision-makers – whether private property owners, groups of resource users, stakeholders, voters, elected officials, or government bureaucrats – are willing to pay to achieve it.

A second implication worth noting about the total cost approach is that effectiveness is a prerequisite to efficiency. If a certain property regime would, under the circumstances, fail to avert the tragedy of open access, then it cannot be an efficient solution. This is because the imposition of any property regime entails substantial transaction costs, costs that cannot be justified unless the property regime would provide offsetting social benefits, in the form of resource conservation. If the property regime would fail to conserve resources, then open access – meaning the absence of property rights – would necessarily remain more efficient.

It is, of course, possible for more than one regime to be effective in a particular situation, which implies that one regime may be *more* effec-tive – providing greater environmental protection – than another. *Relative* effectiveness must, of course, factor into the determination of overall

---

[4] Emphasis added. The source of Dales's pessimism about the ability of economists to de-termine an optimal level of environmental protection is his understanding that economists have no way of accurately measuring social welfare damages: "the economist cannot tell us how to allocate our costs of waste disposal, because he cannot measure welfare dam-ages" (Dales 1968, p. 104). This point may be logically entailed by Arrow's (1951) proof that the social welfare function, if it exists at all, is impossible to specify.

efficiency, but it is not determinative of efficiency. A relatively effective property regime may be more or less efficient than another regime that produces fewer social benefits, in terms of resource conservation. The decisive factor is *the degree of effectiveness* – the amount of conservation or level of environmental quality – *per unit of cost*. Any comparative assessment of property regimes for environmental protection ultimately depends on the answers to two questions, one absolute and the other relative. First, would a certain property regime cost-effectively avert the tragedy of open access? If so, would it avert the tragedy as effectively and efficiently as some alternative property regime? These questions appear straightforward enough, but they are easier to pose than to answer, especially *ex ante*. We are unlikely ever to possess sufficient information, before the fact of any policy decision, to feel confident that it is the right or best decision. Uncertainty enshrouds all our judgments, especially *social* judgments. Knowing this, we should be, but typically are not, modest in criticizing existing institutions and recommending alternatives.

Alternative approaches

This book's total cost criterion differs from other criteria that focus predominantly on the supposed nature of the resource itself. Rose Ann Devlin (2000), for example,[5] offers a framework in which the "optimal" property regime – private, community, or state – is determined by the nature of the good to which it applies. According to Devlin, there are four types of goods: "private," "club," "common-pool," and "public." A "private" good is rivalrous in consumption, meaning that one person's consumption of the resource precludes another's, and excludable, meaning that the resource's physical and biological characteristics make it possible for one person to possess it to the exclusion of others. A "club" good is exclusive but nonrivalrous, which means that several persons can use the resource without interfering with one another's use, but they can still exclude others. A "common-pool" good is rivalrous but nonexclusive. Finally, a "public" good is neither rivalrous nor exclusive.

These labels imply that resources possess certain natural, perhaps immutable, characteristics that uniquely suit them to particular property regimes. Devlin's determinations of which property regimes are best suited for which goods follow intuitively from her characterizations of the goods. Private property is generally best suited to private goods;

---

[5] Another example is McKean (1996).

club goods are appropriately managed with common property regimes;[6] common-pool and public goods are both amenable to either community or state property regimes, depending on the size of the population affected by their management.

Unfortunately, Devlin's framework begs the most important question: how do we determine what counts as a public, common-pool, club, or private good? Devlin does not raise, let alone resolve, this question. She takes it for granted that certain resources have certain natures or characteristics. Indeed, her labels can easily create the misimpression that certain resources or resource types are immutably rivalrous or nonrivalrous, exclusive or nonexclusive. It would be a mistake to conclude, however, that a resource such as land is always and everywhere rivalrous and exclusive, and therefore appropriately a "private" good.

In chapter 6 I showed that land is sometimes treated as a club good, as defined by Devlin, depending on its location and uses. England's open field system, for example, treated agricultural lands as private property for crop raising but common property for pasturage. The land was simultaneously a "private" good and a "club" good. In mountainous regions of South America and Japan, agricultural land could be either a private good or a club good, depending predominantly on its elevation. Moreover, as noted in chapter 5, the extent to which a resource is exclusive and rivalrous can change. Technological innovations may, for example, reduce the costs of enclosure and thereby increase the potential exclusiveness of the resource, so that a resource that is presently nonexclusive may become exclusive. Given this, labels such as "public," "private," and "club" good are not particularly helpful for determining the appropriate property-based approach for managing specific resources or resource amenities. Far more important are the factors on which those labels are based.

The labels "public good," "private good," and "club good" unsurprisingly are determined by the very same factors that determine the "best" property regime for a given resource in a given set of circumstances: the relative costs of exclusion and coordination. These costs are partly, but not solely, determined by the nature or character of the resource. The resource's ecological, technological, and institutional circumstances are also extremely – in some cases, decisively – important. Culture and ideology – factors that are notoriously difficult to model – may also play a crucial role in property regime choice.

[6] Devlin (2000, p. 112) suggests that club goods should be either privately owned, if their use entails few externalities, or community owned, if their use affects large numbers. But her definition of private ownership (p. 111) includes small groups, which brings it within my definition (from chapter 1) of common property.

II   Taking complexity seriously

Stipulating a framework for comparing property regimes is simple enough; applying it to real-world circumstances is another matter. So many factors can influence the effectiveness and efficiency of alternative property regimes, including: the size and location of the resource; the number and varieties of amenities associated with the resource, how those amenities relate one to another, and how they are valued by individuals in society, given their subjective discount rates and time horizons; the availability and cost of enclosure and coordination techologies; and the extent to which existing social institutions protect exclusive property rights and foster cooperation.

Even in seemingly simple, straightforward cases there may be so many variables, so many dimensions of concern, that accurately estimating the sum of exclusion and coordination costs becomes exceedingly difficult, especially *ex ante*. In some cases comparisons of property regimes will not even permit rough judgments to be made about what is "best." It is worth the exercise, however, if only to realize that property regime choice is a complex and rarely obvious matter, which is likely to be determined less by theory than by historical contingency or accident.

Simple cases and complicating factors

Let me begin with a couple of relatively "easy" cases.

Protecting the atmosphere against the tragedy of open access may be the easiest case, simply because our options are strictly limited by technological constraints, at least for the time being. We lack the technical ability to draw boundaries and fence-in the air as private property, rendering the costs of exclusion extremely, if not infinitely, high under either a private/individual property regime or a common property regime. The only viable option to open access, generally speaking, is public/state property.[7] This is not to say that public/state property is a first-best, or even a very good solution. To the extent it is, or becomes, possible to define and protect private air rights, public ownership of the atmosphere may well be an inferior solution.[8]

Another "easy" case involves an ordinary single family home on an ordinary lot in a typical subdivision of Anytown, USA. The land is not a useful habitat for rare or endangered species of plants or animals; no

[7] Some private rights in the atmosphere, such as transferable pollution rights, are feasible, but they are the exceptions that prove the rule, at least for the time being.

[8] This is by no means certain, however. A case can be made that averting the tragedy of open access by public regulation of polluting activities would entail lower transaction costs than millions of private lawsuits against tens of thousands of air polluters.

river runs through the land. In the absence of socially valued resource amenities that private owners are likely to undervalue and, therefore, fail to conserve, a private or family ownership regime would probably entail lower total costs than either a state ownership regime or a larger common ownership regime. In other words, the more closely private costs and benefits of conservation approximate the social costs and benefits, the stronger the argument is for private property rights.

The cases quickly become more complicated, however, as the nature, location, and potential uses and nonuses of resources change. Most agricultural land in the United States is owned by individuals or families, reflecting the relatively low combined exclusion and coordination costs associated with individual or family ownership. In some places and at some times, however, instituting and maintaining an individual ownership regime may prove too costly. The location or size of the land parcel, combined with technological constraints, may make exclusion under a private property regime prohibitively expensive. Consider, for example, the rangelands of the American West, which were maintained in public ownership prior to the invention of barbed wire (see Anderson and Hill 1975), or lands in mountainous regions of Peru, Bolivia, and Japan, where commonfield agriculture is still practiced today (see chapter 6). In some circumstances, the relatively high cost of instituting a private property regime may make common or public property regimes preferable overall, even if they entail marginally higher coordination costs. In other words, the *total* cost of a common or public regime – the sum of exclusion and coordination costs – may be lower than the *total* cost of a private property regime.

Stonehenge: public or private property?

Some lands, such as the Grand Canyon in America and Stonehenge in England, possess unique characteristics that give them great economic *and* extra-economic value for society. It may appear obvious, at first blush, that such monuments should be held in *public* ownership, so that all members of society have access to, and an ownership stake in, the resource. It is not necessarily the case, however, that the Grand Canyon and Stonehenge are better protected under public/state ownership. There is, in fact, some interesting legal history about the status of Stonehenge as property,[9] which illustrates the intrinsic complexity of property regime choice.

At the beginning of the twentieth century the land on which Stonehenge sits was privately owned by Sir Edmund Antrobus. Sir Edmund's

[9] Much of this history comes from Bonyhady (1987, pp. 10–11).

great-great uncle, also Sir Edmund, had purchased the estate, called
Amesbury, in 1824 from the fourth Marquess of Queensberry. The elder
Sir Edmund immediately appointed a guardian to protect the site from
public abuse, which was already threatening the monument. One sarsen
stone had fallen in 1797, and during the nineteenth century "Stonehenge
[became] so busy that an enterprising Amesbury carpenter made a living
selling liquor and refreshments from a smoky hut dug against a stone, and
[the archaeologist William] Stukeley complained of the 'infinite number
of daily visitants'" (Chippindale 1990, p. 15). According to one Victorian
commentator:

Waggonette parties are the bane of Stonehenge. To avoid them you must be up
with the dawn, or you must wait for the evening shadows. Unfortunately I had
stumbled upon the early afternoon, and long before I had reached the stones
I could see that they were ringed with a cordon of waggonettes and flecked with
the light foam of summer blouses. (quoted in Chippindale 1990, p. 31)

The Times of London warned that Stonehenge was "in danger of being vulgarized out of all knowledge and certainly out of all its venerable
charms. To continue to allow this marvellous relic of prehistoric ages
to be ruthlessly disfigured and perish inch by inch would be an eternal
disgrace" (quoted in Chippindale 1990, p. 15).

A second sarsen stone fell in 1900, alarming both Sir Edmund the
younger, who had come into possession of the estate in 1899,[10] and
England's Parliament. The government quickly began drafting plans to
reconstruct the monument and protect it with police guards, under the
1882 Ancient Monuments Act. Its plans were preempted, however, when
Sir Edmund, with the support of the Society of Antiquaries, erected a
barbed-wire fence around the monument and started charging a one-
shilling admission fee.[11] According to Lord Eversley (1910, p. 305),
founder (in 1865) of the Commons Preservation Society and framer of
the 1882 Ancient Monuments Act, Sir Edmund's fence

altered entirely the character of the Monument...rob[bing] it of its peculiar
character – a strange relic of the twilight of the world, standing untouched through
countless centuries – and to convert it into an antiquarian's specimen. It has
lost its solemnity, due to its loneliness in the vast plain. The inhabitants of the
district, who cannot afford to pay one shilling a head for entrance, have lost their
accustomed right of access to it.

Sir Edmund's ostensible reason for enclosing Stonehenge was to
protect it from tourist abuse. He justified the entrance fee as necessary to

[10] Sir Edmund's great-great uncle died in 1926, leaving a future interest in Amesbury to
Sir Edmund following two life tenancies.
[11] There were 3,770 paying visitors the first year (Chippindale 1990, p. 16).

recoup the expenses of enclosing the monument, raising fallen stones, and providing two custodians. This explanation did not satisfy the eminent archaeologist Flinders Petrie, who had surveyed Stonehenge in 1877, or George Shaw-Lefevre and Sir John Brunner, two members of the Commons Preservation Society, on whose behalf the Attorney-General filed a lawsuit designed to force Sir Edmund Antrobus to remove the fences surrounding Stonehenge. The "relators" (the real parties in interest) of the lawsuit wanted the court to declare Stonehenge a public place subject to public rights of access.

The Chancery Division, in a decision by Justice (later Lord Justice) Farwell,[12] dismissed the suit, declaring that Sir Edmund Antrobus was within his rights as owner of the land on which Stonehenge sits to enclose the monument and exclude the public. In Justice Farwell's view, the Attorney-General and the relators were attempting to confiscate Sir Edmund's private property without paying compensation:

I desire to give the relators credit for wishing only to preserve this unique relic of a former age for the benefit of the public, but I fail to appreciate their method for attaining this object. The first claim to dispossess the defendant of his property is simply extravagant, so much so that, although not technically abandoned, no serious argument was addressed to me in support of it.[13]

As for the relators' second claim – that the public had obtained a right-of-way to visit Stonehenge by virtue of its use of existing paths since time out of mind – Justice Farwell concluded that public "access to the circle was incident only to the permission to visit and inspect the stones, and therefore was permissive only . . . The action accordingly fails and ought never to have been brought."[14] The court found it ironic that the relators sought to ensure public access to Stonehenge, when it was public access that constituted the primary threat to the monument. Unimpeded public access "compelled" the defendant "to protect the stones if they were to be preserved," according to the court, and Sir Edmund did "nothing more than [was] necessary for such protection."[15]

Justice Farwell found no evidence to suggest that the Antrobus family or their predecessors in interest intended to dedicate a right-of-way to the public. The fact that they *permitted* the public to visit the site was not, in itself, enough: one can intend to permit visitors without intending to dedicate a right-of-way. Otherwise, Justice Farwell surmised, private property owners would be much less willing to permit any public access. He quoted from an earlier ruling by Lord Justice Bowen:

[12] *Attorney-General v. Antrobus*, 2 Ch. 188 (1905).   [13] *ibid.*, at 208.
[14] *ibid.*   [15] *ibid.*

Nothing worse can happen in a free country than to force people to be churlish about their rights for fear that their indulgence may be abused, and to drive them to prevent the enjoyment of things which, although they are matters of private property, naturally give pleasure to many persons besides the owners, under the fear that their good nature may be misunderstood.[16]

Sir Edmund's enclosure of Stonehenge was, from Justice Farwell's perspective, a success story in the use of private property to avert the tragedy of open access. Indeed, Sir Edmund's fence did protect Stonehenge against public abuse. And Justice Farwell commended the owner for this: "It is only fair to the defendant to say that he is not acting capriciously but on expert advice for the preservation of the stones."

Not all observers agreed with Justice Farwell, however, that Sir Edmund's actions were motivated by a commitment to the public weal, or to the preservation of Stonehenge. According to Lord Eversley (1910, p. 306), Sir Edmund could have protected the stones by bringing the monument within the protection of the Ancient Monuments Act of 1882. Under that law, the monument would have been protected from injury but still publicly accessible without charge (see also Bonyhady 1987, p. 10). Under his private ownership, however, neither public access to, nor preservation of, Stonehenge could be assured at any price. An editorial appearing in the *Times* (London) on April 20, 1905 (p. 7) warned that

if it is within SIR EDMUND'S power to enclose Stonehenge with an open fence and to charge a shilling for the right of entry, it is equally within his power to enclose it with a high park paling or a brick wall, to charge a guinea for admission, or to exclude the public altogether. Thus the most complete and impressive specimen of megalithic work in the British Isles . . . may be altogether closed to the nation, which has had free access to it from time immemorial. (quoted in Bonyhady 1987, p. 11)

Beneath his ostensible public spiritedness, Sir Edmund Antrobus possessed an ulterior, self-interested motive for enclosing Stonehenge. He considered Stonehenge "a dubious asset to the estate, yielding no income yet a source of trouble" (Chippindale 1990, p. 15). His real goal, according to Lord Eversley (1910, p. 304), was to rid himself of this dubious asset by "extorting money for its purchase from the public." Sir Edmund offered to sell Stonehenge to the government for £125,000, threatening, through his agent, that if the government declined his generous offer, he would be forced to "sell the stones to some American millionaire, who would ship them across the Atlantic." The Chancellor of the Exchequer refused, however, to pay the ransom. Sir Edmund later reduced his asking price to £50,000, but the government still balked, claiming that the value

---

[16] *Blount* v. *Layard*, [1891] 2 Ch. 691, n.

of the monument was similar to the value of two ancient abbeys it had recently purchased for £10,000 each (Lord Eversley 1910, pp. 306–7).

Sir Edmund Antrobus's effort to sell Stonehenge to the government for an exorbitant price is most interesting in light of the fact that Parliament could have condemned the monument for public use without compensating Sir Edmund at all. Unlike in America, England's unwritten constitution provides no right to compensation for takings of private property. Although compensation is provided for in ordinary legislation,[17] Parliament can override that legislation by expressing its clear intention to condemn property without compensation.[18] In short, Sir Edmund was attempting to extort compensation from the government without legal leverage. As a matter of historical fact, Parliament has almost always compensated landowners for property rights it has expropriated (Allen 2000, pp. 15–16).[19]

Questions of compensation are beside the point, however, in determining which is the preferred ownership regime for conserving Stonehenge. To argue that the government should simply have taken Stonehenge from Sir Edmund is to beg the most important question: was Stonehenge better left in Sir Edmund's private ownership or appropriated for public use by the government? In other words, was Justice Farwell's decision in the *Antrobus* case the best one from the perspective of public policy? Some additional history may suggest an answer.

In 1915, having failed to sell Stonehenge to the government, the Antrobus family subdivided and sold the entire Amesbury estate. A neighboring landowner, Cecil Chubb, purchased the small triangle of land on which Stonehenge sits for £6,600 (Chippindale 1990, p. 16) – a sum less than the government's earlier estimate of Stonehenge's economic value. Three years later, Mr. Chubb donated Stonehenge to the nation, and received a knighthood for his good deed. It was a case of publicization of private property (as discussed in chapter 3). However, this voluntary – presumptively Pareto-improving – transaction does not necessarily signify that Stonehenge is best managed under public ownership.

Since acquiring Stonehenge, the British government has rarely managed the monument consistently with the goal of long-term preservation.

---

[17] See, for example, *Sisters of Charity of Rockingham* v. *The King* [1922] 2 AC 315 (PC), at 322 (explaining that the entitlement to compensation for a governmental taking of private property for public use must be statutory; there is no common law right to compensation).

[18] As Lord Justice Upjohn explained in *Burmah Oil* v. *Lord Advocate*, [1965] AC 75, at 167: "it is clearly settled that where the executive is authorized by a statute to take the property of a subject for public purposes the subject is entitled to be paid unless the statute has made the contrary intention quite clear."

[19] It is difficult to imagine a plausible public choice explanation for this.

During the exigent circumstances of the First World War, for example, the government located an airfield close to the monument. After the war the airfield was converted into the "Stonehenge pig-farm." Directly across from the monument, a café was built to accommodate tourists, and new cottages were constructed for the monument's custodians. There were even plans to develop a residential community of bungalows close by the stones (Chippindale 1990, p. 16). In the late 1920s a public appeal was launched to raise funds to preserve Stonehenge and its immediate environment from encroaching development. Subsequently, Parliament turned over management of the monument to the National Trust, for preservation in perpetuity (Chippindale 1990, p. 16). This was more easily said than done, however.

After the National Trust accepted responsibility for managing Stonehenge, visitor pressure continued to mount. By 1962 "the grass in the centre of the site had died off. Eventually, the authorities replaced it with orange gravel."[20] By the mid-1970s more than 600,000 people were visiting Stonehenge each year. Starting in 1974 an annual People's Free Festival was organized at the monument, attracting as many as 35,000 people (Chippindale 1990, p. 29).[21] Finally, in 1977 the government was forced to close the monument to visitors, while it belatedly considered methods for preserving the stones against deterioration through overuse.

Ironically, Stonehenge's public managers did precisely what its former private owner, Sir Edmund Antrobus, had done in 1901: they enclosed it behind fences to protect it from the public. At least Sir Edmund had continued to allow the public in for a small fee. When the government closed Stonehenge in 1977, the public was completely excluded, except at the solstices, because Stonehenge's public owners/managers could not agree upon an acceptable way of coordinating access to, and use of, the monument. Apparently, the government never seriously contemplated rationing access to Stonehenge, either by price or by queuing.[22]

The National Trust now manages the lands surrounding Stonehenge, but the monument itself is managed by English Heritage, a government agency created in the National Heritage Act of 1984. English Heritage's

---

[20] Robert Layton and Julian Thomas, "Proposals for a Tunnel at Stonehenge: an Assessment of the Alternatives: a Report to the WAC Executive," at http://www.wac. uct.ac.za/archive/ content/ stonrer.htm.

[21] English Heritage and the National Trust banned the festival in 1985, precipitating the "Battle of Stonehenge." Police, who were later accused of misconduct, arrested 520 annual festival-goers and others who sought to celebrate the solstice at Stonehenge. On the "Battle of Stonehenge" and its aftermath, see Fowler (1990b, pp. 151–5).

[22] The government charges a £3 fee for admission to Stonehenge (see *Financial Times*, 25 September 1995, at p. 6), but that fee only gets the visitor within about 10 meters of the stones; visitors still cannot walk among the stones at any price. For the future, English Heritage plans to abolish the admission fee entirely, although it would retain a car parking fee (*M2 Presswire*, April 2, 1998).

mission is to ensure "the physical well-being of the structure and its environs" (Fowler 1990b, p. 141). Unfortunately, this goal has most often been observed in the breach. The experience of Stonehenge today, for most visitors, is very little different from any other popular tourist destination:

A busy road runs through the north edge of the site, and the main London to Exeter highway a couple of hundred metres to the south. Inescapable demands for visitor facilities – car- and coach-parking, lavatories, a souvenir shop, a café – have been met by a squalid little development, just across the road from Stonehenge. It is on the land that was purchased by national subscription and vested for its safety in the care of the National Trust expressly to prevent its piecemeal conversion into cafés and so on. A grass, and then gravel, surface among the stones could not stand the press of feet, and now visitors cannot normally go into Stonehenge; instead they walk on a tarmac path from which it is very hard properly to appreciate what is there. We have reached the position where so many people try to see Stonehenge that very few see it. (Chippendale 1990, p. 31)

In the late 1980s English Heritage adopted a new management plan, which would remove the roads and facilities presently impinging on Stonehenge.[23] Christopher Chippindale (1990, p. 33) concurs with the goal of this new management plan: "to make open space around Stonehenge, to provide facilities at a better distance, and to let visitors approach Stonehenge on foot, as prehistoric people must have done." English Heritage's plan does little, however, to deal with the problem of too many visitors. In fact, the agency has publicly announced that it has no intention of reducing public access to the monument. In an advertisement it placed in several newspapers on June 5, 1997, English Heritage promised that "[b]y making Stonehenge harder to get to, we would make it more accessible. Visitors would be able to roam freely (and free of charge) among the monuments, unfettered by fences. (Those with disabilities or walking difficulties would be provided with suitable transport.)"[24]

In 1997, Lord St. John of Fawsley raised *the* fundamental question about Stonehenge in Parliament: "One of the profound problems of our time is how to ensure that people have access to our heritage without destroying the very thing they have come to see." Lord Strabolgi added: "We seem totally unable to come to grips with the problem of how to protect a monument of this stature, particularly in the days of mass tourism."[25]

---

[23] On English Heritage's master plan for Stonehenge, see "Stonehenge: the Master Plan," at http://homepages.tcp.co.uk/~ait/masterplan.html.

[24] Quoted in Council for British Archaeology, "The Stonehenge Saga," at http://www.britarch.ac.uk/eba/stone1.html.

[25] The text of the parliamentary discussion is available on the World Wide Web at http://www.parliament.the-stationary-offi...697/ldhansrd/pdvn/lds97/text/ 70630–15.htm.

When Sir Edmund Antrobus fenced in Stonehenge and began charging one shilling for admission in 1901, he was severely criticized. Lord Eversley (1910, p. 310) wrote that

[t]he Monument of Stonehenge has been desecrated and vulgarised by the erection round it of the barbed-wire fencing; and the great majority of the public, who cannot afford to pay one shilling a head for entrance to the inclosure, have been permanently excluded. We may doubt whether in any other country in Europe such treatment of a great historical and national Monument would be permitted.

But today Stonehenge is fenced in by its public owners/managers, and members of the public cannot walk amongst the stones *at any price* during most of the year. The question remains whether Stonehenge is better off under public ownership than it was under Sir Edmund's private/individual ownership.

There are several reasons to suppose that private/individual ownership might deal with at least some of Stonehenge's problems more effectively than public ownership/management. Specifically, a private owner might find it easier than the government to restrict public access. One of the more interesting aspects of Stonehenge's history as property is that Sir Edmund Antrobus's management efforts focused on reducing public access; the government's management, by contrast, has focused on solving coordination problems – the geographical relation of Stonehenge to roads, cafés, and other tourist facilities. In stark contrast to Lord St. John of Fawsley and Lord Stabolgi, English Heritage seems to think, wishfully, that public access is not part of the problem.

It is not as if the government lacks the ability to control public access to publicly owned amenities. They do it all the time. Think of publicly owned zoos or museums, which limit access to animals or art through prices, queuing, or both. Most of the world's art treasures are held in public collections. The Louvre charges an admission fee, most days of the week, for access to the world's largest publicly owned art collection, including the world's single most famous painting, Leonardo's *La Gioconda* (better known as the *Mona Lisa*). In addition, the size of the gallery in which *La Gioconda* hangs restricts access; members of the public who wish to view Leonardo's masterpiece have to crowd around to get a glimpse – often obstructed – of it. This crowding not only restricts access, however. It also reduces the viewing pleasure of many visitors. The French government, which owns the Louvre, might reduce overcrowding by increasing the admission fee or by placing *La Gioconda* in a space specially designed to reduce crowding, for example by moving viewers passed the painting on a slow-moving conveyer belt.[26] Surely, privatization is not necessary to

[26] The French government recently announced plans to divide the Salle des Etats, the gallery in which *La Gioconda* is displayed, in order to give the painting its own, exclusive

solve the access problem. Indeed, privatization of *La Gioconda* is inconceivable (except, perhaps, in the minds of one or two incredibly wealthy collectors and several property rights economists).

Stonehenge is like *La Gioconda* and other famous, publicly owned works of art and artifacts. Although it is not housed in a museum – it is situated, rather, in its natural, historical environment, which contributes substantially to its social value – it is neither impossible nor impracticable to control access to it. Indeed, access to Stonehenge *is* strictly controlled; visitors can approach but not enter the monument.[27] The British government does not charge an admission fee to reduce demand to visit Stonehenge. As the museum analogy suggests, however, it is not unheard of for governments to charge fees and take other measures to protect their most precious public resources. If the French government can protect *La Gioconda* and other masterpieces in the Louvre from "overuse" through an admission fee and queuing, then the British government should be able to similarly regulate access to Stonehenge. Yet, recent management plans specifically designed to preserve Stonehenge fail even to discuss the possibility of an admission fee. Perhaps such a measure is politically infeasible at present in England. If so, that would reflect the existence of a special coordination problem: an inability to settle on a commonly accepted method of regulating access to the publicly owned resource.

Would Stonehenge be managed differently, perhaps better, if it were reprivatized or still privately owned by the Antrobus family? Almost certainly, it would be managed differently. Whether those differences would constitute "better" management depends on one's perspective.

We might predict how a private owner would manage Stonehenge today based in part on the history of Stonehenge's management when Sir Edmund Antrobus owned it. He fenced in the monument and charged an admission fee. We cannot be certain how well this policy would have protected the monument over the long run. We can, however, predict that an admission fee would have some marginal impact on the number of visitors. No doubt Stonehenge's private owner would charge more than

viewing area. The purpose is "to resolve the acute circulation problems created by 6 million annual visitors, many of whom enter the museum for the sole purpose of gazing at the lady with the mysterious smile" (*New York Times*, April 4, 2001, sec. E., p. 1, c. 1).

[27] The same is true for the publicly owned and managed prehistoric cave-paintings in Lascaux, France. The 30,000-year-old paintings were discovered in 1940. Excavation work following the Second World War made the caves publicly accessible. More than 1,000 tourists per day made their way through the caves. Unfortunately, the visitors unintentionally damaged the paintings simply by breathing; the carbon monoxide from their exhalations corroded the rock face and calcite deposits; green algae and mosses began to form upon the paintings. Consequently, in 1963 the French Ministry of Culture closed the cave completely to public access. Since then the public have had to be satisfied with touring a full-scale replica of the site.

one shilling – the 1901 price – for admission in 2001, but, as with all fees, the owner could adjust the level of the fee up or down as needed to obtain a level of access that would be neither too lenient nor overly restrictive.

What fee level would the private owner select? Sir Edmund claimed that the one-shilling admission price he charged was merely to recoup costs. A less publicly minded owner – Sir Edmund himself, if his critics are to be believed – would set the admission fee so as to maximize profits (revenues over management costs). Assuming demand to visit Stonehenge is reasonably elastic, a higher fee would depress the rate of visitation. With a profit-maximizing owner, Stonehenge would have fewer visitors than with a cost-offsetting owner. Whatever else one might conclude about the profit-maximizing owner, her management would avoid the tragedy of overaccess at least as well as the cost-offsetting private owner.

A different private owner might, however, seek to satisfy preferences other than profit-maximizing or cost-offsetting. An owner who happens to be a committed Druid might seek to maximize Stonehenge's spiritual value, even if it means suffering a pecuniary loss. (Ideology matters![28]) She might decide to close Stonehenge to the public, providing free access only to other Druids. Or she might close access to Stonehenge altogether, keeping it as her private, personal sanctuary and altar to the gods. As *The Times* cautioned in 1905, if a private owner of Stonehenge can charge a guinea for admission, then the private owner can also close the monument to public access entirely. From the public's perspective, this would almost certainly constitute an undesirable outcome. On the other hand, Stonehenge would be preserved.

Or would it? If a private owner is free to use their property in any way that does not result in a nuisance, what is to prevent the owner from destroying Stonehenge, carving up or repositioning the stones, or selling them to the Americans, like London Bridge and the *Queen Mary*, as Sir Edmund Antrobus once threatened to do?[29] Whether a private owner would preserve Stonehenge depends on that individual's subjective

---

[28] Anyone who believes otherwise is left to explain, for example, why the Taliban militia recently systematically destroyed ancient Buddhist relics in Afghanistan (see *New York Times*, March 4, 2001, at p. 10).

[29] As Feldman and Weil (1986, § 5.1.1, p. 434) explain, "an eccentric American collector who, for a Saturday evening's amusement, invited his friends to play darts using his Rembrandt portrait as the target would neither violate any public law nor be subject to any private restraint." Anyone who believes that private owners would never actually do such a thing should read Joseph Sax's (1999) *Playing Darts with a Rembrandt: Public and Private Rights in Cultural Treasures*. Sax relates numerous tales of private owners who willfully destroyed or defaced important works of art, including one about the owner of a Toulouse-Lautrec painting who "amused himself by shooting at it with a gun" (p. 7). Because exclusive private ownership can lead to such socially undesirable outcomes, Sax suggests that private ownership of "cultural treasures" should be limited by public rights.

preferences, as well as their subjective discount rate. Chances are, a rational private owner would not intentionally destroy the monument, any more than would public managers. As I have shown, however, a private owner will rationally deplete or destroy a resource when there is an immediate profit to be made, future returns on investments in the resource are expected to be low, and the owner's subjective discount rate is high (Clark 1973a). Even an owner who would never intentionally destroy an asset, however, might not manage it so as to maximize its social, as opposed to private, value.

Returning to the art analogy, there are many important art masterpieces that remain in private ownership, inaccessible to the public. In 1922 Dr. Albert C. Barnes of Philadelphia created a trust to keep his art treasures off-limits in perpetuity to all but a few scholars. His indenture stipulated that the paintings were to be publicly accessible only on the foundation's premises and for "no more than" two days each week.[30] The trustees interpreted this provision as allowing them, at their discretion, to foreclose public access entirely. So, for several decades the Barnes collection was never open to the public.[31] Dozens of art treasures by Picasso, Matisse, Cezanne (57 canvases), Renoir (171 works), and others could not be viewed by members of the public *at any price*. This hardly maximized the economic or extra-economic value of the artworks. But private owners, including trustees, do not always act to maximize their private wealth, let alone social welfare.[32] This story has important implications for historical treasures, such as Stonehenge, with great social value.

Some issues relating to Stonehenge's preservation would likely be beyond the control of any private/individual owner. To the extent the surrounding environment is an important component of Stonehenge's value, substantial coordination problems arise. English Heritage's new management plan grapples with many of these problems, including where roads and visitor services are located with respect to the monument. A single landowner, with limited resources, would be hard pressed to resolve these types of coordination problems, which typically implicate several different properties. Consequently, although a private owner might exercise the right to exclude more effectively, to prevent the tragedy of open access, than public managers, the coordination costs under private ownership could be higher. It is difficult to say whether the total

---

[30] See *Wiegand v. The Barnes Foundation*, 97 A. 2d 81, 86 (Pa. 1953).
[31] See *Commonwealth v. The Barnes Foundation*, 159 A. 2d 500 (Pa. 1960).
[32] Later, in the 1990s, when the Barnes Foundation ran into financial difficulties, its Board of Trustees managed to "amend" the trust, despite strong opposition from devoted Barnes supporters and lengthy litigation, so as to permit limited traveling exhibitions. See *In re: The Barnes Foundation*, 684 A. 2d 123 (Pa. Super. 1995).

costs – exclusion plus coordination costs – of managing Stonehenge under private ownership are less than the total costs of managing Stonehenge under public ownership.

Moreover, the social costs of privatizing Stonehenge may prove insuperable. Consider the thoughtful perspective of the archaeologist Peter Fowler (1990a, pp. 123–6), who feels a real ownership stake, as a member of the public, in Stonehenge:

I do not regard Stonehenge as "belonging" in a general sense to any one person or institution or cult, though I acknowledge that in a strictly legal sense it is owned by a corporation. That corporation is in fact the Government which accepted, on behalf of the nation, the monument as a gift. For practical purposes, the owner has passed the management of the site to another body after nearly 80 years ... Now, the Historic Buildings and Monuments Commission, inheriting an unhappy situation resulting from decades of mismanagement, has to cope with present demands, including mine for educational access, while addressing the major problems arising from its policy decision to improve the care and presentation of Stonehenge ...

... contributions to the cost of the archive, and indeed of looking after the site itself, come from a variety of sources, from income generated on-site and in museums as well as from statutory bodies and private donations, and it is right that this should be so, provided that impersonal public money underpins the system. So, I have a financial stake in the "Stonehenge corpus," enhancing my claim to have access to it as of right; though here again my claim is neither monopolistic nor exclusive. I expect to share the resource, indeed would be disappointed if my interest existed in a social vacuum ...

... I expect [Stonehenge] to be looked after properly and I think I have a right to expect that such will be the case in the hands of whoever has the responsibility for its conservation. Like many others, I am far from convinced that this responsibility has been properly discharged in recent decades ...

It goes without saying that these several claims as of right carry with them equally strong obligations to contribute as well as consume, to give as well as take.

Dr. Fowler's perspective on Stonehenge is not obviously idiosyncratic. Lord Eversley and Flinders Petrie certainly shared his view. Doubtless many, if not most, other Britons do as well. Stonehenge is, after all, part of the national patrimony. But recognizing this does not resolve the problem of determining how best to manage the monument.

There appears, finally, to be no first-best, property-based solution for Stonehenge. By all accounts, public ownership and management have not adequately protected the monument from degradation resulting from too much public access. It is possible that a new public management plan could improve the situation, but there is always reason for concern over the commitment of public resource managers and the consistency of management policies that are subject to the political trade winds. Private/individual ownership might more effectively protect the monument from too much public access, by virtue of the right to exclude. But private ownership would violate the widely shared sentiment, articulated by Peter Fowler, that Stonehenge belongs to no single individual, and should not be managed according to any single individual's preferences. Stonehenge possesses social values that might not be respected – let alone maximized – by an individual owner. Moreover, some of the management problems besetting Stonehenge, such as the location of tourist facilities and roads, would be outside the control of any single property owner.

Ultimately, the case for either public or private ownership of Stonehenge is underdetermined. Either regime would experience management difficulties, though perhaps of different kinds and magnitudes; and all practicable solutions to those difficulties would be contestable.

To end this discussion on a note of stark realism: speculating about reprivatizing Stonehenge is like whistling in the wind. There is no chance – zero – that Stonehenge will be privatized. Even at the height of Thatcherite privatization in Britain during the 1980s, the prospect was never raised. All management policies for preserving Stonehenge will have to be implemented under public ownership. This is not to say, however, that private property rights will play no role in any management solution. Some form of limited privatization – for example, the granting of a private concession to secure and control access to the monument – could well be part of an overall management plan instituted by Stonehenge's public owners.

For all its complexity, the Stonehenge case *is* comparatively simple. It involves a single, socially valued attribute – the monument itself – in a fairly small, contained environment. Significantly, the monument does not move, which limits the extent of acreage involved in its preservation. This distinguishes Stonehenge from so-called "fugitive" resources that move across, under, or over broad reaches of territory. As the number of socially valued resource amenities increase, and as the amount of territory they require expands, it becomes even more difficult to determine the "best" property regime for protecting those amenities from depletion and degradation.

Returns to scale in resource conservation

Economists have long recognized that the appropriate scale of economic organization – including the ownership structure – is both circumstantial and consequential (see, for example, Heal 1999). Large-scale organization is sometimes more efficient in production than small-scale organization;[33] in other circumstances, the converse is true. Returns to scale are important not only for production, however. They can also be crucial in resource conservation.

Ecologists, such as Reed Noss, Rodger Schlickeisen, and Allen Cooperrider (1994, p. 141), point out that ecosystem conservation requires large, contiguous blocks of undeveloped, roadless areas that limit human access. This obviously bears on the choice of property regime, as the discussions of wildlife preservation in chapters 2 and 5 have illustrated. Dean Lueck's (1989) comparison of wildlife ownership regimes in the United States and England suggests that larger species with larger habitats are more likely to be protected under public property regimes, especially when private/individual landholdings are relatively small. Lueck's findings are hardly counterintuitive. The more space a species requires to survive, especially a species that has little or no commodity value, the less likely it is that private owners of relatively small land parcels can or will effectively coordinate their activities to protect its critical habitat.

The fact of the matter, however, is that endangered species habitat is more extensive than even public/state ownership, alone, can manage. In the United States, nearly 90 percent of endangered species have some or all of their critical habitat on private lands (General Accounting Office 1993); more than half have at least 81 percent of their habitat on non-federal land; and between one-third and one-half are found *exclusively* on private property (Wilcove et al. 1996). This is not good news for endangered species preservation. According to a study by the Environmental Defense Fund (Wilcove et al. 1996):

endangered species on private land appear to be faring much worse than their counterparts on federal land. For listed plants and animals found entirely on federal land, approximately 18 percent are judged to be improving; the ratio of declining species to improving species is approximately 1.5 to 1. In contrast, for species found entirely on private property (excluding property owned by non-profit conservation groups) only 3 percent are improving, and the ratio of declining species to improving species is 9 to 1. Even more troubling is the fact that the Fish and Wildlife Service does not know the status of over half of the species found exclusively on private land, perhaps a reflection of the reluctance of many private landowners to allow conservation officials onto their land to assess how endangered species there are faring.

The evidence suggests that public/state ownership protects endangered species and their habitat better than private ownership. However,

---

[33] Ellickson (1993, p. 1332) notes that group ownership of land is sometimes preferable to individual ownership because of "increasing returns to scale and the desirability of spreading risks." See also Dagan and Heller (2001, p. 572).

recognizing that returns to scale generally favor public/state ownership of endangered species habitat does not resolve the problem. The fact remains that most endangered species habitat is on privately owned lands, giving rise to a perplexing coordination problem.

Private owners of lands with economic development potential cannot be expected willingly to sacrifice that development potential in order to provide critical habitat for endangered species with little or no commodity value. This makes it highly unlikely that private property alone can serve the purpose of endangered species preservation. On the other hand, the state cannot afford to take title to, and pay compensation for, large enough contiguous land masses to comprise the critical habitat for many large and mobile endangered species. Endangered species protection, therefore, necessarily implicates numerous properties, with different owners, which inevitably raises coordination costs.

Coordination becomes especially difficult in this case because of the existence of conflicting ownership regimes: private ownership of the habitat and public/state ownership of the wildlife. This and other problems associated with property regime conflicts will be addressed in the next chapter. In the meantime, it should be clear that scale issues in endangered species protection can greatly complicate the determination of a viable property-based solution. It seems inevitable that practicable solutions to the problem of endangered species preservation (some of which are discussed in the next chapter) must involve an admixture of public/state and private (individual or common) rights.

History and culture matter

Property arrangements are also influenced and sometimes determined by historical, cultural, even religious factors. It would be a mistake to presume, however, that such factors necessarily impede efficient resource conservation.

Consider cattle. Throughout the West the cow is a commodity resource. The market values the species and ensures its perpetuation, as free-market environmentalists would predict. So long as consumers in their millions demand beef, leather, and other goods provided by cows, there is little chance, apart from some natural, unpreventable catastrophe, that the bovine species will become extinct. There are, however, alternative ways of ensuring the perpetuation of cattle, without markets. It is common knowledge that cows are sacred in Hindu culture. Religious injunctions against harming, let alone eating, cattle not only prevent the species from becoming a commodity resource but also ensure its preservation – a combined result free-market environmentalists can hardly comprehend. If Americans displayed a similar religious, cultural, or ideological attachment to, say, the red-cockaded woodpecker (*Picoides borealis*), it would never require legal protection under the Endangered Species Act.[34]

However irrational such religious or ideological attachments may seem, they sometimes embody economically rational policies. Stephen Toulmin (2001, pp. 60–2) tells an instructive story of the disaster that resulted on the Island of Bali when the National Government of Indonesia and the Asian Development Bank engaged in large-scale socioeconomic engineering of agricultural production. Balinese farmers traditionally irrigated their rice paddies following a strict schedule established and supervised by "water temple" priests. Economists and engineers from the Asian Development Bank, convinced that such a religious institution could have no economic relevance, presumed to improve rice yields by introducing modern agricultural techniques. "As one frustrated American irrigation engineer declared, 'These people don't need a high priest, they need a hydrologist!' " In their arrogance, the bank's engineers and economists failed to perceive that the irrigation schedules of Bali's water temple priests were based on centuries of experience. The priests had learned what worked to ensure satisfactory rice yields while minimizing pestilence. When the old system was first replaced, rice yields did increase, but "[b]efore long, the farmers of Bali were afflicted with all the biblical plagues of Egypt." Pest and fungus infestations quickly reached crisis proportions, and Balinese farmers clamored for a return to the old system. In the end, the Indonesian government was forced to "strik[e] a compromise between the older water temple schedules" and modern agricultural techniques.

The case of the Balinese water temples stands as a cautionary tale to those who would casually replace traditional, supposedly inefficient institutions with new, *theoretically* more efficient policies. History and local knowledge, embodied in traditional religious or cultural practices, should not be disregarded but carefully considered and evaluated. Before offering solutions, outside "experts" should ask questions. To be sure, technological innovations and novel, theory-based institutions can generate tremendous improvements in both production and resource conservation; but they do not do so invariably. Traditional social institutions – including property regimes – methods of production, and conservation policies should be amended or replaced with caution.

---

[34] In fact, the red-cockaded woodpecker *is* listed as an endangered species, indicating that Americans do not revere it as Hindus do cows.

III   Still "in the nature of social experiments"

The inherent complexity of real-world circumstances does not render theoretical modeling useless, but should make us circumspect about prescribing theory-based solutions to real-world resource conservation problems. More than thirty years ago the economist J. H. Dales (1968, p. 77) sagely noted that each attempt to protect the environment is "in the nature of a social experiment." Since then, societies have learned some valuable lessons about *what works (or doesn't work) when* for certain pollution and resource conservation problems. Still, our efforts to avert tragedies of open access remain *in the nature of social experiments.*

Throughout this book, I have shown that various approaches – all of them property-based – to environmental protection are useful, but within limits. No single approach universally protects against the tragedy of open access better than the others. Neither socialism – the complete public/state ownership of natural resources – nor "free-market environmentalism" – the complete privatization of all natural resources – can suffice. What is required, instead, is generally what we have: a multiplicity of institutions, embodying various property-based approaches, that deal, by design or by historical/cultural contingency, with particular aspects of environmental problems. Admixtures of private, public, and common property regimes are likely to be more effective in staving off the tragedy of open access over the broad range of cases than any singular approach.

Eventually, we may learn enough about how the world works to predict, within a substantial margin for error, how well or poorly alternative property arrangements work to avert the tragedy of open access in various circumstances. First, however, we must get beyond the simplistic notion that our environmental problems are all the result of either too much or too little private or public property. Second, we must closely attend to the strengths and weaknesses of alternative property arrangements, the costs of exclusion and coordination (given the ecological, institutional, technological, and cultural circumstances), and historical experience.

8   When property regimes collide: the "takings" problem

I have shown that various property regimes – individual, common, and public – may be vested in a single resource or resource amenity at the same time; or they may be vested in different resources or resource amenities that overlap. For example, publicly owned waters or wildlife may cross privately owned lands. In these circumstances property regimes may come into conflict. When they do, it may become impossible to enforce one set of rights in the resource or resource amenity without violating others.

The most prominent example of the type of problems that can arise when property regimes collide is the so-called "takings" claim.[1] Section 1 of this chapter provides a summary introduction to the law of takings. Section 2 reframes takings disputes as conflicts between existing public and private property regimes. And section 3 briefly considers the implications for takings doctrine and public policy.

In contrast to the preceding chapters in this book, the analysis in this chapter is almost entirely legal and heavily doctrinal. Takings doctrine does, of course, carry social and economic implications. The purpose here, however, is not to assess the social value of takings law but more simply to highlight a neglected problem in takings doctrine and jurisprudence, which relates to issues discussed throughout this book.

I   An introduction to takings law

Governments in most countries possess the power of *eminent domain*, which literally means *highest ownership of land*. According to *Webster's New Collegiate Dictionary* (1975), the phrase "eminent domain" refers to "a right of a government to take private property for public use by virtue of the superior dominion of the sovereign power over all lands within its jurisdiction." The constitutions of most, but not all, countries require the government to provide compensation when it takes land from

---

[1] Richard Lazarus first pointed out to me the fact that takings cases typically arise where property regimes collide.

private owners by eminent domain. The Fifth Amendment to the US Constitution, for example, provides: "nor shall private property be taken for public use, without just compensation."

For more than a century after the Fifth Amendment was enacted in 1891, the Takings Clause was of minor importance, coming into play only when the federal government or state[2] took title to private property for, usually uncontroversial, public uses such as road-building. Few cases were litigated under the clause (see Bosselman et al. 1973, ch. 7), and there was no such thing as a "regulatory taking" – a claim for compensation based on government regulation of private land uses – although state and local governments had been regulating private land uses, sometimes quite stringently, since the colonial era (see Treanor 1995; Hart 1996).

In 1922 the Constitution's Taking Clause rose momentarily to prominence. This was the year the Supreme Court ruled in *Pennsylvania Coal Co.* v. *Mahon*[3] that government regulations of private land uses *could* constitute compensable takings, *if* the regulated land use does not amount to a nuisance *and* the government's regulation deprives the landowner of nearly all of the value of his landholding. The *Pennsylvania Coal Co.* ruling was of little immediate consequence, however. The Court did not find another regulatory taking of private property for more than half a century, despite the continued proliferation of government land-use regulations. Finally, in the 1980s the Takings Clause returned to a more lasting prominence. It has remained ever since an active subject of litigation.

Instead of a detailed account of recent developments in takings jurisprudence,[4] it is enough for present purposes to summarize, with a bit of interpretive commentary, where that law stands at the start of the twenty-first century. During the last twenty-five years the Supreme Court has employed at least four distinct rules of taking law.

Permanent physical occupations

The oldest and most well-settled rule of takings law is that the government must compensate private owners when it permanently occupies their land or authorizes the permanent physical occupation of one person's land by another. The Supreme Court reaffirmed this rule in *Loretto* v. *Teleprompter Manhattan CATV Corp.*,[5] in which the Court held that a New York law requiring landlords to permit the installation of cable television facilities

---

[2] The 5th Amendment's Takings Clause applies to the states through the 14th Amendment.
[3] *Pennsylvania Coal Co.* v. *Mahon*, 260 US 393 (1922).
[4] Detailed accounts of the development of takings law can be found in Fischel (1995) and Laitos (1998), among others.
[5] 458 US 419 (1982).

on their properties constituted a compensable taking. The Court, in an opinion by Justice Thurgood Marshall, observed that "we have long considered a physical intrusion by government to be a property restriction of an unusually serious character for purposes of the Takings Clause. Our cases further establish that when the physical intrusion reaches the extreme form of a permanent physical occupation, a taking has occurred."[6]

The police power/nuisance exception and its problems

When the government regulates or eradicates a nuisance, it acts pursuant not to its eminent domain power but its "police power." Like eminent domain, the police power is an inherent power of government, not requiring explicit constitutional authorization (see Freund 1904, §§ 5 and 8). Unlike eminent domain, however, the Constitution imposes no express compensation requirement for police power regulations, where the government is regulating what amounts to an unlawful activity. This makes sense as a matter of both equity and efficiency. If the government had to compensate for restricting land uses such as prostitution and illicit drug-making, its regulations would lose their deterrent effect. By the same token, if the government had to compensate for pollution regulations, those regulations would fail to serve the purpose of internalizing externalities.

Whatever the formal and functional justifications for the police power/nuisance exception, the formal distinction between eminent domain takings and police power regulations has proven problematic in application. It can be extremely difficult for the courts to determine whether the government is exercising one power as opposed to the other. Ernst Freund (1904, § 511) attempted to clarify the matter by distinguishing between government actions designed to *confer public benefits* – eminent domain – and those designed to *prevent public harms* – police power. As many authors (such as Michaelman 1967, pp. 1196–7 and Fischel 1995, p. 354) have noted, however, Freund's distinction does not solve the problem. Almost any activity that confers public benefits can be described as preventing public harm, and vice versa. When the government restricts development of a pristine area in order to preserve a scenic vista, for example, it is conferring a public benefit by preserving the scenic vista *and* it is preventing public harm by restricting development that would destroy the scenic vista.[7]

---

[6] 458 US at 426.
[7] Justice William Brennan made the same point in his opinion dissenting from the Court's ruling in *San Diego Gas & Electric Co. v. San Diego*, 450 US 621, 652 (1981): "From the government's point of view, the benefits flowing to the public from preservation of

The problem of distinguishing between compensable eminent domain takings and noncompensable police power regulations is compounded by the structure of government decision-making. Under the police power, the legislature traditionally has had broad discretion to decide what constitutes a public harm to be regulated or eradicated. The legislative decision must not be arbitrary,[8] but that is a minimal constraint. It would be very difficult for a court to find that any decision agreed to by a majority of several hundred legislators was "arbitrary." For most of US history, the courts have felt institutionally constrained to accept the legislature's own determination of what constitutes a compensable eminent domain taking, as opposed to a noncompensable police power regulation. But as the "regulatory state" burgeoned, initially during the progressive era and even more rapidly following the Second World War, the courts became increasingly suspicious of legislative motives in regulating private land uses, and decreasingly reluctant to assert their own authority.

Oliver Wendell Holmes was among the earliest judicial skeptics of the state's police power. In his 1872 review of Thomas Cooley's *A Treatise on the Constitutional Limitations Which Rest Upon the Legislative Power of the States of the American Union* (pp. 141–2), Holmes wrote that the police power "was invented to cover certain acts of the legislature which are seen to be unconstitutional, but which are believed to be necessary." Seventeen years later, as a Justice on the Massachusetts Supreme Judicial Court, Holmes authored the majority opinion in *Rideout* v. *King*,[9] upholding a state statute that prohibited landowners from constructing fences higher than 6 feet. Holmes concluded that this prohibition was a proper exercise of the state's police power, but he expressly sought to limit the scope of the government's regulatory authority to "small limitations" designed to prevent "manifest evil." Larger limitations, he suggested, even those intended to prevent public harm, could not be justified under the police power, but required the exercise of eminent domain and payment of just compensation.

In his *Rideout* opinion, Holmes noted that the difference between "smaller" and "larger" limitations is a matter "of degree" (p. 392). This

---

open space through regulation may be equally great as from creating a wildlife refuge through formal condemnation or increasing electricity production through a dam project that floods private property." Similarly, Justice Scalia's majority opinion in *Lucas* v. *South Carolina Coastal Council*, 505 US 1003, 1024 (1992), noted that "the distinction between 'harm-preventing' and 'benefit-conferring' regulation is often in the eye of the beholder . . . the distinction between regulation that 'prevents harmful use' and that which 'confers benefits' is difficult, if not impossible, to discern on an objective, value-free basis."

[8] See *Reinman* v. *Little Rock*, 237 US 171, 176 (1915); *Hadachek* v. *Sebastian*, 239 US 394 (1915).

[9] 19 NE 390 (1889).

foreshadowed his opinion thirty-three years later, as an Associate Justice of the US Supreme Court, in *Pennsylvania Coal*. By then, Holmes had grown even more distrustful of legislative motives. While still acknowledging that the legislature's judgment must be accorded "[t]he greatest weight,"[10] in *Pennsylvania Coal* Justice Holmes expressed his concern that the police power was subject to abuse: "When the seemingly absolute protection [of private property] is found to be qualified by the police power, the natural tendency of human nature is to extend the qualification more and more until at last private property disappears."[11]

Justice Holmes's qualms about the police power were as nothing, however, compared to the hostility exhibited precisely seventy years after *Pennsylvania Coal* by Supreme Court Associate Justice Antonin Scalia in *Lucas* v. *South Carolina Coastal Council*: "Since ... a [police power] justification can be formulated in practically every case, this amounts to a test of whether the legislature has a stupid staff."[12] Scalia's unmistakable implication is that if the government can avoid paying compensation by describing its actions as police power regulations, rather than eminent domain takings, it will do so. Rational legislators have incentives to impose regulatory costs on a few discrete landowners, which is the case if they regulate without compensation under the police power, rather than on all taxpayers/voters, which would be the case if they took title to property by eminent domain and paid compensation. Because of their incentive structure, legislators simply cannot be trusted to honestly and sincerely distinguish between police power regulations and eminent domain takings.

In *Lucas*, the State of South Carolina may have merited Justice Scalia's distrust. The case arose after the state enacted legislation regulating beachfront development to prevent beach erosion. The law prevented Mr. Lucas from building on two beachfront lots he owned. The Court ruled that because the law completely wiped out Mr. Lucas's investment, it constituted a compensable taking.[13] The state subsequently settled with Mr. Lucas, paying $850,000 for his two lots. It then sought to recoup the expense by selling the lots to the highest bidder *for development*.

---

[10] Holmes was not disingenuous about this. He strongly opposed judicial meddling in legislative determinations of social welfare – witness his dissent in *Lochner* v. *New York*, 198 US 45 (1905). Ironically, the majority opinion in *Lochner* (at 64) displayed a rather Holmesian distrust of the state's police power: "It is impossible for us to shut our eyes to the fact that many of the laws of this character, while passed under what is claimed to be the police power for the purpose of protecting the public health or welfare are, in reality, passed from other motives." Holmes did not address this point in his dissent.

[11] 260 US at 415.   [12] 505 US at 1025 n. 12.

[13] This decision is under the diminution-in-value test, which is addressed in the next subsection.

This alone does not necessarily imply that the state was acting in bad faith. A sense of fiscal responsibility, or even state law, may explain South Carolina's decision to recoup its expenses resulting from the Supreme Court's ruling – expenses which it arguably should never have been forced to bear.

The Court's ruling in *Lucas* remains controversial. In the first place, the case arguably was not ripe for judicial review because Mr. Lucas did not exhaust his administrative remedies prior to filing suit.[14] Also, there is reason to believe that Mr. Lucas did not suffer an extreme diminution in value, let alone a complete wipe out, of his investment. According to one newspaper account (*Charleston Post and Courier*, August 27, 1993, at 1-B), one of Mr. Lucas's neighbors, Andy Guagenti, bid $315,000 for one of the lots, which he intended to keep undeveloped to preserve the unobstructed views from his house. This constitutes evidence, albeit after the fact of the Court's ruling, that Mr. Lucas's land held substantial economic value in its undeveloped state.

However, Mr. Guagenti's $315,000 bid also constitutes evidence that the State of South Carolina merited Justice Scalia's distrust in *Lucas*. The state rejected his bid, which would have kept at least one of the lots undeveloped, in favor of a construction company's bid of $785,000 for both lots. As Gideon Kanner (1996, p. 310) has scathingly remarked,

once it found itself picking up the tab, the state abandoned its claims of threats to life and property. It was unwilling to forego even $77,000 to assure that one of Lucas's lots would remain vacant – precisely what the state told three levels of courts it wanted to accomplish as vitally necessary.

Whether or not the State of South Carolina merited Justice Scalia's distrust of legislative motives in the *Lucas* case, his distrust remains difficult to square with the regular behavior of other legislative bodies, such as Britain's Parliament. In contrast to American legislatures, Parliament is under no constitutional obligation to compensate landowners when it takes their property for public use. Parliament has nevertheless imposed upon itself, by legislation, compensation requirements from which it almost never deviates. It typically compensates for actual takings of private property, but not for regulatory takings (see Allen 2000, p. 21). Parliament must, of course, decide what is and is not a compensable taking. But there is virtually no judicial oversight of its decisions, even in cases involving exactions (see Grant 1996). Legislators in Britain, therefore, have greater discretion than their American counterparts to determine what constitutes a police power regulation, as opposed to an eminent domain taking. Yet, Parliament *does* regularly provide compensation.

---

[14] See 505 US at 2906–7 (Blackmun, J., dissenting).

Like Britain's Parliament, several American states have imposed superconstitutional compensation requirements upon themselves by enacting takings statutes. In Texas, the state must compensate for any land-use regulations that reduce property values by 25 percent or more.[15] Florida's takings law requires the state to compensate for any regulation that "inordinately burdens" the use of private property.[16] A burden is "inordinate" if the landowner is "permanently unable to attain the reasonable, investment-backed expectations" for the property, or "bears permanently a disproportionate share of a burden imposed for the good of the public, which in fairness should be borne by the public at large." Texas and Florida both exempt regulations of common-law nuisances, however, from the ambit of their takings laws.[17]

Such legislative remedies for regulatory takings raise questions about the increasing level of judicial distrust of democratically elected legislators. There is no reason to suppose that legislative bodies in Britain, Texas, and Florida are better able to distinguish between police power regulations and eminent domain takings than other American legislatures.[18] It seems unlikely that they are, for institutional or cultural reasons, more trustworthy with private property rights. How then, can we explain their self-imposed compensation requirements for takings? Would Justice Scalia dare suggest that the Texas and Florida legislatures, let alone Parliament, offer compensation when their regulations substantially reduce property values simply because their staffs are "stupid"? Takings statutes in Britain, Texas, and Florida support William Fischel's (1995) argument that private property rights are, for most purposes, sufficiently protected through the political process.

Warranted or not, the judicial distrust of legislative motives, exhibited to different degrees by Justices Holmes and Scalia, has led the Supreme Court to enunciate a third takings rule, which delimits the nuisance exception.

The diminution-in-value test for regulatory takings

In his majority opinion in *Pennsylvania Coal* (1922), Justice Holmes altered the focus of takings analysis from property *rights* to property *value*.

---

[15] Tex. Gov't Code Ann. 2007.041, 2007.002.   [16] Fla. Stat. Ann. 70.001(2), (3)(e).
[17] Tex. Gov't Code Ann. 2007.003(b); Fla. Stat. Ann. 70.001(3)(e).
[18] According to Allen (2000, p. 24), "[i]n England the supremacy of Parliament makes it unnecessary to distinguish between its sovereign powers over property. Hence, there has been no real need for the courts to refine the presumptions of interpretation to distinguish between the purposes that require compensation and those that do not." This is correct, so far as the courts are concerned. Parliament, however, requires some such distinction, in order to determine when and when not to offer compensation.

In cases where the government purports to be regulating under the police power, it must pay compensation, just as if it had taken the property pursuant to eminent domain, *if* (a) the regulated landowner's activity does not constitute an actionable nuisance and (b) the regulation greatly diminishes the value of the landowner's property. The government can still regulate nuisances out of existence; and it can still regulate non-nuisance-causing land uses to "a certain extent," under its police power, without paying compensation. But if the regulation "goes too far" – when its effect on the economic *value* of the landowner's property "reaches a certain magnitude" – the government must pay compensation. The Court thus pares down what was formerly a general police power exception into a more limited nuisance exception.

Justice Holmes's diminution-in-value test was an exercise in bald "judicial activism." The rule has no basis in either the text or original understanding of the Fifth Amendment's Takings Clause. He invented it out of whole cloth. As Fred Bosselman, David Callies, and John Banta (1973, p. 124) put it, Justice Holmes's decision in *Pennsylvania Coal* constituted a "rewriting" of the Constitution. But to what end? As noted above, Justice Holmes distrusted legislative motives. But that cannot be the whole explanation because in 1915, just seven years before he invented the diminution-in-value test in *Pennsylvania Coal*, Justice Holmes voted with a majority of his brethren to uphold a Municipal Ordinance that shut down a brick-making operation in Los Angeles, as a legitimate nuisance regulation.[19] Was the Los Angeles City Council somehow more trustworthy than the Pennsylvania legislature? If not, how might we explain Justice Holmes's votes in the two cases?

Justice Holmes created the diminution-in-value test in *Pennsylvania Coal* not only because he distrusted legislative motives but also because he was concerned with fundamental fairness. Towards the end of his opinion he wrote, "the question at bottom is upon whom the loss of the changes desired should fall."[20] In answering this question, Justice Holmes makes clear his sense that it would be unfair to impose the loss on the private property owner who had bargained and paid for resources later rendered nearly valueless by government regulation.[21] In this respect,

---

[19] *Hadachek v. Sebastian*, 239 US 394 (1915).   [20] 260 US at 416.

[21] Justice Holmes's expressed concern with fundamental fairness in *Pennsylvania Coal* is in stark contrast to his usual elevation of the public welfare over the interests of individuals. Consider, for example, his opinion in *Buck v. Bell*, 274 US 200, 207 (1927), a ruling that upheld a Virginia statute permitting the involuntary sterilization of those deemed mentally incompetent. Holmes wrote, "We have seen more than once that the public welfare may call upon the best citizens for their lives. It would be strange if it could not call upon those who already sap the strength of the State for these lesser sacrifices." But

the diminution-in-value test is in the nature of an equitable gloss on the Constitution,[22] akin to English common law's ancient concept of equity on the statute (see Plucknett 1956, pp. 334–5; Manning 2001).

For centuries England's common-law judges have been molding or adapting – sometimes to the point of rewriting – general parliamentary enactments in order to do "justice" in individual cases. As Manning (2001, p. 8) explains, "English judges . . . often extended statutes beyond their plain terms in order to make them more coherent expressions of purpose, and cut back others to avoid inequitable results that did not serve the statutory purpose." This is precisely what Justice Holmes did with the US Constitution's Takings Clause in *Pennsylvania Coal*.[23]

In 1992 the Supreme Court reaffirmed and expanded on its *Pennsylvania Coal* ruling in the *Lucas* case. The *Lucas* Court was particularly concerned to clarify, as much as it could, the proper distinction between noncompensable police power regulations and compensable eminent domain takings. Justice Scalia, writing for the majority, refined Justice Holmes's test as follows: when the government regulates private land uses, it must pay compensation, as if it had taken the property pursuant to eminent domain, *if* (a) the regulated landowner's activity does not constitute an actionable private or public nuisance *under state common law* and (b) the regulation greatly diminishes or wipes out the value of the landowner's property. The key change is in the highlighted phrase, "under state common law," which constitutes a further limitation of the nuisance exception. In contrast to Justice Holmes, who, despite his distrust of legislative motives, hardly limited at all the legislature's authority to determine what constituted a nuisance, Justice Scalia sought to limit the legislature's ability to expand the scope of nuisance law:

Where the State seeks to sustain regulation that deprives land of all economically beneficial use, we think it may resist compensation only if the logically antecedent inquiry into the nature of the owner's estate shows that the proscribed use interests were not part of his title to begin with . . .

Any limitation so severe [as to be confiscatory] cannot be newly legislated or decreed (without compensation), but must inhere in the title itself, in the restrictions that background principles of the State's law of property and nuisance already place upon land ownership. A law or decree with such an effect must, in

---

then, as Holmes's philosophical mentor Ralph Waldo Emerson (1909, p. 66) wrote, "a foolish consistency is the hobgoblin of little minds," and Holmes's mind was capacious.

[22] On the concept of "constitutional equity," see Wedgwood (1994).

[23] The notion that the diminution-in-value test is in the nature of an equitable gloss on the Constitution is further supported by the Supreme Court's decision in *Armstrong v. United States*, 364 US 40, 49 (1960). The Court stated that the Fifth Amendment is "designed to bar Government from forcing some people alone to bear public burdens which, in all fairness and justice, should be borne by the public as a whole." See also *First English Evangelical Lutheran Church v. County of Los Angeles*, 482 US 304, 318–19 (1987).

other words, do no more than duplicate the result that could have been achieved in the courts – by adjacent landowners (or other uniquely affected persons) under the State's law of private nuisance, or by the State under its complementary power to abate nuisances that affect the public generally, or otherwise.[24]

Justice Scalia's expansion of Justice Holmes's diminution-of-value test is noteworthy, given the former's reputation as a strict constitutional constructionist. Justice Scalia has associated himself with both "originalism" (1989) – interpretation of the Constitution based on what the framers intended when they wrote it – and "textualism" (1997) – interpretation of the Constitution based on the "plain meaning" of the text. As noted earlier, however, the diminution-in-value test for regulatory takings has no basis in either the text or the original understanding of the Takings Clause. In his *Lucas* opinion, Justice Scalia makes a weak effort to support his conclusions with a textual analysis: "the text of the Clause can be read to encompass regulatory as well as physical deprivations."[25] But this is disingenuous. The text of the fifth Amendment says nothing about takings based on reductions in property *values*. In the *Lucas* case, at least, Justice Scalia's jurisprudence is better described as "functionalist" or "instrumentalist," rather than "textualist" or "originalist."

A chief effect of the Court's rulings in *Pennsylvania Coal* and *Lucas* was to shift the final say about the source of government regulatory power – noncompensable police power regulation or compensable eminent domain taking – from the legislatures to the courts. This arguably constitutes a judicial usurpation of legislative authority under the Constitution (see Humbach 1993). However, the Court is now the final arbiter of what is a legitimate police power regulation and what is an eminent domain taking.

Substantive due process review for "exactions"

The fourth and, so far, final rule of takings law applies only in highly specialized circumstances. This rule intermingles traditional takings analysis with a form of analysis developed under another provision of the Fifth Amendment: the Due Process Clause.

It has become common for state and local government agencies with land-use permitting and regulatory authority to require "exactions" of land – uncompensated conveyances of private property into public ownership – as a condition for approving large-scale land-development activities, such as new subdivisions (see, for example, Bosselman and Stroud 1985). Regulatory authorities typically justify these exactions as compensation

---

[24] 505 US at 1027–9.   [25] 505 US at 1028, n. 15.

for the increased pressure that new developments place on public services, including schools, roads, parks, police, fire, water, and sewer. In some cases, however, public agencies have required exactions that seem out of all proportion to the pressure on public services resulting from the development. Land developers alleged that such exactions constituted takings of their property without just compensation. In the late 1980s the Supreme Court began applying a novel form of takings analysis to resolve these disputes.

The takings rule governing exaction cases is currently as follows: a state or local government land-use permitting agency may require an "exaction" without paying compensation only *if* (a) the exaction substantially furthers a legitimate state interest,[26] *and* (b) the burden imposed on the developer by the exaction is "roughly proportional" to the public harm resulting from his land-development activities.[27] Every exaction that does not meet these requirements constitutes, in essence, a permanent physical occupation requiring compensation.

Perspectives on takings law

Commentators of virtually all ideological stripes deplore the state of takings law. At one extreme, property rights advocates such as Richard Epstein (1985) and Ellen Frankel Paul (1988) argue that *all* government regulations, except those narrowly tailored to deal with common-law nuisances, should be treated as compensable takings. From their perspective, the diminution-in-value test is insufficient because it allows the government to impose substantial burdens on private property owners. It requires compensation only if those burdens "go too far." But why should the government be able to avoid compensating for regulations that affect property rights, just because those regulations reduce property values by only 50 percent, rather than 90-plus percent? At the other end of the political spectrum, supporters of social welfare regulation decry the Supreme Court's recent takings jurisprudence for restricting the government's ability, under the police power, to protect public values against the harmful effects of private development activities. Douglas Kendall and Charles Lord (1998, p. 510), for example, see developments in takings law as part of a "a large and increasingly successful campaign by conservatives and libertarians to use the federal judiciary to achieve an anti-regulatory, anti-environmental agenda."

[26] *Nollan v. California Coastal Commission*, 483 US 825 (1987).
[27] *Dolan v. City of Tigard*, 512 US 374 (1994).

In the vast middle ground between highly politicized extremes, scholars voice various complaints about takings law. Molly McUsic (1998, pp. 592–3) has concisely summarized their complaints:

> how is one to understand a doctrine that provides compensation for losses of one dollar[28] but not for losses of millions of dollars,[29] that protects the right to bequeath property[30] but not the right to sell property,[31] that finds a taking when the government requires landlords to allow installation of cable television[32] but not when the government requires them to charge below market rents?[33] The literature offers a wide range of explanations for the Court's inconsistencies – the Justices read the history wrong, they ignore words in the Clause, they cannot agree on what the purpose of property protection is, they select the wrong purpose, or perhaps they select the right purpose but do not pursue it diligently – and just as many suggestions for correcting Court mistakes.[34]

Because of the seeming inconsistency of the Court's application of the Takings Clause, it has become increasingly difficult for parties, including government agencies *and* private property owners, to predict judicial outcomes and organize their behavior accordingly.

The Supreme Court has acknowledged these deficiencies in its takings jurisprudence. Justice Brennan, writing for the majority in *Penn Central Transportation Company* v. *New York City*,[35] noted that "this Court, quite simply, has been unable to develop any 'set formula' for determining when 'justice and fairness' require that economic injuries caused by public action be compensated by the government, rather than remain disproportionately concentrated on a few persons."[36] Indeed, we have frequently observed that whether a particular restriction will be rendered invalid by the government's failure to pay for any losses proximately caused by it depends largely "upon the particular circumstances [in that] case." However, to the extent that regulatory takings law is an equitable gloss on the Constitution's Taking Clause, as I suggested earlier, rather than a conventional legal rule, this lack of consistency and coherence may be inevitable.

In addition to what Carol Rose (1984) calls the "muddle" of takings doctrine, some scholars complain about the increasing insinuation of the courts into the legislative/regulatory process. John Humbach (1993), for

---

[28] *Loretto* v. *Teleprompter Manhattan CATV Corp.*, 458 US 419 (1982).
[29] *Penn Central Transportation Co.* v. *New York City*, 438 US 104 (1978).
[30] *Hodel* v. *Irving*, 481 US 704 (1987).   [31] *Andrus* v. *Allard*, 444 US 51 (1979).
[32] *Loretto*, again.   [33] *Pennell* v. *City of San Jose*, 485 US 1 (1988).
[34] Some citations omitted.   [35] 438 US 104, 124 (1978) (citations omitted).
[36] Also see *Palazzolo* v. *Rhode Island*, 533 US 606 (2001), 121 S.Ct. 2448 at 2466 (O'Connor, J., concurring) ("The concepts of 'fairness and justice' that underlie the Takings Clause, of course, are less than fully determinate").

example, argues that the Supreme Court has usurped legislative authority by taking upon itself the ultimate determination whether some government action is under the police power or the eminent domain power (also see Bork 1990, p. 229–30). William Fischel (1995) offers a more nuanced version of the same general argument. He suggests that the courts should defer, more than they have done in recent years, to legislative determinations of compensable takings and noncompensable nuisance regulations, because private property owners are generally capable of protecting their interests in the political process. This process-based claim is consistent with Britain's experience of substantial property rights protection in the absence of a constitutional just compensation requirement, as well as the recent proliferation of takings legislation in American states. Fischel would generally restrict judicial intervention to cases where the political process is likely to fail, something he believes is more likely to happen at lower levels of government.

There is one additional failing of takings doctrine that few scholars have recognized: many, if not most, takings claims arise when existing public property regimes bump up against private property regimes. This presents an important boundary issue: where do the private property rights end and the public rights begin? Unfortunately, the courts typically neglect this boundary question in their takings decisions.

II   Takings as conflicts between public and private property regimes

Takings are conventionally understood as government-imposed restrictions on preexisting private property rights. But this is myopic. A cursory examination of actual takings cases reveals that disputes arise when existing public *and* private property rights collide. In many, if not most, takings cases, the government is not just imposing on private property rights but attempting to vindicate public property rights, for which no compensation should be required. This presents a boundary issue: where do private property rights end and public property rights begin?

Public and private property rights in the air

The notion of takings cases as conflicts between private and public property regimes is well illustrated by the demise of the old common-law rule *Cujus est Solum, ejus est usque ad coelum,* according to which private property boundaries are deemed to extend upwards from the land to the heavens and downwards to the center of the earth (see Blackstone [1766]

1979, p. 18). In *United States* v. *Causby*[37] the Supreme Court ruled that the US military's use of airspace above the Causbys' farm constituted a compensable taking. The conflict arose during the Second World War, when the federal government leased for military use an airport near Greensboro, North Carolina. The glide path to one of the airport's runways passed directly over the Causbys' chicken farm. In fact the runway was just 2,220 feet from their barn, and another 55 feet from their house. Military aircraft, including bombers, transports, and fighters, frequently flew over the Causbys' land, often "in considerable numbers and rather close together." When descending to land, the aircraft came close enough to "blow the old leaves off the trees." The noise from the planes literally frightened the Causbys' chickens to death, so production "fell off." "The result was the destruction of the use of the property as a commercial chicken farm."

Causby was not a simple case of government trespass into privately owned airspace. The Court did *not* rule that the government had to compensate the Causbys because of the *Cujus est Solum* rule. To the contrary, the Court expressly declared that the old common-law rule "has no place in the modern world."[38] The real issue in the case concerned the relative air rights of private landowners and the public. Landowners retained sufficient rights in the air above to protect their interest in the land below:

it is obvious that if the landowner is to have full enjoyment of the land, he must have exclusive control of the immediate reaches of the enveloping atmosphere. Otherwise buildings could not be erected, trees could not be planted, and even fences could not be run. The principle is recognized when the law gives a remedy in case overhanging structures are erected on adjoining land. The landowner owns at least as much of the space above the ground as he can occupy or use in connection with the land.[39]

But the landowner's rights are more limited than the old common-law rule recognized. A private landowner can still sue her neighbor for erecting an overhanging building or fence, but her property rights no longer extend all the way to the heavens. She cannot, for example, prevent civil or commercial aviation activities:

The airplane is part of the modern environment of life, and the inconveniences which it causes are normally not compensable under the Fifth Amendment. The airspace, apart from the immediate reaches above the land, is part of the public domain. We need not determine at this time what those precise limits are. Flights over private land are not a taking, unless they are so low and so frequent as to be a direct and immediate interference with the enjoyment and use of the land.[40]

---

[37] 328 US 256 (1946).   [38] *United States* v. *Causby*, 328 US 256, 261 (1946).
[39] ibid. at 264 (citation omitted).   [40] ibid. at 266.

Even more significantly for present purposes, the Supreme Court in *Causby* made it clear that navigable airspace is of necessity public, rather than private, property:

The air is a public highway, as Congress has declared. Were that not true, every transcontinental flight would subject the operator to countless trespass suits. Common sense revolts at the idea. To recognize such private claims to the airspace would clog these highways, seriously interfere with their control and development in the public interest, and transfer into private ownership that to which only the public has a just claim.[41]

In other words, the costs of coordinating commercial aviation would be enormously high under private ownership of airspace. Conceived of as a "public highway," managed by the federal government, however, those coordination costs are much lower.

The real issue in *Causby* concerned the *extent* of public air rights as against the rights of the private landowner. The Court reasonably concluded that where the public use destroys completely the utility of the land, it is tantamount to a physical occupation of the land, and therefore constitutes a compensable taking. In other words, private landowners possess such rights in the air as are necessary to secure their land rights. Beyond that, the public "owns" the air.

Where private lands meet public waters

Many of the Supreme Court's most important recent takings decisions arose where privately owned land met publicly owned water. In *Lucas v. South Carolina Coastal Council*,[42] for instance, the state regulated Mr. Lucas's land because it was beachfront property. The ostensible purpose was not so much to protect the state's interest in publicly owned ocean resources, as to control beach erosion. However, because the state owns the beds and banks of navigable waterways up to the mean high-tide line,[43] it possesses a significant ownership interest in the beach itself. The Court in *Lucas* said nothing about the state's ownership interest in the beachfront, focusing entirely on rescuing Mr. Lucas's investment in the two beachfront lots.

Likewise in *Nollan v. California Coastal Commission*, the Court ignored public property rights in the beachfront in deciding that the State of California had unconstitutionally taken Mr. and Mrs. Nollan's private property rights without just compensation. The State Coastal Commission had granted the Nollans a building permit, but on the condition that

[41] ibid. at 261.   [42] 505 US 1003 (1992).
[43] See *Shively v. Bowlby*, 152 US 1 (1894).

the landowners would allow public passage along the beach below a sea wall that separated their house from the Pacific Ocean. The Court treated this cursorily as a dedication of private land to public use, even though the State of California claimed in its brief that the land subject to the condition was state-owned to begin with because it was frequently below the mean high-tide line.[44] As Justice Brennan pointed out in his dissent from the majority decision, the Court simply ignored the state's ownership claim.[45] Rather than seriously attempting to determine the proper boundary between publicly and privately owned property where the land met the ocean, the Court focused exclusively on the private property rights and values at issue. Consequently, the Court's ruling may have had the perverse effect of requiring the state to pay for the privilege of preventing the Nollans from destroying state property.

Most recently, Justice Antonin Scalia, in an intemperate concurring opinion in *Palazzolo v. Rhode Island*,[46] labeled the government of Rhode Island a "thief" for preventing a private landowner from filling coastal salt marshes that the Court simply presumed were part of his property. The Court ruled that Mr. Palazzolo *might* have a claim for compensation against the government, *if* the trial court finds on remand that the state's wetlands regulations had too great an impact on his reasonable, investment-based expectations, or greatly diminished the total value of his property. Neither Justice Scalia nor Justice Kennedy, who authored the majority opinion, mentioned the possibility that the state might have retained substantial property rights in the coastal marshes that were subject to regular tidal flooding. To be fair, the issue was not properly before the Court because it had not been a basis for the Rhode Island Supreme Court's decision, which was on appeal. But the Supreme Court could have recognized at least that the issue was central to the determination of the case on remand. At the very least, Justice Scalia might have avoided prejudging the issue, as he seems to have done. Did the state *steal* Mr. Palazzolo's property, as Justice Scalia suggests, or was it merely protecting the public's own, preexisting property rights in coastal tidelands?

The argument for preexisting public property rights is straightforward. "It is well settled in Rhode Island that pursuant to the public trust doctrine the State maintains title in fee to all soil within its boundaries that lies below the high-water mark, and it holds such land in trust for the use of

---

[44] See Government's Brief at 6, *Nollan v. California Coastal Commission*, 483 US 825 (1987) (No. 86–133); Motion of Appellee California Coastal Commission to Dismiss at 3, *Nollan v. California Coastal Commission*, 233 Cal. Rptr. 28 (Cal. Ct. App. 1986) (Civ. B-004663). Also see Kendall and Lord (1998, p. 555).

[45] 483 US at 847–55 (Brennan, J. dissenting).

[46] — US —, 121 S.Ct. 2448, 2468 (2001) (Scalia, J., concurring).

the public."[47] In theory, the mean high-tide line "can be located wherever a tidal effect can be found" (Maloney and Ausness 1974, p. 207). In this case the elevations recorded on the 1980 assessor's plat "suggest that a substantial amount – if not most – of the property is below the mean high-water mark and thus belongs to the State rather than to petitioner."[48]

Justice Stevens's dissent from the Court's ruling in *Palazzolo* recognizes that public property rights are at stake in the case. He mentions the possibility that Mr. Palazzolo does not own the property alleged to have been taken: "the property issue at stake in this litigation is the right to fill the wetlands on the tract that petitioner owns. Whether either he or his predecessors in title ever owned such an interest, and if so, when it was acquired by the State, are questions of state law."[49] Stevens did not, however, attempt to resolve the issue, which was not properly before the Court. His comments were in the nature of a hint to Rhode Island's courts about how they might resolve the case on remand.

In contrast to the Supreme Court's disregard for existing public property rights in *Nollan* and *Palazzolo*, consider *Just* v. *Marinette County*,[50] a takings case in which the Wisconsin Supreme Court took seriously the boundary issue. In 1961 the Justs purchased 36.4 acres of land fronting along the south shore of Lake Noquebay, a navigable body of water located in Marinette County, Wisconsin. They subdivided the land into several parcels, some of which they sold, and some of which they intended to retain for personal use. The local US Geological Survey Map designated the Justs' land as swamps or marshes, which brought the land within the local conservancy district as wetlands. Consequently, in order to fill in any of the marshes for development, the Justs had to first obtain a conditional use permit from the county zoning administrator.

In 1967, six years after the Justs had purchased their land on Lake Noquebay, Marinette County adopted a shore land zoning ordinance, the purpose of which was, in the words of the Court, "to protect navigable waters *and the public rights therein* from the degradation and deterioration which results from uncontrolled use and development of the shore lands."[51] The ordinance conformed with the state's 1965 Water Quality Act and its Navigable Waters Protection Act, which was intended to "aid

---

[47] *Greater Providence Chamber of Comm.* v. *Rhode Island*, 657 A. 2d 1038, 1042 (R.I. 1995); *Hall* v. *Nascimento*, 594 A. 2d 874, 877 (R.I. 1991).

[48] Brief of the National Conference of State Legislatures, National League of Cities, National Governors' Association, US Conference of Mayors, Council of State Governments, National Association of Counties, and International City/County Management Association as Amici Curiae in Support of Respondents, *Palazzolo* v. *Rhode Island*, 99–2047, 1999 US Briefs 2047, January 3, 2001, at 24. Also see Brief of Save the Bay – People for Narragansett Bay, Amicus Curiae in Support of Respondents, *Palazzolo* v. *Rhode Island*, 99–2047, 1999 US Briefs 2047, January 3, 2001.

[49] 121 S.Ct. at 2472.   [50] 56 Wis. 2d 7 (1972).   [51] ibid. at 10 (emphasis added).

in the fulfillment of the state's role as trustee of its navigable waters and to promote public health, safety, convenience and general welfare."

Six months after Marinette County enacted its shore land zoning ordinance, Ronald Just filled in an area 20 feet wide and 600 feet long, including more than 500 square feet of designated wetlands, without first obtaining a conditional use permit. The county brought an action against the Justs, who countered that the county's shore land zoning ordinance was unconstitutional because it took their land without just compensation.

The Wisconsin Supreme Court ruled that there was no taking. In his opinion for a unanimous court, Justice Hallows appropriately focused on the conflict between private property rights in the land and existing public property rights in the neighboring waterways and associated wetlands:

> The exercise of the police power in zoning must be reasonable and we think it is not an unreasonable exercise of that power to prevent harm to *public rights* by limiting the use of private property to its natural uses . . .

> This is not a case of an isolated swamp unrelated to a navigable lake or stream, the change of which would cause no harm to *public rights*. Lands adjacent to or near navigable waters exist in a special relationship to the state.[52]

Among the more interesting features of the *Just* ruling is Justice Hallows's response to Justice Holmes's famous assertion in *Pennsylvania Coal,* that "a strong desire to improve the public condition is not enough to warrant achieving the desire by a shorter cut than the constitutional way of paying for the damage":[53]

> This observation refers to the improvement of the public condition, the securing of a benefit not presently enjoyed and to which the public is not entitled. The shore land zoning ordinance preserves nature, the environment, and natural resources as they were created and to which *the people have a present right.*[54]

More significant than which side prevailed in *Just v. Marinette County* is the fact that the Wisconsin Supreme Court treated the dispute appropriately as a boundary conflict between a private property regime and a public property regime. Whether or not the Court achieved a proper balance between public and private rights is, however, another, inevitably contestable issue.

Public wildlife on private lands

As with water resources, wildlife are for the most part public property, as chapter 2 has shown. Whenever wildlife habitat exists on privately owned land, a property regime conflict is likely to arise.

[52] ibid. at 17–18 (emphasis added).   [53] 260 US at 416.   [54] 56 Wis. 2d at 23–4.

The US Endangered Species Act[55] prohibits private landowners from using or developing their land in ways that harm endangered or threatened species of plants or animals known to be present.[56] This constitutes a potentially widespread limitation on land development for, as chapter 7 has shown, most endangered species habitat is located on privately owned lands. Although there are no recorded cases where landowners have been prevented from building houses on their land because of endangered species, implementation of the Act has led to a few takings claims.

Consider, for example, the case of Richard P. Christy, a herder who grazed 1,700 sheep on land he leased from the Blackfeet Indian Tribe near Glacier National Park in Montana. During a single eight-day period in 1982, grizzly bears from the park killed twenty of Christy's sheep, at a cost to Christy of at least $1,200. On the eighth day, when two grizzly bears came out of the forest and threatened Christy's sheep, he shot and killed one of the bears. Mr. Christy knew, of course, that grizzly bears are protected from harm as a "threatened" species under the Endangered Species Act.[57] The government fined Christy $2,500 for killing the bear/ protecting his sheep. Christy subsequently claimed that the enforcement of the Endangered Species Act against him constituted a taking of his property (the sheep). Both the Federal District Court in Montana and the US Court of Appeals for the Ninth Circuit rejected Christy's claim. As Judge Alarcon wrote for a unanimous appellate panel,[58] "[n]umerous cases have considered, and rejected, the argument that the destruction of private property by protected wildlife constitutes a governmental taking." More significantly, in light of this book's thesis that government regulation constitutes an assertion of public property rights over otherwise unowned resources, Judge Alarcon added, "[t]he federal government does not 'own' the wild animals it protects, nor does the government control the conduct of such animals."[59] For reasons set out in chapter 2, Judge Alarcon's statement should not be taken to mean that the public possesses no property rights at all in wildlife.[60] However, by declaring that the federal government does not "own" endangered species, the court avoided treating the case realistically as a conflict between public property in wildlife and private property in domestic livestock.

---

[55] 16 USC § 1538.
[56] See *Babbit* v. *Sweet Home Chapter of Communities for a Greater Oregon*, 515 US 867 (1995).
[57] 50 CFR § 17.11(h) (1987).
[58] *Christy* v. *Hodel*, 857 F. 2d 1324, 1334 (9th Cir. 1988), *cert. denied* 490 US 1114 (1989).
[59] ibid. at 1335.
[60] Also see *Toomer* v. *Witsell*, 334 US 385, 399 (1948), in which the Supreme Court observed that "fish and game are the common property of all citizens of the governmental unit and that the government, as a sort of trustee, exercises this 'ownership' for the benefit of its citizens."

Most recently, in *Tulare Lake Basin Water Storage District* v. *United States*,[61] the US Court of Federal Claims, which specializes in monetary claims against the federal government, ordered the government to compensate California water users after it restricted their water rights under the Endangered Species Act. The US Fish and Wildlife Service sought to prevent the extinction of two endangered fish species, the delta smelt and the winter-run chinook salmon, by restricting out-of-stream diversions in order to ensure sufficient instream flows. The plaintiffs, California water users, claimed that those restrictions violated the Fifth Amendment by taking without compensation their contractually conferred rights to use the water, and the court agreed. This did not mean, however, that there were no public property rights in the water. The court noted that the California State Water Resources Board had the authority, under the doctrines of reasonable use and public trust,[62] to alter the terms of plaintiffs' contract-based water rights without compensation.[63] In other words, the state could require an increase in instream flows to protect the endangered fish species without committing a compensable taking. The implication is that the public property rights at issue in the case belong to the State of California, rather than the federal government.

III   Jurisprudential and policy implications

American society relies on multiple and mixed property regimes that are designed to serve a variety of objectives, on the theory that all property systems work better in some circumstances, for some purposes, than in others. The Supreme Court's takings jurisprudence, however, presumes that only private property rights are at stake. The Court has been willfully oblivious to the fact that many, though by no means all,[64] of the regulatory takings cases it decides arise where existing public and private rights collide. In *Nollan* and *Palazzolo*, parties specifically briefed the Court on the *public* property rights at stake, and argued that the government regulations at issue were designed to protect those existing public rights. You would never learn about those claims, however, by reading the majority and concurring opinions in either *Nollan* or *Palazzolo*.[65] It is quite

---

[61] 49 Fed. Cl. 313, 2001 US Claims LEXIS 72 (2001).
[62] On the public trust doctrine, see chapter 2.   [63] See chapter 2.
[64] Not all takings cases involve boundary contests between private and public property regimes. *Pennsylvania Coal* did not involve conflicting property regimes. Neither did *Eastern Enterprises* v. *Apfel*, 524 US 498 (1998), in which the Supreme Court found a compensable taking when Congress enacted a law that applied retroactively to require a defunct coal company to pay additional medical benefits to its former workers.
[65] This is not to say that those arguments should necessarily prevail, but only that the Court should at least seriously treat those claims, as they do the private property claims at stake.

unusual for the Court simply to ignore potentially dispositive arguments that are explicitly raised in briefs, but that is precisely what the Court did in those two cases. This raises a question about the motivations and trustworthiness of the Court in takings cases that is every bit as relevant as Justice Scalia's concern about the motivations and trustworthiness of legislative bodies.

But what difference would it make if the Supreme Court seriously considered the boundary issue? Would the outcomes of actual cases be any different if the Court reframed its approach to takings cases and treated them as public–private boundary disputes? Potentially, yes. If the Court in *Nollan* had seriously considered the State of California's public property claim, the case might have been decided differently. Instead of a government "exaction" of private property rights, the Court might have found that the land-use condition imposed on the Nollans related only to land already owned by the State of California. There would have been no taking at all.[66] On the other hand, a serious consideration of public property rights in *Christy* might have forced the US Court of Appeals for the Ninth Circuit to forthrightly confront the claims of private property owners for damages caused by publicly owned wildlife.

To the extent, however, that takings cases are really about constitutional *equity* – who should bear the costs arising from land-use conflicts – rather than constitutional *law* – who possesses what rights – an analysis of competing public and private property rights would be relevant only to the Court's balancing of the equities. A private property owner might have a stronger equitable claim to compensation where no public property rights are implicated, but a weaker claim if the state is merely seeking to protect public entitlements.

In the *Christy* case, the fairness issue concerned who bore the costs of endangered species protection, the individual sheep herder or the taxpayers. Under current rules, individual property owners bear virtually all the costs of protecting endangered species on private lands, mostly in the form of reduced property uses and values. The Endangered Species Act, meanwhile, is designed to benefit all of society. This does not conform with traditional notions of equity, according to which those who receive the benefits from the law should share proportionately in its costs. That is the basis for the diminution-in-value test fashioned by Justice Holmes in *Pennsylvania Coal* and extended by Justice Scalia in *Lucas*. It was also the basis for Justice Byron White's dissent from the Supreme Court's decision not to grant certiorari in the *Christy* case. Even if the government

---

[66] *Palazzolo* is yet to be decided on remand, and it is entirely possible that the Rhode Island courts will ultimately decide that Mr. Palazzolo never had title to most of the lands affected by the state regulations.

does not "own" the grizzly bears as the Ninth Circuit maintained, Justice White wrote, that hardly means the government should be able to force Mr. Christy to sacrifice his property for the public benefit of preserving endangered species.[67] Justice White may be right about this as a matter of equity, but whether such payments should be in the form of "compensation" for a taking under the Fifth Amendment is another matter.

The conclusion that a "taking" has occurred presumes that the government's scheme for protecting publicly owned wildlife has interfered with some preexisting private property "right." Such a presumption might not be warranted, however. There is no reason to suppose that a private property owner's bundle of rights includes the "right" to harm endangered species. If not, then no existing "right" has been taken when the government prohibits the private property owner from harming endangered species that wander onto his land. Even if no specific "right" has been taken, however, it is clear that Endangered Species Act regulations can and do seriously affect the value of private *investments* in land. This is why Justice Holmes shifted the focus in takings doctrine in *Pennsylvania Coal* from formal legal analysis of property *rights* to the equitable analysis of property *values*. The shift from law to equity embodied in the diminution-in-value test implicitly recognizes that formal legal analysis, focusing on "rights," is incapable of effectively resolving property regime conflicts. But criticisms of the diminution-in-value test itself, recounted earlier in this chapter, indicate that it is not a very effective approach either.

Better mechanisms may lie outside the judicial/constitutional "takings" regime altogether. For example, private property owners such as Mr. Christy could be paid for assisting in endangered species preservation, though not as "compensation" for property rights taken. Instead, payments could be in the form of quasi-contractual consideration or even insurance. In an insurance scheme, the government could establish a fund, financed by taxes, to settle claims by ranchers and others who suffer property losses resulting from endangered species and habitat preservation efforts. Under such a system, Mr. Christy would have been able to file a claim for the lost market value of the sheep that were slaughtered by the grizzly bears. The economic risks created by endangered species regulations would then be spread among the whole of society, which benefits from those regulations.

Some nongovernmental organizations, such as Defenders of Wildlife, have been experimenting with payment schemes designed to alter the incentives of landowners who come into contact with endangered species. In 1987 Defenders established a fund to pay ranchers for verified livestock

[67] 490 US at 1116 (White, J., dissenting).

losses resulting from wolf recovery programs. It established a similar trust fund to pay ranchers for grizzly bear depredation ten years later.

Here's how Defenders' programs work. If a rancher believes a grizzly bear or wolf has killed livestock, he or she notifies the appropriate state, tribal or federal agency. A trained specialist, usually on the scene within 24 hours, investigates to determine if wolves or grizzly bears were responsible for the death of the livestock. They rely on necropsy techniques (all predators have unique styles for killing their prey) and the presence of tracks, hair or scat. If the investigator verifies that wolves or grizzly bears killed the livestock, a report is sent to Defenders of Wildlife.

A Defenders' staff member from the region then calls the rancher to discuss the incident, explain our compensation program and agree on a payment amount.

In nine out of ten cases, Defenders of Wildlife pays what the livestock producer suggests. In case of a difference of opinion, the program relies on county extension agents to determine fair market value, but that rarely happens.

Defenders tries to send a check to the rancher within two weeks of receiving verification of a livestock loss.[68]

Between 1987 and 2000, Defenders of Wildlife paid out more than $206,000 to ranchers for livestock lost due to wolf and grizzly bear predation.[69]

Bills have been introduced into Congress, but not yet enacted, that would achieve the same result of rewarding landowners for protecting endangered species, but without recognizing preexisting private property rights to harm them. In 1997 a bipartisan-sponsored bill to amend the Endangered Species Act was introduced into the Senate, which would have established a $10 million federal fund to provide grants of up to $25,000 to private landowners for their assistance in implementing endangered species recovery plans.[70] Such policy innovations hold out the hope of a fairer and less antagonistic system of endangered species protection. They wisely avoid the need to reconcile legal conflicts arising from collisions between publicly owned wildlife and privately owned land, while resolving associated equity concerns.

IV   Conclusion

So long as society relies on multiple property systems and admixtures of property systems for environmental protection – likely a very, very long time – those systems will occasionally collide, raising issues about primacy – which system prevails over another – and who bears the costs

[68] "Defenders Pays $62,000 in Wolf/Grizzly Compensation During 2000," available on the World Wide Web at http://www.defenders.org/releases/pr2001/pr011801.html.
[69] ibid.
[70] A BILL to reauthorize the Endangered Species Act, S. 1180, 105th Congress; 1st Session (1997), § 5.

arising from property regime conflicts. To date, the US Supreme Court has focused on the second issue, while completely ignoring the first. But ignoring the fact that takings cases often involve conflicts between property regimes will not make those conflicts go away. When deciding whether some public land-use regulation constitutes a taking of private property, the Court should at least consider the public property rights at stake.

9   Final thoughts

Since the downfall of communism in Eastern Europe, private/individual property has been widely and rightly celebrated as a guarantor of personal liberty (see Pipes 1999) and an engine of social prosperity (see Bethell 1998; De Soto 2000). The arguments advanced in this book do not suggest otherwise. Where environmental protection is concerned, however, celebrations of private property are at least premature and arguably utopian.

Private property regimes do not guarantee effective or efficient environmental protection. The reason is not simply the absence of completely defined property rights in all resources but the costs of coordination and exclusion under private property regimes in some ecological, technological, and institutional circumstances. Sometimes, as shown in chapter 7, public/state or common property regimes are preferable. The most we can legitimately claim about private ownership of environmental goods, then, is that it has substantial but not unlimited utility for conservation.

This conclusion is hardly surprising. We have only just begun, after all, to understand the rich complex of interconnected and ever-changing ecological systems that comprise our world. The notion that a single, sociolegal institution – private property – is both necessary and sufficient to resolve all environmental problems is not just highly improbable but fantastic. It is every bit as unrealistic as Marx's belief that the complete social ownership of the means of production would eradicate pollution and other unwanted byproducts of economic activity (see Cole 1998, p. 160). An unconditional, theory-based commitment to either socialism or "free-market environmentalism" cannot avert the tragedy of open access. What is required, instead, is a pragmatic, case-by-case approach with a large toolbox.

Private/individual property will be one, very useful tool. In some cases, however, common or public/state property tools may be expected to work better. Each property-based tool has distinct advantages and disadvantages. As discussed in chapter 5, private/individual property tends to minimize coordination costs but often entails higher exclusion costs than other property regimes. In addition, environmental protection regimes based on private/individual property may raise concerns about the discount rates, time horizons, and unaccountable preferences of individual owners. In chapter 6 I showed that common property regimes sometimes entail lower exclusion costs than private property regimes, and embody a greater social consensus about what should be done. But common property regimes may be susceptible to changes in, or threats to, the constitution and cohesiveness of the ownership group. In other words, co-ordination costs may be or become quite high under a common property regime. Moreover, powerful individuals may dominate the common ownership group, so that the common property regime reflects not the preferences of the group but those of discrete individuals, just like private property. Public property regimes, which were the subject of chapter 2, can expand the range of decision-making beyond individual and small-group preferences, which may be preferable where the social value of a resource or resource amenity exceeds its private value. Public ownership can also minimize exclusion costs and maximize returns to scale. But environmental goods under public property regimes will always be subject to potential political abuse and bureaucratic mismanagement. Finally, as chapters 3 and 4 showed, mixed public and private property regimes, such as tradeable pollution permits and conservation easements, combine various advantages and disadvantages of those two systems.

As Coase (1964, p. 195) has noted (albeit in a very different context), society's various mechanisms for organizing social relations – in this case relations concerning environmental goods – are all "more or less failures." The goal, in this second-best world, is to structure those relations in ways that, *under the circumstances*, are least likely to fail or are likely to fail the least. Admittedly, this book has offered little guidance for making that determination. The rudimentary model offered in chapter 7 – *exclusion costs + coordination costs = total costs* – provides only general direction. The various complicating factors identified in that chapter would likely make a mockery of our designs, no matter how elaborate our model. Hence, this book's more modest aspiration: to clearly and realistically frame the relations between environmental protection and property systems.

References

Ackerman, Bruce A. and Hassler, William T. 1981, *Clean Coal/Dirty Air: Or How the Clean Air Act Became a Multibillion-Dollar Bail-Out for High-Sulfur Coal Producers and What Should Be Done About It*, New Haven: Yale University Press.

Ackerman, Bruce A. and Stewart, Richard B. 1985, "Reforming Environmental Law," *Stanford Law Review* 37: 1333–65.

Alchian, Armen A. 1950, "Uncertainty, Evolution, and Economic Theory," *Journal of Political Economy* 58: 211–21.

Allen, Tom 2000, *The Right to Property in Commonwealth Constitutions*, Cambridge: Cambridge University Press.

American Law Institute 1963–7, *Restatement (2d) Torts*, St. Paul, Minn.: American Law Institute Publishers.

American Law Institute 2001, *A Concise Restatement of Property*, St. Paul, Minn.: American Law Institute Publishers.

Anderson, Terry L. 1994, "Enviro-Capitalism vs. Enviro-Socialism," *Kansas Journal of Law and Public Policy* 4: 35–40.

Anderson, Terry L. and Hill, Peter J. 1975, "The Evolution of Property Rights: a Study of the American West," *Journal of Law and Economics* 12: 163–79.

Anderson, Terry L. and Hill, Peter J. 1983, "Privatizing the Commons: an Improvement?," *Southern Economics Journal* 50: 438–50.

Anderson, Terry L. and Leal, Donald R. 1991, *Free Market Environmentalism*, Boulder, Col.: Westview Press.

Anderson, Terry L. and Leal, Donald R. 1992, "Free Market Versus Political Environmentalism," *Harvard Journal of Law and Public Policy* 15: 297–310.

Andrews, Richard N. L. 1999, *Managing the Environment, Managing Ourselves: a History of American Environmental Policy*, New Haven: Yale University Press.

Antal-Mokos, Zoltan 1998, *Privatization, Politics, and Economic Performance in Hungary*, Cambridge: Cambridge University Press.

Aristotle 1941, "Politica," trans. B. Jowett, in Richard McKeon (ed.), *The Basic Works of Aristotle*, New York: Random House, pp. 1113–316.

Arnold, Frank S. 1995, *Economic Analysis of Environmental Policy and Regulation*, New York: Wiley.

Arrow, Kenneth 1951, *Social Choice and Individual Values*, New York: Wiley.

Arthur, W. Brian 1989, "Competing Technologies, Increasing Returns and Lock-in by Historical Events," *Economic Journal* 99: 116–31.

Ault, Warren O. 1965, "Open Field Husbandry and the Village Community," *Transactions of the American Philosophical Society* 55: 5–102.

Ault, W. O. 1972, *Open-Field Farming in Medieval England/ a Study of Village By-Laws*, London: Allen and Unwin.

Baden, John and Stroup, Richard 1990, "Natural Resource Scarcity, Entrepreneurship, and the Political Economy of Hope," in Walter E. Block (ed.), *Economics and the Environment: a Reconciliation*, Vancouver, BC: Fraser Institute, pp. 117–36.

Baldwin, Melissa Waller 1997, "Conservation Easements: a Viable Tool for Land Preservation," *Land and Water Law Review* 32: 89–123.

Barnes, David W. 1982–3, "Enforcing Property Rights: Extending Property Rights Theory to Congestible and Environmental Goods," *Environmental Affairs* 10: 583–638.

Barzel, Yoram 1989, *Economic Analysis of Property Rights*, Cambridge: Cambridge University Press.

Baumol, William J. and Oates, Wallace E. 1971, "The Use of Standards and Prices for Protection of the Environment," in Peter Bohm and Allen V. Kneese (eds.), *The Economics of Environment: Papers from Four Nations*, New York: St. Martin's Press, pp. 53–65.

Baumol, William J. and Oates, Wallace E. 1988, *The Theory of Environmental Policy*, Cambridge: Cambridge University Press.

Beerman, Jack M. 1991, "Interest Group Politics and Judicial Behavior: Macey's Public Choice," *Notre Dame Law Review* 67: 183–229.

Bell, George Joseph 1899, *Principles of the Law of Scotland*, Edinburgh: Law Society of Scotland/Butterworths.

Berkes, Fikret 1992, "Success and Failure in Marine Coastal Fisheries of Turkey," in Daniel W. Bromley (ed.), *Making the Commons Work*, San Francisco: Institute for Contemporary Studies, pp. 161–82.

Berkes, F., Feeny, D., McCay, B. J. and Acheson, J. M. 1989, "The Benefits of the Commons," *Nature* 340 (July 13): 91–3.

Bethell, Tom 1998, *The Noblest Triumph: Property and Prosperity Through the Ages*, New York: St. Martin's Griffin.

Black, Bernard S., Krakman, Rainer and Tarassova, Anna 2000, "Russian Privatization and Corporate Governance: What Went Wrong?," *Stanford Law Review* 52: 1731–808.

Blackie, Jeffrey A. 1989, "Conservation Easements and the Doctrine of Changed Conditions," *Hastings Law Journal* 40: 1187–222.

Blackstone, William [1766] 1979, *Commentaries on the Laws of England*, vol. II, Chicago: University of Chicago Press.

Block, Walter E. 1990, "Environmental Problems, Private Property Rights Solutions," in Walter E. Block (ed.), *Economics and the Environment: a Reconciliation*, Vancouver, BC: Fraser Institute, pp. 281–332.

Blumm, Michael C. 1992, "The Fallacies of Free Market Environmentalism," *Harvard Journal of Law & Public Policy* 15: 371–89.

Bohi, Douglas R. 1994, "Utilities and State Regulators are Failing to Take Advantage of Emission Allowance Trading," *Electricity Journal* 7(2): 20–7.

Bonyhady, Tim 1987, *The Law of the Countryside: the Rights of the Public*, Milton Park Estate, Abingdon, UK: Professional Books.

Borcherding, Thomas E. 1990, "Natural Resources and Transgenerational Equity," in Walter E. Block (ed.), *Economics and the Environment: a Reconciliation*, Vancouver, BC: Fraser Institute, pp. 95–115.

Bork, Robert H. 1990, *The Tempting of America: the Political Seduction of the Law*, New York: Free Press.

Bosselman, Fred, Callies, David, and Banta, John 1973, *The Taking Issue: an Analysis of the Constitutional Limits of Land Use Control*, Washington, DC: US Government Printing Office.

Bosselman, Fred P. and Stroud, Nancy E. 1985, "Pariah to Paragon: Developer Exactions in Florida 1975–85," *Stetson Law Review* 14: 527–63.

Brenner, Joel Franklin 1974, "Nuisance Law and the Industrial Revolution," *Journal of Legal Studies* 3: 403–33.

Brimblecombe, Peter 1987, *The Big Smoke: a History of Air Pollution in London Since Medieval Times*, London: Methuen.

Bromley, Daniel W. 1989, *Economic Interests and Institutions: the Conceptual Foundations of Public Policy*, Oxford: Basil Blackwell.

Bromley, Daniel W. 1991, *Environment and Economy: Property Rights and Public Policy*, Oxford: Basil Blackwell.

Bromley, Daniel W. (ed.) 1992, *Making the Commons Work: Theory, Practice, and Policy*, San Francisco: Institute for Contemporary Studies.

Brunet, Edward 1992, "Debunking Wholesale Private Enforcement of Environmental Rights," *Harvard Journal of Law and Public Policy* 15: 311–24.

Buchanan, James and Tullock, Gordon 1962, *The Calculus of Consent*, Ann Arbor: University of Michigan Press.

Buchanan, James and Tullock, Gordon 1975, "Polluters' 'Profit' and Political Response," *American Economic Review* 65: 139–47.

Burtraw, Dallas 1996, "Cost Savings Sans Allowance Trades? Evaluating the SO2 Emission Trading Program to Date," Discussion Paper 95-30-REV, Washington, DC: Resources for the Future.

Burtraw, Dallas, Krupnick, Alan J., Mansur, Erin, Austin, David and Farrell, Deirdre 1997, "The Costs and Benefits of Reducing Acid Rain," Discussion Paper 97-31-REV, Washington, DC: Resources for the Future.

Calabresi, Guido and Melamed, A. Douglas 1972, "Property Rules, Liability Rules, and Inalienability: One View of the Cathedral," *Harvard Law Review* 85: 1089–128.

Callander, Robin 1998, *How Scotland is Owned*, Edinburgh: Canongate.

Campbell, Bruce M. S. and Godoy, Ricardo A. 1992, "Commonfield Agriculture: the Andes and Medieval England Compared," in Daniel W. Bromley (ed.), *Making the Commons Work*, San Francisco: Institute for Contemporary Studies, pp. 99–127.

Carl Bro International 1984, *An Evaluation of Livestock Management and Production with Special References to Communal Areas*, Glostrup, Denmark: Carl Bro International.

Carlson, Curtis, Burtraw, Dallas, Cropper, Maureen and Palmer, Karen L. 2000. "Sulfur-Dioxide Control by Electric Utilities: What are the Gains from Trade?," *Journal of Political Economy* 108: 1292–326.

Carson, Rachel 1962, *Silent Spring*, Boston: Houghton Mifflin.

Castle, Emery N. 1965, "The Market Mechanism, Externalities, and Land Economics," *Journal of Farm Economics* 47: 542–56.

Chambers, J. D. 1964, *Laxton: the Last English Open Field Village*, London: HMSO.

Cheever, Frederico 1996, "Public Good and Private Magic in the Law of Land Trusts and Conservation Easements: a Happy Present and a Troubled Future," *Denver University Law Review* 73: 1077–102.

Chertow, Marian R. and Esty, Daniel C. (eds.) 1997, *Thinking Ecologically: the Next Generation of Environmental Policy*, New Haven: Yale University Press.

Cheung, Steven N. S. 1986, *Will China Go Capitalist?*, Hobart Paper 94, London: Institute of Economic Affairs.

Cheung, Steven N. S. 1998, "The Transaction Costs Paradigm," *Economic Inquiry* 36: 514–21.

Chippindale, Christopher 1990, "The Stonehenge Phenomenon," in Christopher Chippindale, Paul Devereux, Peter Fowler, Rhys Jones, and Tim Sebastian (eds.), *Who Owns Stonehenge?*, London: Batsford, pp. 9–34.

Church, Albert M. 1982, *Conflicts Over Resource Ownership*, Lexington, Mass.: Lexington Books.

Ciriacy-Wantrup, S. V. and Bishop, Richard C. 1975, "'Common Property' as a Concept in Natural Resources Policy," *Natural Resources Journal* 15: 713–27.

Clark, Colin W. 1973a, "Profit Maximization and the Extinction of Animal Species," *Journal of Political Economy* 81: 950–61.

Clark, Colin W. 1973b, "The Economics of Overexploitation," *Science* 181: 630–34.

Clawson, Marian and Held, Burnell 1957, *The Federal Lands: their Use and Management*, Baltimore: Johns Hopkins University Press for Resources for the Future.

Coase, Ronald H. 1937, "The Theory of the Firm," *Economica* 4: 386–405.

Coase, Ronald H. 1959, "The Federal Communications Commission," *Journal of Law and Economics* 2: 1–40.

Coase, Ronald H. 1960, "The Problem of Social Cost," *Journal of Law and Economics* 3: 1–44.

Coase, Ronald H. 1964, "Discussion: the Regulated Industries," *American Economic Review* 54: 194–7.

Coase, Ronald H. 1984, "How Should Economists Choose?," in R. H. Coase, *Essays on Economics and Economists*, Chicago: University of Chicago Press, pp. 15–33.

Coase, Ronald H. 1988, *The Firm, the Market and the Law*, Chicago: University of Chicago Press.

Coase, Ronald H. 1994, *Essays on Economics and Economists*, Chicago: University of Chicago Press.

Coggins, George Cameron, Wilkinson, Charles F. and Leshy, John D. 1993, *Federal Public Lands and Resources Law*, Westbury, NY: Foundation Press.

Cohen, Felix 1970 [1944], "Indian Claims," in Lucy Kramer Cohen (ed.), *The Legal Conscience: Selected Papers of Felix S. Cohen*, New York: Archon Books, pp. 264–72.

Cohen-Tanugi, Laurent 1985, *Le droit sans l'état: sur la démocratie en France et en Amérique*, Paris: Presses Universitaires de France.

Cole, Daniel H. 1998, *Instituting Environmental Protection: From Red to Green in Poland*, Basingstoke: Macmillan.

Cole, Daniel H. 1999, "New Forms of Property Rights: Property Rights in Environmental Goods," in Boudwijn Bouckaert and Gerrit de Geest (eds.), *Encyclopedia of Law and Economics*, vol. II, Cheltenham: Edward Elgar, pp. 274–314.

Cole, Daniel H. 2000a, "The Importance of Being Comparative: the M. Dale Palmer Professorship Inaugural Lecture," *Indiana Law Review* 33: 921–36.

Cole, Daniel H. 2000b, "Clearing the Air: Four Propositions on Property Rights and Environmental Protection," *Duke Environmental Law and Policy Forum* 10: 103–30.

Cole, Daniel H. and Grossman, Peter Z. 1999, "When is Command-and-Control Efficient? Institutions, Technology, and the Comparative Efficiency of Alternative Regulatory Regimes for Environmental Protection," *Wisconsin Law Review*: 887–938.

Cole, Daniel H. and Grossman, Peter Z. (forthcoming a), "The Meaning of Property Rights: Law vs. Economics," *Land Economics* 78(3).

Cole, Daniel H. and Grossman, Peter Z. (forthcoming b), "Toward a Total-Cost Approach to Environmental Instrument Choice," in Timothy Swanson (ed.), *Research in Law and Economics*, Stamford, Conn.: JAI Press.

Cordell, John and McKean, Margaret A. 1992, "Sea Tenure in Bahia, Brazil," in Daniel W. Bromley (ed.), *Making the Commons Work*, San Francisco, Institute for Contemporary Studies, pp. 183–205.

Cox, Susan J. B. 1985, "No Tragedy on the Commons," *Environmental Ethics* 7: 49–61.

Crocker, Thomas D. 1966, "The Structuring of Atmospheric Pollution Control Systems," in Harold Wolozin (ed.), *The Economics of Air Pollution*, New York: Norton, pp. 61–86.

Cropper, Maureen L., Evans, William N., Berardi, Stephen J., Ducla-Soares, Maria M. and Portney, Paul R. 1992, "The Determinants of Pesticide Regulation: a Statistical Analysis of EPA Decision Making," *Journal of Political Economy* 100: 175–97.

Dagan, Hanoch and Heller, Michael 2001, "The Liberal Commons," *Yale Law Journal* 110: 549–623.

Dahlman, Carl. J. 1979, "The Problem of Externality," *Journal of Law and Economics* 22: 141–62.

Dahlman, Carl. J. 1980, *The Open-Field System and Beyond: Property Rights Analysis of an Economic Institution*, Cambridge: Cambridge University Press.

Dales, J. H. 1968, *Pollution, Property and Prices: an Essay in Policy-Making and Economics*, Toronto: University of Toronto Press.

Daniels, Tom and Bowers, Deborah 1997, *Holding Our Ground: Protecting America's Farms and Farmland*, Washington, DC: Island Press.

Dasgupta, Partha 1982, *The Control of Resources*, Cambridge, Mass.: Harvard University Press.

Davies, Clarence J. and Mazurek, Jan 1998, *Pollution Control in the United States: Evaluating the System*, Washington, DC: Resources for the Future.

Davis, Otto A. and Kamien, Morton I. 1969, "Externalities, Information, and Alternative Collective Action," in Joint Economic Committee, United States Congress, *The Analysis and Evaluation of Public Expenditures: The PPB System*, vol. I, Washington, DC: US Government Printing Office, pp. 67–86.

Dellapenna, Joseph W. 2000, "The Importance of Getting Names Right: the Myth of Markets for Water," *William and Mary Environmental Law and Policy Review* 25: 317–77.

Demsetz, Harold 1964, "The Exchange and Enforcement of Property Rights," *Journal of Law and Economics* 7: 11–26.

Demsetz, Harold 1967, "Toward a Theory of Property Rights," *American Economic Review* 57: 347–59, reprinted in Harold Demsetz, *Ownership, Control and the Firm*, vol. I, *The Organization of Economic Activity*, Cambridge: Basil Blackwell, 1988, pp. 104–16.

Demsetz, Harold 1968, "The Costs of Transacting," *Quarterly Journal of Economics* 82: 33–53.

Demsetz, Harold 1969, "Information and Efficiency: Another Viewpoint," *Journal of Law and Economics* 12: 1–22.

Demsetz, Harold 1988, *Ownership, Control and the Firm*, vol. I, *The Organization of Economic Activity*, Oxford: Basil Blackwell.

Denman, D. R. 1978, *The Place of Property: a New Recognition of the Function and Form of Property Rights in Land*, The Keep, Berkmansted, Herts., UK: Geographical Publications.

Dennis, Jeanne M. 1993, "Smoke for Sale: Paradoxes and Problems of the Emissions Trading Program of the Clean Air Act Amendments of 1990," *UCLA Law Review* 40: 1101–1144.

De Soto, Hernando 2000, *The Mystery of Capital: Why Capitalism Triumphs in the West and Fails Everywhere Else*, New York: Basic Books.

Devlin, Rose Ann 2000, "Property Rights, Tenure Systems and Managing Natural Capital," in Michael D. Kaplowitz (ed.), *Property Rights, Economics, and the Environment*, Stamford, Conn.: JAI Press, pp. 103–19.

Diehl, Janet and Barrett, Thomas S. 1988, *The Conservation Easement Handbook*, Washington, DC: Land Trust Alliance.

Downing, Paul B. and Kimball, James N. 1982, "Enforcing Pollution Control Laws in the US," *Policy Studies Journal* 1: 55–65.

Downs, Anthony 1957, *An Economic Theory of Democracy*, New York: Harper.

Driesen, David M. 1998, "Is Emissions Trading an Economic Incentive Program?: Replacing the Command and Control/Economic Incentive Dichotomy," *Washington and Lee Law Review* 55: 289–350.

Eggertsson, Thráinn 1990, *Economic Behavior and Institutions*, Cambridge: Cambridge University Press.

Eggertsson, Thráinn 1996, "The Economics of Control and the Cost of Property Rights," in Susan S. Hanna, Carl Folke and Karl-Gören Mäler (eds.), *Rights to Nature: Ecological, Economic, Cultural, and Political Principles of Institutions for the Environment*, Washington, DC: Island Press, pp. 157–75.

Ellickson, Robert C. 1991, *Order Without Law: How Neighbors Settle Disputes*. Cambridge, Mass.: Harvard University Press.

Ellickson, Robert C. 1993, "Property in Land," *Yale Law Journal* 102: 1315–400.

Emerson, Ralph Waldo 1909, "Self-Reliance," in Ralph Waldo Emerson, *Essays and English Traits*, New York: P. F. Collier.

Engel, Kirsten 1997, "State Environmental Standard-Setting: Is There a 'Race' and Is It 'To the Bottom?,'" *Hastings Law Journal* 48: 271–376.

Ensminger, Jean 1990, "Co-Opting the Elders: the Political Economy of State Incorporation in Africa," *American Anthropologist* 92: 662–75.

Enterprise for the Environment 1998, *The Environmental Protection System in Transition: Toward a More Desirable Future*, Washington, DC: Center for Strategic and International Studies.

Epstein, Richard A. 1985, *Takings: Private Property and the Power of Eminent Domain*, Cambridge, Mass.: Harvard University Press.

Epstein, Richard 1994, "On the Optimal Mix of Private and Common Property," in Ellen Frankel Paul, Fred D. Miller Jr. and Jeffrey Paul (eds.), *Property Rights*, Cambridge: Cambridge University Press, pp. 17–41.

Epstein, Richard 1995, *Simple Rules for a Complex World*, Cambridge, Mass.: Harvard University Press.

Ercmann, Sevine 1996, "Enforcement of Environmental Law in United States and European Law: Realities and Expectations," *Environmental Law* 26: 1213–39.

Lord Ernle 1968, *English Farming, Past and Present*, London: Heinemann.

Evans, David 1992, *A History of Nature Conservation in Britain*, New York: Routledge.

Lord Eversley 1910, *Commons, Forests and Footpaths: the Story of the Battle During the Last Forty-Five Years for Public Rights over the Commons, Forests and Footpaths of England and Wales*, London: Cassell and Co.

Farber, Daniel A. and Frickey, Philip P. 1991, *Law and Public Choice: a Critical Introduction*, Chicago: University of Chicago Press.

Featherstone, Allen M. and Goodwin, Barry K. 1993, "Factors Influencing a Farmer's Decision to Invest in Long-Term Conservation Improvements," *Land Economics* 69: 67–81.

Feeny, D., Berkes, F., McCay, B. J. and Acheson, J. M. 1990, "The Tragedy of the Commons: Twenty-Two Years Later," *Human Ecology* 18: 1–19.

Feeny, David, Hanna, Susan, and McEvoy, Arthur F. 1996, "Questioning the Assumptions of the 'Tragedy of the Commons' Model of Fisheries," *Land Economics* 72: 187–205.

Feldman, Franklin and Weil, Stephen E. 1986, *Art Law*, Boston: Little, Brown.

Fenner, Randee Gorin 1980, "Land Trusts: an Alternative Method of Preserving Open Spaces," *Vanderbilt Law Review* 33: 1039–99.

Fenoaltea, Stefano 1988, "Transaction Costs, Whig History, and the Common Fields," *Politics and Society* 16: 171–240.

Fidzanù, N. H. 2000, "The Botswana Tribal Grazing Land Policy: a Property Rights Study," in Jennifer Rietbergen-McCracken and Hussein Abaza (eds.), *Economic Instruments for Environmental Management*, London: Earthscan for the United Nations Environment Programme, pp. 19–30.

Field, Barry 1989, "The Evolution of Property Rights," *Kyklos* 42: 319–45.

Fischel, William A. 1995, *Regulatory Takings: Law, Economics, and Politics*, Cambridge, Mass.: Harvard University Press.

Foster, Vivien and Hahn, Robert W. 1995, "Designing More Efficient Markets: Lessons from Los Angeles Smog Control," *Journal of Law and Economics* 38: 19–48.

Fowler, Peter 1990a, "Stonehenge: Academic Claims and Responsibilities," in Christopher Chippindale, Paul Devereux, Peter Fowler, Rhys Jones and Tim Sebastian (eds.), *Who Owns Stonehenge?*, London: Batsford, pp. 120–38.

Fowler, Peter 1990b, "Stonehenge in a Democratic Society," in Christopher Chippindale, Paul Devereux, Peter Fowler, Rhys Jones, and Tim Sebastian (eds.), *Who Owns Stonehenge?*, London: Batsford, pp. 139–59.

Fraschini, Angela and Cassone, Alberto 1994, "Instrument Choice in Water Pollution Policy in Italy," in Hans Opschoor and Kerry Turner (eds.), *Economic Incentives and Environmental Policies*, Dordrecht: Kluwer Academic Publishers, pp. 89–112.

Freeman, A. Myrick 1982, *Air and Water Pollution Control: a Benefit-Cost Assessment*, New York: Wiley.

Freund, Ernst, 1904, *The Police Power: Public Policy and Constitutional Rights*, Chicago: Callaghan and Co.

Funk, William 1992, "Free Market Environmentalism: Wonder Drug or Snakeoil?," *Harvard Journal of Law and Public Policy*: 511–16.

Furubotn, Eirik G. and Richter, Rudolf 1998, *Institutions and Economic Theory: the Contribution of the New Institutional Economics (Economics, Cognition and Society)*, Ann Arbor: University of Michigan Press.

Gaines, Sanford E. and Westin, Richard A. 1991, *Taxation for Environmental Protection: a Multinational Legal Study*, New York: Quorum Books.

Garrett, Kemble Hagerman 1984, "Conservation Easements: the Greening of America?," *Kentucky Law Journal* 73: 255–73.

Geisler, Charles 2000, "Property Pluralism," in Charles Geisler and Gail Daneker (eds.), *Property and Values: Alternatives to Public and Private Ownership*, Washington: Island Press, pp. 65–87.

Gerhardt, Paul H. 1969, "Incentives to Air Pollution Control," in Clark Havighurst (ed.), *Air Pollution Control*, Dobbs Ferry, NY: Oceana, pp. 162–72.

Goetze, David 1987, "Identifying Appropriate Institutions for Efficient Use of Common Pools," *Natural Resources Journal* 27: 187–99.

Goodstein, Eban 1995, "The Economic Roots of Environmental Decline: Property Rights or Path Dependence?," *Journal of Economic Issues* 29: 1029–43.

Gordon, H. Scott 1954, "The Economic Theory of a Common Property Resource: the Fishery," *Journal of Political Economy* 62: 122–42.

Gordon, Scott 1958, "Economics and the Conservation Question," *Journal of Law and Economics* 1: 110–21.

Grant, Malcolm 1996, "If Tigard Were an English City: Exactions Law in England Following the *Tesco* Case," in David L. Callies (ed.), *Takings: Land-Development Conditions and Regulatory Takings After Dolan and Lucas*, Chicago: Section of State and Local Government Law, American Bar Association, pp. 332–53.

Grapel, William (trans.) 1994 (reprint), *The Institutes of Justinian, with the Novel as to Successions*, Holmes Beach, Fla.: Wm. W. Gaunt and Sons.

Green, Donald P. and Shapiro, Ian 1994, *Pathologies of Rational Choice Theory: a Critique of Applications in Political Science*, New Haven: Yale University Press.

Grossman, Margaret Russo 2000, "Leasehold Interests and the Separation of Ownership and Control in US Farmland," in Charles Geisler and Gail Daneker (eds.), *Property and Values: Alternatives to Public and Private Ownership*, Washington, DC: Island Press, pp. 119–48.

Gustanski, Julie Ann 2000, "Protecting the Land: Conservation Easements, Voluntary Actions, and Private Lands," in J. A. Gustanski and R. H. Squires (eds.), *Protecting the Land: Conservation Easements Past, Present, and Future*, Washington, DC: Island Press, pp. 9–25.

Hagevik, George 1969, "Legislating for Air Quality Management: Reducing Theory to Practice," in Clark Havighurst (ed.), *Air Pollution Control*, Dobbs Ferry, NY: Oceana, pp. 173–202.

Hahn, Robert W. 1990, "The Politics and Religion of Clean Air," *Regulation: Cato Review of Business and Government* (winter): 21–30.

Hahn, Robert W. and Hester, Gordon L. 1989a, "Where Did All the Markets Go? An Analysis of EPA's Emissions Trading Program," *Yale Journal on Regulation* 6: 109–53.

Hahn, Robert W. and Hester, Gordon L. 1989b, "Marketable Permits: Lessons for Theory and Practice," *Ecology Law Quarterly* 16: 361–406.

Hahn, Robert W. and Noll, Roger G. 1982, "Designing a Market for Tradeable Emissions Permits," in Wesley A. Magat (ed.), *Reform of Environmental Regulation*, Cambridge, Mass.: Ballinger Publishing, pp. 119–46.

Hamilton, James T. 1995, "Pollution as News: Media and Stock Market Reactions to the Toxics Release Inventory Data," *Journal of Environmental Economics and Management* 28: 98–113.

Hanna, Susan, Folke, Carl, and Mäler, Karl-Gören 1996, "Property Rights and the Natural Environment," in Susan Hanna, Carl Folke, and Karl-Gören Mäler (eds.), *Rights to Nature: Ecological, Economic, Cultural, and Political Principles of Institutions for the Environment*, Washington, DC: Island Press, pp. 1–10.

Hanna, Susan and Munasinghe, Mohan 1995, "An Introduction to Property Rights and the Environment," in Susan Hanna and Mohan Munasinghe (eds.), *Property Rights and the Environment: Social and Ecological Issues*, Washington, DC: Beijer International Institute of Ecological Economics and the World Bank, pp. 3–11.

Hardin, Garrett 1968, "The Tragedy of the Commons," *Science* 162: 1243–8.

Hardin, Garrett 1978, "Political Requirements for Preserving our Common Heritage," in H. P. Brokaw (ed.), *Wildlife and America*, Washington, DC: Council on Environmental Quality, pp. 310–17.

Harrison, David, Jr. and Portney, Paul R. 1981, "Making Ready for the Clean Air Act," *AEI Journal on Government and Society* (Mar./Apr.): 24–31.

Hart, John 1996, "Colonial Land Use Law and its Significance for Modern Takings Doctrine," *Harvard Law Review* 109: 1252–300.

Heal, Geoffrey (ed.), 1999, *The Economics of Increasing Returns*, Cheltenham: Edward Elgar.

Heaton, Herbert 1948, *Economic History of Europe*, London: Harper and Row.

Heinzerling, Lisa 1995, "Selling Pollution, Forcing Democracy," *Stanford Environmental Law Journal* 14: 300–44.

Heller, Michael A. 1998, "The Tragedy of the Anticommons: Property in the Transition from Marx to Markets," *Harvard Law Review* 111: 621–88.

Hines, N. William 1966, "Nor Any Drop to Drink: Public Regulation of Water Quality," *Iowa Law Review* 52: 186–235.

Hohfeld, Wesley Newcomb 1913, "Some Fundamental Legal Conceptions as Applied in Judicial Reasoning," *Yale Law Journal* 23: 16–59.

Hohfeld, Wesley Newcomb 1917, "Fundamental Legal Conceptions as Applied in Judicial Reasoning," *Yale Law Journal* 26: 710–70.

Holmes, Oliver Wendell 1872, "Book Review," *American Law Review* 6: 140–2.

Honoré, Toni 1961, "Ownership," in Anthony Gordon Guest (ed.), *Oxford Essays in Jurisprudence*, Oxford: Oxford University Press, pp. 107–47.

Horwitz, Morton J. 1977, *The Transformation of American Law, 1780–1860: the Crisis of Legal Orthodoxy*, Oxford: Oxford University Press.

Hotelling, Harold 1931, "The Economics of Exhaustible Resources," *Journal of Political Economy* 39: 137–75.

Howe, Charles W. 1979, *Natural Resource Economics*, New York: Wiley.

Huffman, James L. 1994, "The Inevitability of Private Rights in Public Lands," *University of Colorado Law Review* 65: 241–77.

Humbach, John A. 1993, "Evolving Thresholds of Nuisance and the Takings Clause," *Columbia Journal of Environmental Law* 18: 1–29.

Hurst, James Willard 1984, *Law and Economic Growth: the Legal History of the Lumber Industry in Wisconsin, 1836–1915*, Madison: University of Wisconsin Press.

Hyde, William F. 1981, "Compounding Clearcuts: the Social Failures of Public Timber Management in the Rockies," in John Baden and Richard Stroup (eds.), *Bureaucracy Versus the Environment*, Ann Arbor: University of Michigan Press, pp. 186–202.

Jahnke, James A. 1993, *Continuous Emission Monitoring*, New York: Wiley.

Jodha, N. S. 1985, "Population Growth and the Decline of Common Property Resources in Rajasthan, India," *Population and Development Review* 11: 247–64.

Jung, Chulho, Krutilla, Kerry and Boyd, Roy 1996, "Incentives for Advanced Pollution Abatement Technology at the Industry Level: an Evaluation of Policy Alternatives," *Journal of Environmental Economics and Management* 30: 95–111.

Kamiński, Bartłomiej and Sołtan, Karol 1989, "The Evolution of Communism," *International Political Science Review* 10: 371–91.

Kanner, Gideon 1996, "Not with a Bang, but a Giggle: the Settlement of the *Lucas* Case," in David Callies (ed.), *Takings: Land-Development Conditions and Regulatory Takings after Dolan and Lucas*, Chicago: Section of State and Local Government Law, American Bar Association, pp. 308–11.

Kantor, Shawn Everett 1998, *Politics and Property Rights: the Closing of the Open Range in the Postbellum South*, Chicago: University of Chicago Press.

Kendall, Douglas T. and Lord, Charles P. 1998, "The Takings Project: a Critical Analysis and Assessment of the Progress So Far," *BC Environmental Affairs Law Review* 25: 509–87.

Keohane, Nathaniel O., Revesz, Richard L. and Stavins, Robert N. 1997, "The Positive Political Economy of Instrument Choice in Environmental Policy," Resources for the Future Discussion Paper No. 97–25, Washington, DC: Resources for the Future.

Kerr, William 1927, *Kerr On Injunctions*, London: Sweet and Maxwell.

Kirby, Chester 1933, "The English Game Law System," *American Historical Review* 38(2): 240–62.

Klyza, Christopher McGrory 1996, *Who Controls Public Lands?: Mining, Forestry, and Grazing Policies, 1870–1990*, Chapel Hill: University of North Carolina Press.

Komesar, Neil K. 1994, *Imperfect Alternatives: Choosing Institutions in Law, Economics, and Public Policy*, Chicago: University of Chicago Press.

Konar, Shameek and Cohen, Mark A. 1997, "Information as Regulation: the Effect of Community Right to Know Laws on Toxic Emissions," *Journal of Environmental Economics and Management* 32: 109–24.

Kornai, János 1986, "The Soft Budget Constraint," *Kyklos* 39: 3–30.

Korngold, Gerald 1984, "Privately Held Conservation Servitudes: a Policy Analysis in the Context of in Gross Real Covenants and Easements," *Texas Law Review* 63: 433–94.

Krier, James 1970, "Environmental Litigation and the Burden of Proof," in M. Baldwin and J. Page (eds.), *Law and the Environment*, New York: Walker and Co., pp. 105–22.

Krier, James A. 1974, "The Irrational National Air Quality Standards: Macro- and Micro-Mistakes," *UCLA Law Review* 22: 323–42.

Krupnick, Alan J. 1986, "Costs of Alternative Policies for the Control of Nitrogen Dioxide in Baltimore," *Journal of Environmental Economics and Management* 13: 189–97.

Laitos, Jan 1975, "Legal Institutions and Pollution: Some Intersections Between Law and History," *Natural Resources Journal* 15: 423–51.

Laitos, Jan 1985, *Natural Resources Law: Cases and Materials*, St. Paul, Minn.: West Publishing.

Laitos, Jan 1998, *Law of Property Rights Protections: Limitations on Governmental Powers*, New York: Aspen Publishers.

Land Trust Alliance 1994, Special Report: the 1994 National Land Trust Survey.

Larson, Bruce A. and Bromley, Daniel W. 1990, "Property Rights, Externalities, and Resource Degradation: Locating the Tragedy," *Journal of Development Economics* 33: 235–62.

Le Goff, Pierrick B. 1997, "The French Approach to Corporate Liability for Damage to the Environment," *Tulane European and Civil Law Forum* 12: 39–135.

Leman, Christopher K. 1984, "How the Privatization Revolution Failed, and Why Public Land Management Needs Reform Anyway," in John G. Francis and Richard Ganzel (eds.), *Western Public Lands*, Totowa, N.J.: Rowman and Allanheld, pp. 110–28.

Lewis, James A. 1980, "Landownership in the United States, 1978," Economics, Statistics, and Cooperatives Service, Agriculture Information Bulletin No. 435, Washington, DC: United States Department of Agriculture.

Libecap, Gary D. 1981, *Locking up the Range: Federal Land Controls and Grazing*, Cambridge, Mass.: Ballinger Publishing.

Libecap, Gary D. 1989, *Contracting for Property Rights*, Cambridge: Cambridge University Press.

Libecap, Gary D. 1996, "Environmental Regulation and Federalism," *Arizona Law Review* 38: 901–7.

Lieberman, Alvin and Schipma, Peter 1969, *Air Pollution-Monitoring Instrumentation: a Survey*, Washington, DC: Technology Utilization Division, National Aeronautics and Space Administration.

Liroff, Richard A. 1986, *Reforming Air Pollution Regulation: the Toil and Trouble of EPA's Bubble*, Washington, DC: Conservation Foundation.

Lockwood, Jeffrey A. 1998, "The Intent and Implementation of the Endangered Species Act: a Matter of Scale," in Jason F. Shogren (ed.), *Private Property and the Endangered Species Act*, Austin, Tex.: University of Texas Press, pp. 70–91.

Luckin, Bill 1986, *Pollution and Control: a Social History of the Thames in the Nineteenth Century*, Bristol: Adam Hilger.

Lueck, Dean 1989, "The Economic Nature of Wildlife Law," *Journal of Legal Studies* 18: 291–324.

Lueck, Dean 1991, "Ownership and the Regulation of Wildlife," *Economic Inquiry* 29: 249–60.

Lueck, Dean and Michael, Jeffrey 2000, "Preemptive Habitat Destruction Under the Endangered Species Act," unpublished working paper on file with the author.

Lund, Thomas A. 1975, "British Wildlife Law Before the American Revolution: Lessons from the Past, *Michigan Law Review* 74: 49–74.

Mackaay, Ejan 1999, "On Property Rights and Their Modification," in Walter Kanning and Donald A. Walker (eds.), *Economics, Welfare Policy and the History of Economic Thought – Essays in Honor of Arnold Heertje*, Cheltenham: Edward Elgar, pp. 245–64.

Magat, Wesley A. 1982, "Reform of Environmental Regulation: an Introduction," in Wesley A. Magat (ed.), *Reform of Environmental Regulation*, Cambridge, Mass.: Ballinger Publishing, pp. 1–12.

Maloney, Frank E. and Ausness, Richard C. 1974, "The Use and Legal Significance of the Mean High Tide Water Line in Coastal Boundary Mapping," *North Carolina Law Review* 53: 185–273.

Maloney, Michael T. and McCormick, Robert E. 1982, "A Positive Theory of Environmental Quality Regulation," *Journal of Law and Economics* 25: 99–121.

Maloney, Michael T. and Yandle, Bruce 1984, "Estimation of the Cost of Air Pollution Control Regulation," *Journal of Environmental Economics and Management* 11: 244–63.

Manning, John F. 2001, "Textualism and the Equity of the Statute," *Columbia Law Review* 101: 1–127.

Marchak, M. Patricia 1998, "Who Owns Natural Resources in the United States and Canada?" Land Tenure Center, North America Series, Working Paper No. 20, University of Wisconsin-Madison.

Mayo, Todd D. 2000, "A Holistic Examination of the Law of Conservation Easements," in J. A. Gustanski and R. H. Squires (eds.), *Protecting the Land:*

Conservation Easements Past, Present, and Future, Washington, DC: Island Press, pp. 26–54.

Mazurek, Henry E. 1994, "The Future of Clean Air: the Application of Futures Markets to Title IV of the 1990 Amendments to the Clean Air Act," *Temple Environmental Law and Technology Journal* 13: 1–33.

McCay, Bonnie J. 1996, "Common and Private Concerns," in Susan Hanna, Carl Folke, and Karl-Gören Mäler (eds.), *Rights to Nature: Ecological, Economic, Cultural, and Political Principles of Institutions for the Environment*, Washington, DC: Island Press, pp. 111–26.

McCay, Bonnie J. 2000, "Property Rights, the Commons, and Natural Resource Management," in Michael D. Kaplowitz (ed.), *Property Rights, Economics, and the Environment*, Stamford, Conn.: JAI Press, pp. 67–82.

McCay, Bonnie J. and Acheson, James M. (eds.) 1987, *The Question of the Commons: the Culture and Ecology of Communal Resources*, Tuscon: University of Arizona Press.

McGee, Robert W. and Block, Walter E. 1994, "Pollution Trading Permits as a Form of Market Socialism and the Search for a Real Market Solution to Environmental Pollution," *Fordham Environmental Law Journal* 6: 51–77.

McKean, Margaret 1986, "Management of Traditional Common Lands (*Iriachi*) in Japan," in *Proceedings of the Conference on on Common Property Resource Management*, National Research Council, Washington, DC: National Academy Press, pp. 533–89.

McKean, Margaret 1992, "Management of Traditional Common Lands (*Iriachi*) in Japan," in Daniel W. Bromley (ed.), *Making the Commons Work*, San Francisco: Institute for Contemporary Studies, pp. 63–98.

McKean, Margaret 1996, "Common-Property Regimes as a Solution to Problems of Scale and Linkage," in Susan S. Hanna, Carl Folke, and Karl-Gören Mäler (eds.), *Rights to Nature: Ecological, Economic, Cultural, and Political Principles of Institutions for the Environment*, Washington, DC: Island Press, pp. 223–43.

McUsic, Molly S. 1998, "Looking Inside Out: Institutional Analysis and the Problem of Takings," *Northwestern University Law Review* 92: 591–664.

Meidinger, Errol 1985, "On Explaining the Development of 'Emissions Trading' in US Air Pollution Regulation," *Law and Policy* 7: 447–79.

Meiners, Roger E. and Yandle, Bruce 1988, "The Common Law: How it Protects the Environment," PERC Policy Series, Issue Number PS-13, Bozeman: Political Economy Research Center.

Mendelsohn, Robert 1980, "An Economic Analysis of Air Pollution from Coal-Fired Power Plants," *Journal of Environmental Economics and Management* 7: 30–43.

Menell, Peter S. 1991, "The Limitations on Legal Institutions for Addressing Environmental Risks," *Journal of Economic Perspectives* 5: 93–111.

Menell, Peter S. 1992, "Institutional Fantasylands: From Scientific Management to Free Market Environmentalism," *Harvard Journal of Law and Public Policy* 15: 489–510.

Menell, Peter S. and Stewart, Richard B. 1994, *Environmental Law and Policy*, Boston: Little, Brown.

Mercuro, Nicholas and Medema, Steven G. 1997, *Economics and the Law: From Posner to Post-Modernism*, Princeton, N.J.: Princeton University Press.

Michaelman, Frank 1967, "Property, Utility and Fairness: Comments on the Ethical Foundations of 'Just Compensation' Law," *Harvard Law Review* 80: 1165–1258.

Michaelman, Frank 1982, "Ethics, Economics, and the Law of Property," in J. R. Pennock and J. W. Chapman (eds.), *Nomos 24: Ethics, Economics, and the Law*, New York: New York University Press, pp. 3–40.

Miller, Kathleen A. 1996, "Water Banking to Manage Supply Variability," *Advances in Economics of Environmental Resources* 1: 185–210.

Mostaghel, Deborah M. 1995, "State Reactions to the Trading of Emissions Allowances Under Title IV of the Clean Air Act Amendments of 1990," *Boston College Environmental Affairs Law Review* 22: 201–24.

National Society for Clean Air 1983, *The History of Air Pollution and its Control in Great Britain*, Brighton: National Society for Clean Air.

Nef, J. U. 1977, "An Early Energy Crisis and its Consequences," *Scientific American* (October): 141–51.

Nellis, John 2000, "Time to Rethink Privatization in Transition Economies?," International Finance Corporation Working Paper No. 38, Washington, DC.

Nelson, Robert H. 1995, *Public Lands and Private Rights: the Failure of Scientific Management*. Lanham, Md.: Rowman and Littlefield.

Netting, Robert M. 1976, "What Alpine Peasants Have in Common: Observations on Communal Tenure in a Swiss Village," *Human Ecology* 4: 135–46.

Niskanen, William A., Jr. 1971, *Bureaucracy and Representative Government*, Chicago: Aldine-Atherton.

Noll, Roger C. 1989, "Economic Perspectives on the Politics of Regulation," in Richard Schmalensee and Robert D. Willig (eds.), *Handbook of Industrial Organization*, Amsterdam: North-Holland, pp. 1253–87.

North, Douglass C. 1990, *Institutions, Institutional Change, and Economic Performance*, Cambridge: Cambridge University Press.

North, Douglass C. and Thomas, Robert C. 1973, *The Rise of the Western World: a New Economic History*, Cambridge: Cambridge University Press.

Noss, Reed F., Schlickeisen, Rodger and Cooperrider, Allen Y. 1994, *Saving Nature's Legacy: Protecting and Restoring Biodiversity*, Washington, DC: Island Press.

Oakland, William H. 1987, "Theory of Public Goods," in Alan H. Averbach and Martin Feldstein (eds.), *Handbook of Public Economics*, vol. II, Amsterdam: North-Holland, pp. 485–535.

Olson, Mancur, Jr. 1965, *The Logic of Collective Action*, New York: Schocken Books.

Opschoor, J. B. and Vos, Hans B. 1989, *Economic Instruments for Environmental Protection*, Paris: Organization for Economic Cooperation and Development.

Organization for Economic Cooperation and Development 1995, *Environmental Performance Reviews: Poland*, Paris: OECD.

Orts, Eric W. 1995, "Reflexive Environmental Law," *Northwestern University Law Review* 89: 1227–340.

Orzechowski, William 1977, "Economic Models of Bureaucracy: Survey, Extensions, and Evidence," in T. C. Borcherding (ed.), *Budgets and Bureaucrats: the Sources of Government Growth*, Durham, N.C.: Duke University Press, pp. 199–259.

Ostrom, Elinor 1990, *Governing the Commons: the Evolution of Institutions for Collective Action*, Cambridge: Cambridge University Press.

Ostrom, Elinor, Burger, Joanna, Field, Christopher B., Norgaard, Richard B. and Policansky, David 1999, "Rivisiting the Commons: Local Lessons, Global Challenges," *Science* 284 (9 Apr.): 278–82.

Ostrom, Elinor and Gardner, Roy 1993, "Coping with Asymmetries in the Commons: Self-Governing Irrigation Systems Can Work," *Journal of Economic Perspectives* 7: 93–112.

Ovid 1992, *Metamorphoses V–VIII*, trans. D. E. Hill, Warminster, Wiltshire, UK: Aris and Phillips.

Palmer, A. R., Mooz, W. E., Quinn, T. H. and Wolf, K. A. 1980, "Economic Implications of Regulation of Clorofluorocarbon Emissions from Nonaerosol Applications," Rand Corp. Report No. R-2524-EPA, prepared for the US Environmental Protection Agency, Santa Monica: Rand Corporation.

Palmer, Craig T. 1993, "Folk Management, 'Soft Evolutionism,' and Fishers' Motives: Implications for the Regulation of the Lobster Fisheries of Maine and Newfoundland," *Human Organization* 52: 414–20.

Pashigian, B. Peter 1985, "Environmental Regulation: Whose Self-Interests Are Being Protected?," *Economic Inquiry* 23: 551–84.

Paul, Ellen Frankel 1988, *Property Rights and Eminent Domain*, New Brunswick: Transaction Books.

Percival, Robert, Miller, Alan S., and Schroeder, Christopher H. 1996, *Environmental Regulation: Law, Science, and Policy*, Boston: Little, Brown.

Petersen, William F., Jr. 1994, "The Limits of Market-Based Approaches to Environmental Protection," *Environmental Law Reporter* 24: 10173–6.

Peterson, Andrea L. 1989, "The Takings Clause: in Search of Underlying Principles Part I – a Critique of Current Takings Clause Doctrine," *California Law Review* 77: 1301–63.

Pigou, A. C. [1920] 1960, *The Economics of Welfare*, London: Macmillan.

Pipes, Richard 1999, *Property and Freedom: the Story of How Through the Centuries Private Ownership Has Promoted Liberty and the Rule of Law*, New York: Knopf.

Plucknett, Theodore F. T. 1956, *A Concise History of the Common Law*, Boston: Little, Brown.

Polesetsky, Matthew 1995, "Will a Market in Air Pollution Clean the Nation's Dirtiest Air? A Study of the South Coast Air Quality Management District's Regional Clean Air Incentives Market," *Ecology Law Quarterly* 22: 359–411.

Poole, Robert W., Jr. 1996, "Privatization for Economic Development," in Terry L. Anderson and Peter J. Hill (eds.), *The Privatization Process: a Worldwide Perspective*, Lanham, Md.: Rowman and Littlefield, pp. 1–18.

Portney, Paul R. 1990, "Air Pollution Policy," in Paul R. Portney (ed.), *Public Policies for Environmental Protection*, Washington, DC: Resources for the Future, pp. 27–96.

Posner, Richard A. 1992, *Economic Analysis of Law*, Boston: Little, Brown.

Pound, Diana draft 1999, "'Thanet Coast – An Asset for All?,' Consensus Building Process: a Review" (typescript).

Power, Thomas Michael 1996, *Lost Landscapes and Failed Economies: the Search for a Value of Place*, Washington, DC: Island Press.

Power, Thomas Michael 1997, "Ideology, Wishful Thinking, and Pragmatic Reform: a Constructive Critique of Free-Market Environmentalism," in John Baden and Donald Snow (eds.), *The Next West: Public Lands, Community, and Economy in the American West*, Washington, DC: Gallatin Institute and Island Press.

Randall, Alan and Castle, Emery N. 1985, "Land Resources and Land Markets," in Allen V. Kneese and James L. Sweeney (eds.), *Handbook of Natural Resource and Energy Economics*, vol. II, Amsterdam: Elsevier Science Publishers, 571–620.

Rasker, Raymond 1994, "A New Look at Old Vistas: the Economic Role of Environmental Quality in Western Public Lands," *University of Colorado Law Review* 65: 369–99.

Rasker, Raymond, Martin, Michael V. and Johnson, Rebecca L. 1992, "Economics: Theory Versus Practice in Wildlife Management," *Conservation Biology* 6: 338–49.

Reitze, Arnold W., Jr. 1999, "The Legislative History of US Air Pollution Control," *Houston Law Review* 36: 679–741.

Repetto, Robert 1983, "Air Quality Under the Clean Air Act," in Thomas C. Schelling (ed.), *Incentives for Environmental Protection*, Cambridge, Mass.: MIT Press, pp. 221–90.

Revesz, Richard L. 1996a, "The Control of Interstate Environmental Externalities in a Federal System," *Arizona Law Review* 38: 883–99.

Revesz, Richard L. 1996b, "Federalism and Interstate Environmental Externalities," *University of Pennsylvania Law Review* 144: 2341–416.

Roach, F., Kolstad, C., Kneese, A. V., Tobin, R. and Williams, M. 1981, "Alternative Air Quality Policy Options in the Four Corners Region," *Southwestern Review* 1: 29–58.

Roberts, Marc 1982, "Some Problems of Implementing Marketable Permit Schemes: the Case of the Clean Air Act," in Wesley A. Magat (ed.), *Reform of Environmental Regulation*, Cambridge, Mass.: Ballinger Publishing, 93–117.

Rose, Carol M. 1984, "*Mahon* Reconstructed: Why the Takings Issue is Still a Muddle," *Southern California Law Review* 57: 561–99.

Rose, Carol M. 1990, "Energy and Efficiency in the Realignment of Common-Law Water Rights," *Journal of Legal Studies* 19: 261–96.

Rose, Carol M. 1994, *Property and Persuasion: Essays on History, Theory and Rhetoric of Ownership*, Boulder, Col.: Westview Press.

Rose, Carol 1998, "Canon's of Property Talk, or, Blackstone's Anxiety," *Yale Law Journal* 108: 601–32.

Rosenberg, Adam J. 1994, "Emissions Credit Futures Contracts on the Chicago Board of Trade: Regional and Rational Challenges to the Right to Pollute," *Virginia Environmental Law Journal* 13: 501–36.

Ruderman, Henry, Levine, Mark, and McMahon, James 1987, "Energy-Efficiency Choice in Purchase of Residential Appliances," in Willett Kempton and Max Neiman (eds.), *Energy Efficiency: Perspectives on Individual Behavior*, Washington, DC: American Council for an Energy-Efficient Economy, pp. 41–50.

Russell, Clifford, Harrington, Winston, and Vaughn, William J. 1986, *Enforcing Pollution Control Laws*, Washington, DC: Resources for the Future.

Russell, Clifford S. and Powell, Philip T. 1996, *Choosing Environmental Policy Tools: Theoretical Cautions and Practical Considerations*, Washington, DC: Inter-American Development Bank.

Samuels, Warren J. 1999, "Theories of Property," *Journal of Economic Issues* 33: 183–8.

Samuelson, Paul A. 1980, *Economics*, 11th edn, New York: McGraw-Hill.

Sanchez, Nicolas and Nugent, Jeffrey B. 1994, "When Common Property Rights Can Be Optimal: Nineteenth-Century Cattle Grazing in the Semiarid American West," in Terry L. Anderson and Peter J. Hill (eds.), *The Political Economy of the American West*, Lanham, Md.: Rowman and Littlefield, pp. 43–67.

Sapp, William W. 1995, "The Supply-Side and Demand-Side of Wetlands Mitigation Banking," *Oregon Law Review* 74: 951–93.

Savage, Howard 1998, "What We Have Learned About Properties, Owners, and Tenants from the 1995 Property Owners and Managers Survey," Census Bureau, Current Housing Reports: Housing and Household Economic Statistics, H121/98-1.

Sax, Joseph L. 1999, *Playing Darts with a Rembrandt: Public and Private Rights in Cultural Treasures*, Ann Arbor: University of Michigan Press.

Scalia, Antonin 1989, "Originalism: the Lesser Evil," *University of Cincinnati Law Review* 57: 849–65.

Scalia, Antonin 1997, *A Matter of Interpretation: Federal Courts and the Law*, Princeton: Princeton University Press.

Schlager, Edella and Ostrom, Elinor 1992, "Property-Rights Regimes and Natural Resources: a Conceptual Analysis," *Land Economics* 68: 249–62.

Schmalensee, Richard, Joskow, Paul L., Ellerman, A. Denny, Montero, Juan Pablo and Bailey, Elizabeth M. 1998, "An Interim Evaluation of Sulfur Dioxide Emissions Trading," *Journal of Economic Perspectives* 12: 53–68.

Schmid, A. Allan 1999, "Government, Property, Markets . . . In That Order . . . Not Government Versus Markets," in Nicholas Mercuro and Warren J. Samuels (eds.), *The Fundamental Interrelationships Between Government and Property*, Stamford, Conn.: JAI Press, pp. 233–7.

Schroder, Robert L. and Johnson, S. Lee 1997, "Using Market Forces to Reduce Pollution: Michigan's Emissions Reduction Credit and Emission Averaging Rules," *Michigan Bar Journal* 76: 70–3.

Scott, Anthony D. 1955, "The Fishery: the Objectives of Sole Ownership," *Journal of Political Economy* 63: 203–15.

Seabright, Paul 1993, "Managing Local Commons: Theoretical Issues in Incentive Design," *Journal of Economic Perspectives* 7: 113–34.

Seskin, Eugene P., Anderson, Robert J., and Reid, Robert O. 1983, "An Empirical Analysis of Economic Strategies for Controlling Air Pollution," *Journal of Environmental Economics and Management* 10: 112–24.

Shanks, Bernard 1981, "Dams and Disasters: the Social Problems of Water Development Policies," in John Baden and Richard L. Stroup (eds.),

Bureaucracy vs. Environment: the Environmental Costs of Bureaucratic Government, Ann Arbor: University of Michigan Press, pp. 108–23.

Shapiro, Sidney A. and McGarity, Thomas O. 1991, "Not So Paradoxical: the Rationale for Technology-Based Regulation," *Duke Law Journal*: 729–52.

Shogren, James F. and Hayward, Patricia H. 1998, "Biological Effectiveness and Economic Impacts of the Endangered Species Act," in James F. Shogren (ed.), *Private Property and the Endangered Species Act*, Austin: University of Texas Press, pp. 48–69.

Smith, Adam [1776] 1994, *The Wealth of Nations*, New York: Modern Library.

Smith, Henry 2000, "Semi-Common Property Rights and Scattering in the Open Fields," *Journal of Legal Studies* 29: 131–69.

Sohn, David and Cohen, Madeline 1996, "From Smokestacks to Species: Extending the Tradeable Permit Approach from Air Pollution to Habitat Conservation," *Stanford Environmental Law Journal* 15: 405–51.

Solow, Robert M. 1974, "Richard T. Ely Lecture: the Economics of Resources or the Resources of Economics," *American Economic Association* 64: 1–14.

Spofford, Walter O., Jr. 1984, "Efficiency Properties of Alternative Source Control Policies for Meeting Ambient Air Quality Standards: an Empirical Application to the Lower Delware Valley," Resources for the Future Discussion Paper No. D-118, Washington DC: Resources for the Future.

Squillace, Mark 1992, *Environmental Law: Air Pollution*, Cincinnati: Anderson Publishing.

State Utility Forecasting Group 1991, *Indiana Electricity Demand: the 1990 Forecast*, West Lafayette, Ind.: State Utility Forecasting Group.

Stavins, Robert 1993, "Transaction Costs and the Performance of Markets for Pollution Control," Resources for the Future Discussion Paper No. QE93-16, Washington, DC: Resources for the Future.

Stavins, Robert 1998, "What We Can Learn from the Grand Policy Experiment? Lessons from SO$_2$ Allowance Trading," *Journal of Economic Perspectives* 12(3): 69–88.

Stavins, Robert N. and Whitehead, Bradley W. 1992, "Dealing With Pollution: Market-Based Incentives for Environmental Protection," *Environment* 34: 7–42.

Steinzor, Rena 1998, "Reinventing Environmental Regulation: Back to the Past By Way of the Future," *ELR News and Analysis* 28: 10361–72.

Stevenson, Glenn G. 1991, *Common Property Economics: a General Theory and Land Use Applications*, Cambridge: Cambridge University Press.

Stewart, Richard B. 1981, "Regulation, Innovation, and Administrative Law: a Conceptual Framework," *California Law Review* 69: 1259–377.

Stewart, Richard B. 1993, "Environmental Regulation and International Competitiveness," *Yale Law Journal* 102: 2039–106.

Stewart, Richard B. 1996, "The Future of Environmental Regulation: United States Environmental Regulation: a Failing Paradigm," *Journal of Law and Commerce* 15: 585–96.

Stewart, Richard B. and Krier, James E. 1978, *Environmental Law and Policy: Readings, Materials and Notes*, Indianapolis: Bobbs-Merrill.

Story, Joseph [1884] 1988, *Commentaries on Equity Jurisdiction*, Birmingham, Ala.: Legal Classics Library.

Stroup, Richard L. and Baden, John A. 1973, "Externality, Property Rights and the Management of Our National Forests," *Journal of Law and Economics* 16: 303–12.

Stroup, Richard L. and Baden, John A. 1983, *Natural Resources: Bureaucratic Myths and Environmental Management*, San Francisco: Pacific Institute for Public Policy Research.

Stroup, Richard L. and Goodman, Sandra L. 1992, "Property Rights, Environmental Resources, and the Future," *Harvard Journal of Law and Public Policy* 15: 427–41.

Sutherland, Douglas 1988, *The Landowners*, London: Muller.

Svendsen, Gert Tingaard 1998, *Public Choice and Environmental Regulation*, Cheltenham: Edward Elgar.

Swift, Byron 1997, "The Acid Rain Test," *Environmental Forum* 14: 17–25.

Taylor, Michael 1992, "The Economics and Politics of Property Rights and Common Pool Resources," *Natural Resources Journal* 32: 633–48.

Terrebonne, R. Peter 1993, "Privatizing the Commons: the Distribution of Total Product," *Eastern Economic Journal* 19: 165–71.

Thirsk, Joan 1964, "The Common Fields," *Past and Present* 29: 3–25.

Thompson, Andrew Mcfee 1996, "Free Market Environmentalism and the Common Law: Confusion, Nostalgia, and Inconsistency," *Emory Law Journal* 45: 1329–72.

Thompson, Barton H. 1993, "Institutional Perspectives on Water Policy and Markets," *California Law Review* 81: 673–764.

Thompson, Barton H. 1996, "The Search for Regulatory Alternatives," *Stanford Environmental Law Journal* 15: 8–21.

Thompson, Barton H. 2000, "Tragically Difficult: the Obstacles to Governing the Commons," *Environmental Law* 30: 241–78.

Tietenberg, Thomas 1985, *Emissions Trading: an Exercise in Reforming Pollution Policy*, Washington, DC: Resources for the Future.

Tietenberg, T.H. 1991, "Economic Instruments for Environmental Protection," in Dieter Helm (ed.), *Economic Policy Towards the Environment*, Oxford: Basil Blackwell, pp. 86–110.

Tipton, Carrie A. 1995, "Protecting Tomorrow's Harvest: Developing a National System of Individual Transferable Quotas to Conserve Ocean Resources," *Virginia Environmental Law Journal* 14: 381–421.

Toulmin, Stephen 2001, *Return to Reason*, Cambridge, Mass.: Harvard University Press.

Treanor, William Michael 1995, "The Original Understanding of the Takings Clause and the Political Process," *Columbia Law Review* 95: 782–887.

Tripp, James T. B. and Dudek, Daniel J. 1989, "Institutional Guidelines for Designing Successful Transferable Rights Programs," *Yale Journal on Regulation* 6: 369–91.

Wade, Robert 1987, "The Management of Common Property Resources: Collective Action as an Alternative to Privatisation or State Regulation," *Cambridge Journal of Economics* 11: 95–106.

Warming, Jens 1911, "Om 'grundrente' af fiskegrunde," *Nationalokonomisk Tidsskrift*, 495–506, translated in P. Andersen 1983, "On Rent of Fishing Grounds: a Translation of Jens Warming's 1911 Article, with an Introduction," *History of Political Economy* 15: 391–6.

Wedgwood, Ruth 1994, "Constitutional Equity," *Yale Law Journal* 104: 33–7.

Wijewardana, Don 1990, "Sale of the Century: NZ Forestland for Sale; in a Controversial Move, the New Zealand Government is Offering for Sale its Stock of Plantation Forest as Part of a Privatization Program to Reduce National Debt," *World Wood* 31(Feb.): 24–5.

Wilkove, David S., Bean, Michael J., Bonnie, Robert and McMillan, Margaret 1996, "Rebuilding the Ark Toward a More Effective Endangered Species Act for Private Land," New York: Environmental Defense Fund, available on the World Wide Web at http://www.edf.org/pubs/Reports/help-esa/index.html#problem.

Williamson, Oliver 1975, *Markets and Hierarchies: Analysis and Antitrust Implications*, New York: Free Press.

Williamson, Oliver 1983, "Credible Commitments: Using Hostages to Support Exchange," *American Economic Review* 83: 519–40.

Williamson, Oliver 1985, *The Economics Institutions of Capitalism*, New York: Free Press.

Willick, D. and Windle, T. 1973, "Rule Enforcement by the Los Angeles Country Air Pollution Control District," *Ecology Law Quarterly* 3: 507–34.

Wittman, Donald A. 1995, *The Myth of Democratic Failure: Why Political Institutions are Efficient*, Chicago: University of Chicago Press.

Wolozin, Harold 1969, "The Economics of Air Pollution: Central Problems," in Clark Havighurst (ed.), *Air Pollution Control*, Dobbs Ferry NY: Ocean Publications, pp. 31–42.

Yandle, Bruce 1992, "Escaping Environmental Feudalism," *Harvard Journal of Law and Public Policy* 15: 517–39.

Yandle, Bruce 1993, "Bootleggers and Baptists – Environmentalists and Protectionists: Old Reasons for New Coalitions," in Terry L. Anderson (ed.), *NAFTA and the Environment*, San Francisco: Pacific Research Institute for Public Policy, pp. 91–103.

Yandle, Bruce 1997, *Common Sense and Common Law for the Environment: Creating Wealth in Hummingbird Economies*, Lanham, Md.: Rowman and Littlefield.

Young, Robert A. and Haveman, Robert H. 1985, "Economics of Water Resources: a Survey," in Allen V. Kneese and James L. Sweeney (eds.), *Handbook of Natural Resource and Energy Economics*, vol. II, Amsterdam: North-Holland, pp. 465–529.

Youngman, Joan 1993, "Concepts of Property and Taxation," in Gene Wunderlich (ed.), *Land Ownership and Taxation*, Boulder, Col.: Westview Press., pp. 45–59.

Zupko, Ronald E. and Laures, Robert A. 1996, *Straws in the Wind: Medieval Urban Environmental Law*, Boulder, Col.: Westview Press.

Żylicz, Tomasz 1995, "Will New Property Right Regimes in Central and Eastern Europe Serve the Purposes of Nature Conservation?," in Susan Hanna and Mohan Munasinghe (eds.), *Property Rights in a Social and Ecological Context:*

Case Studies and Design Applications, Washington, DC: Beijer International Institute of Ecological Economics and the World Bank, pp. 63–74.

GOVERNMENT REPORTS

Council on Environmental Quality 1971, *The President's 1971 Environmental Program*. Washington, DC: Government Printing Office.

Council on Environmental Quality 1990, *Environmental Quality: The Twentieth Annual Report of the Council on Environmental Quality Together with the President's Message to Congress*. Washington, DC: Government Printing Office.

Department of Commerce 1997, *Environmental Industry of the United States*, Washington, DC: US Department of Commerce, International Trade Administration, Environmental Technologies Exports.

Department of the Environment 1992, *The UK Environment*, London: HMSO.

Energy Information Administration 1997, *The Effects of Title IV of the Clean Air Act Amendments of 1990 on Electric Utilities: an Update*, Washington, DC: United States Department of Energy.

Environmental Protection Agency 1980, *Emissions Reduction Banking and Trading Update*. Washington, DC: Environmental Protection Agency.

Environmental Protection Agency 1987, *EPA's Use of Benefit-Cost Analysis: 1981–1986*, Washington, DC: Environmental Protection Agency.

Environmental Protection Agency 1990, *Environmental Investments: the Cost of a Clean Environment*. Washington, DC: Environmental Protection Agency.

Environmental Protection Agency 1997, *The Benefits and Costs of the Clean Air Act, 1970–1990*, Washington, DC: Environmental Protection Agency.

Forest Service, US Department of Agriculture, 1996, *Land Areas of the National Forest System*, Washington, DC.

General Accounting Office 1993, *Endangered Species Act: Information on Species Protection on Nonfederal Lands*, GAO/RCED-95-16, Washington, DC: US General Accounting Office.

General Accounting Office 1994, *Report to the Chairman, Environment, Energy, and Natural Resources Subcommittee, Committee on Government Operations, House of Representatives, Air Pollution: Allowance Trading Offers an Opportunity to Reduce Emissions at Less Cost*. Washington, DC: US General Accounting Office.

Khana, Seretse 1975, "National Policy on Tribal Grazing Land," Government White Paper No. 2, Gaborone, Botswana: Botswana Government Printer.

National Academy of Sciences, National Research Council 1977, *Environmental Monitoring, Vol. IV of Analytical Studies for the US Environmental Protection Agency*, Washington, DC: Government Printing Office.

National Commission on Air Quality 1981, *To Breathe Clean Air*, Washington, DC: The Commission.

National Research Council 1993, *Setting Priorities for Land Conservation*, Washington, DC: National Academy Press.

Office of Technology Assessment 1995, *Environmental Policy Tools: a User's Guide*, Washington, DC: Government Printing Office.

Royal Commission on Environmental Pollution 1971, *First Report*, London: HMSO.

State Inspectorate for Environmental Protection 1998, *The State of the Environment in Poland*, Warsaw: PIOŚ.

US Census Bureau 1999, *American Housing Survey for the United States: 1999*, available on the World Wide Web at http://www.census.gov/hhes/ www/housing /ahs/ahs99/tab315.html.

US Department of Agriculture (Rev. Dec. 2000), Summary Report, 1997 National Resources Inventory.

PERIODICALS

BNA Daily Environment Report, August 12, 1996.

BNA National Environment Daily, December 16, 1998.

BNA National Environment Daily, June 29, 1998.

BNA National Environment Daily, December 16, 1998.

Charleston Post and Courier, August 27, 1993.

Economist, February 5, 1994.

Financial Times (London), September 25, 1995.

Guardian, May 19, 1994.

M2 Presswire, April 2, 1998.

New York Times, March 4, 2001.

New York Times, April 4, 2001.

Scotland on Sunday, May 29, 1994.

The Times, April 20, 1905.

Utility Environment Report, March 14, 1997.

Index